Throughout the 1980s and 1990s Asia's economic growth astonished the world. The region's stock markets soared to new heights, unprecedented economic growth rates were recorded and an acquisitive new middle class emerged. Then overnight, it all fell apart. The question now being asked is: Who brought the party to an end?

In this penetrating and thoughtful account, Philippe Delhaise points the finger squarely at Asia's antiquated banking and financial systems. Everything else - the currency panics, the social and political shocks - is simply a stream of consequences flowing from the main source. What is exceptional about the crisis is not that it happened but the manner in which it came about, inflicting indiscriminate devastation to all.

The story of the Asian Crisis is a tale of greed and sorrow, of intelligent people making unforgivable mistakes and of a collective misunderstanding about the management of economic expansion. Asia will undoubtedly recover but the speed and strength of its re-emergence will depend on how well it has learned its lessons. The concluding chapter of the book outlines the many issues that need to be addressed and provides a template for the future development of the region's finance industry.

Asia in Crisis

The Implosion of the Banking and Finance Systems

Asia in Crisis

The Implosion of the Banking and Finance Systems

Philippe Delhaise

John Wiley & Sons (Asia) Pte Ltd

Singapore • New York • Chichester • Brisbane • Toronto • Weinheim

Other Wiley Editorial Offices

John Wiley & Sons, Inc., 605 Third Avenue, New York, NY 10158-0012, USA
John Wiley & Sons Ltd, Baffins Lane, Chichester, West Sussex PO19 1UD, England
John Wiley & Sons (Canada) Ltd, 22 Worcester Road, Rexdale, Ontario M9W 1L1, Canada
Jacaranda Wiley Ltd, 33 Park Road (PO Box 1226), Milton, Queensland 4046, Australia
Wiley-VCH, Pappelallee 3, 69469 Weinheim, Germany

Library of Congress Cataloging-in-Publication Data:
Delhaise, Philippe, 1948-
    Asia in crisis : the implosion of the banking and finance systems/Philippe Delhaise/
    p. cm.
    Includes bibliographical references and index.
    ISBN 0-471-83193-X (alk. paper). — ISBN 0-471-83450-5 (pbk. : alk. paper)
    1. Banks and banking—Asia—Case studies.   2. Finance—Asia—Case studies.
    3. Business cycles—Asia—Case studies.   I. Title.
    HG3252.D45   1998
    332.1'095—dc21   98-42024
                                                                               CIP

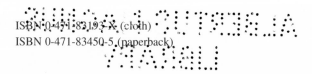

ISBN 0-471-83193-X (cloth)
ISBN 0-471-83450-5 (paperback)

Typeset in 10/12 point, Times by Linographic Services Pte Ltd
Printed in Singapore by Kyodo Printing Co (S'pore) Pte Ltd
10 9 8 7 6 5 4 3 2 1

To Anne-Sophie Delhaise and Elizabeth Delhaise
who spent the best part of their young lives in Asia

CONTENTS

ACKNOWLEDGEMENTS

D uring the 10 weeks I spent writing this book, Asia never stopped moving the goal posts. Currencies and stock markets went up and down, the general mood switched back and forth between hope and despair, while daily developments took place that affected my views on the crisis.

I wish to express my thanks to Thomson BankWatch and Thomson Financial Services for their support and for having agreed to let me draw from the group's huge wealth of data.

Particular thanks go to Jonathan Golin, Thomson BankWatch Asia Vice President, who volunteering his own time, agreed to act as a mirror for my opinions and as a guardian of stylistic correctness. He is a talented writer who could probably have penned this book himself.

My gratitude also goes to Mark Jones and Paul Grela, Thomson BankWatch Asia Vice Presidents, and their teams, who assessed my opinions on the five distressed countries.

My task would have been immensely more difficult if not for the support of Natasha Penner who coordinated the compilation of the very rich Thomson BankWatch data and the preparation of historical information.

I must also stress how grateful I am to several analysts previously associated with my work. In 1986, Lionel Desjardins invited me to establish Capital Information Services, Asia's first regional bank rating agency. He had the prescience to foresee the spectacular expansion of Asia's banking systems. The firm we created was prompt at denouncing the horrendous condition of most of the banks and it acquired considerable respect for its opinions. This culminated in courtship from several of the world's largest rating agencies and, ultimately, in the acquisition of the company's rating business by Thomson BankWatch in 1994.

We detected the first serious cracks in Asia's banking systems well before anyone else and, among the many analysts who translated those worries into rating suggestions, particular credit must go to Damien Wood, Tony Watson and Andrew Seiz.

My thanks go to John Wiley & Sons (Asia) Pte Ltd, in particular Nick Wallwork and Gael Lee for their invaluable insight and advice; and to Jane Cotter at Cotter Communications for her editorial eye.

Last but not least, the reader deserves some gratitude and apologies. I often write for specialists who want shortcuts to professional conclusions and can follow the most succinct developments. In spite of my efforts, I may have at times skipped some steps in my reasoning. But this is not all. My native language is French, the language of love and philosophy, the heir to the clarity of classical Greek. Years of writing in English have yet to allow the transposition of my thoughts in as fluent and clear a prose as perhaps my French would have. No amount of editing, however creative, can substitute for the fluency of a native English-language writer.

Philippe Delhaise
June 1998

INTRODUCTION

The economic, financial and political turmoil that struck Asia in mid-1997 represents both a crisis and a panic. The crisis was one of fundamentals. It is a growth crisis. At its core were antiquated financial systems that relied almost exclusively on commercial banks to provide capital for economic expansion. These institutions, very highly leveraged and poorly regulated for the most part, could no longer support the high growth that most of the region had sustained for nearly two decades. Everything else was panic: the currency crises, the debt crises, the social crises and even the political crises are but a string of consequences flowing from the main source. This book concentrates on the crisis, not the panic.

Asia's financial systems have had to rely on what Professor Merton Miller of the University of Chicago has called "19th century technology" because there was no alternative.[1] Capital markets were poorly developed. As is inevitably the case, banks expanded credit excessively on the upside of the business cycle, misallocated capital and employed weak credit controls. When the Thai baht was devalued on July 2, 1997, panic spread among both foreign and domestic creditors and investors. Instead of realizing that what was needed were some modest reforms in the financial systems in much of the region, lenders, investors and domestic punters believed that the Asian miracle was over or indeed that it had never existed. Likened to being trapped in a burning building, they rushed to the exit, all at the same time, bringing down currencies and stock markets.

The story of the crisis then is one of greed and sorrow, of intelligent people making unjustifiable but understandable mistakes, and of a collective misunderstanding about economic growth. All that Asia needs for harmonious growth, it has in abundance. The economies of Asia will resume their growth after the present period of consolidation. The banking systems throughout much of the region have now imploded and the capital funds needed to rehabilitate the banks exceed 20% of GDP.[2]

This book is a modest attempt at understanding what went wrong, focusing on banking and financial systems, and at guessing how and how fast Asia will come out of its predicament.

The panic that swept through the region like a brush fire or a contagious epidemic devastated the region's currencies and equities well beyond what was reasonable. None of the countries deserved the wild adjustments that took place. But the contagion fed on itself and the crisis blew out of all reasonable proportion. While serious changes were called for, the implosion of the banking systems was not necessary. Fractional reserve banks are always vulnerable to panics, as by their nature such institutions hold fewer liquid funds than potential claims upon them. It is therefore unsurprising that banks crashed and burned throughout the region. Indeed, in some cases, it was inevitable and, certainly, the blow was welcome as an opportunity to weed out inefficient players. The panic did have its origins, as I have alluded to, in a crisis of fundamentals. This book focuses on that underlying crisis rather than on the more visible panic that resulted from the corresponding loss of confidence.

A Crisis of Growth

Growth rates have been extraordinarily high in Asia over the past three decades. But Asia's financial systems have not grown with Asia. They are extraordinarily fragile. In actuality, it is a miracle that they did not fall apart earlier than they did. Many countries are distressed in Asia today, but a set of five (Thailand, Korea, Indonesia, Malaysia and the Philippines) suffered a collapse of their currencies and stock markets. All five at various degrees — and many of those which have escaped disaster so far,[3] for that matter — exhibit flaws in their financial systems that would have, at one point in the near future, led to a crisis. But, absent the panic, it would have been a string of domestic crises, not a regional collapse. What is exceptional about the Asian crisis is not that it happened, but that it happened the way it did at the time it did, inflicting indiscriminate devastation to all. The truth is, looking at fundamentals, that none of those countries was in any immediate danger, save Thailand.

The main reason why the banking systems are so weak lies in the quality of financial management. Most commercial banks of Asia are run like pawnshops. Proper credit culture, meaning lending upon the basis of reasoned credit and cash flow analysis, is minimal. Rather collateral is king, and the primary factor in the lending decision. The other reason is the relationship between bank and customer. At best, the focus on relationship results in "name lending", or making credit decisions primarily on the basis of the bank officer's assumed knowledge of the customer in question. Such knowledge may involve a real understanding of the customer's business and the character of managers. At its worst, name lending deteriorates into related party lending and crony capitalism. Under such circumstances, depositors and minority shareholders tend to get short shrift. Bank owners milk deposits, friends of friends of the well connected get loans and creative accounting becomes an art form.

Asian bankers are not entirely to blame for the situation. Both history and culture have had an impact. In Asia prior to independence, banking was left to colonial banks that did little to groom local talent. It was not until major American banks became active in the region that local bankers received proper training. To this day, the best bankers in Asia have usually spent some time with a major American name.[4] Very few have learned their trade with British banks, in spite of their long presence in Asia.

Another phenomenon that makes Asia different is a cultural one that reflected the nascent state of economic development in the region not long ago. Brilliant managers would not work for companies unless they owned them. This is very Asian: if you are any good, why would you want to work for someone else? Create your own firm, and be your own boss. The same mentality applies to first-rank bankers, with the difference that most of them can hardly own a bank. Self-made industrialists and traders have often seen banks both as status symbols and as a cheap means of financing their empires, often at the expense of depositors. The result is that Asia is littered with rags-to-riches and riches-to-rags stories that often include a venture into banking, with mixed results.

Other writers have come out with sophisticated theories about the causes and the consequences of the crisis. Sachs, Miller, Krugman, Radelet, Wade and some other analysts are brilliant.[5] Lesser writers have fuzzy opinions. There is little consensus among them, and often the conclusions are hedged. Worse, some of those with the grandest theories are those with the least understanding as to how the institutions that are the chess pieces in their hypotheses actually operate. In the end, what the reader wants is an opinion, or at the very least a likely explanation for what happened. This will be my modest contribution to the debate. I have studied Asian banks for 20 years, first as a banker, then as a bank financial analyst.

This experience has given me what I believe is the key to the crisis. While I concede a danger in attributing causes to that which one knows best, I will demonstrate that there is ample justification to blame the crisis, in the aggravated manifestation that we have seen, on the weaknesses of Asia's banking systems in a context of high growth. We have witnessed nothing other than an implosion of the banking and financial systems. This was no surprise. But the rest of the story, in particular the panic, was.

The Business of Banking and a Disclaimer

Once the veil of respectability and rectitude that clothe the profession are parted, the business of banking can be seen as one of the easiest professions on earth and as one least deserving of the propriety and status that it enjoys. But these accouterments accomplish their purpose in mystifying the trade of money lending with a grandeur that it seldom deserves. It impresses the depositors who trust the banker with their hard-earned funds.

I should know; I was once a bank manager. The main quality of a banker is to be trustworthy. Superior intellectual skills are not an absolute pre-requisite. Thankfully, there are quite a number of brilliant bankers who, incidently, would have been brilliant in any other professions. Whoever met John Reed or Maurice Lauré, among many others, would agree. What does it take to be a good banker? A basic understanding of accounting, a bit of flair and, above all, a fair amount of luck are all one needs. Banks do employ rocket scientists who can trot out the most arcane value-at-risk formulations on a moment's notice, but they are confined to secondary positions. In the better banks, there is a subtle harmony and a resulting synergy between the streetwise credit managers and the rocket scientists. In other banks, all decisions are very amateurish. With more revenue than they need, some banks can afford to be profligate and to make monstrously stupid decisions. Every year, a large chunk of the operating revenue painfully amassed by thousands of bank employees — often at the expense of a suffering public — is swallowed by wrong credit decisions made by a few 'often ill-informed' managers.

Thirty years ago in Europe, bank managers were selected on an obscure basis that gave more relevance to family connections than to technical ability. Many of them, of impeccable pedigree — or so they claimed — were in fact barely educated. The more lucid recognized their limits and consequently devoted the best of their meager abilities to concealing their stupidity. Some were so dumb that even they themselves could not figure it out. I once worked with a baron-banker whose greatest ability was that he knew how to button up a three-piece suit. He was congenitally stupid.

But this is not the right place for generalizations. It would be too simplistic and too unfair. After all, not all Bulgarians carry poisonous umbrellas, and not every English solicitor is dishonest. In this book, we shall inevitably poke fun at some banks. No one should feel offended. Alas, some of us are not blessed with much of a sense of humor. They should rest assured that this will be done without dark intentions.

The Purpose of this Book

The purpose of this book is to sit back at a distance and to examine why the Asian crisis of 1997 happened. Crisis, critical, criticize, critic, critique. The words come from the Greek verb *krinein*, meaning to assess, to appraise or to evaluate.[6] Strictly speaking, what we experienced was an Asian panic, not a crisis. It is a crisis to the extent that we can pause and react to the events. This is what this book attempts to do. We shall see how it came to happen, how to possibly resolve it and what the future may hold. The weakness of the banking systems is the ultimate source, not the consequence of the crisis, although the severity of the turmoil and the contagion effect have forced an implosion of the banking systems. Such implosion should have been less devastating. We shall therefore examine the various banking systems of the region to clarify that point.

The crisis has brought suffering to the masses in several Asian countries. This is no joking matter. But the best way forward is to arm one's mind with a solid sense of humor. Short of that, there is nothing to do but sit and cry. Asia deserves better than that. Good brains, high education, hard work, beauty and smiles: Asia has it all. Asia offers the best growth story of this century. The century may be over, the growth story is not. This crisis is merely a pause.

Methods and Approach

There are some technical pages, but this particular book is not a technical analysis of the crisis. This would be too boring. The reader will find elsewhere hundreds of comprehensive studies on this or that aspect of the problem, thousands of tables and charts, and a myriad of opinions as to the key reasons for the Asian crisis. All opinions are debatable and statistical information is only a tool that can be used in support of them. If figures, ratios and general statistics had been giving clear and undisputed signals, there would have been a consensus prior to the crisis on the impending dangers facing Asia. Very few observers saw the warning signs and fewer still made use of them to announce potential problems, but the world would not have listened anyway. As usual, everybody was riding on the wave of unfettered optimism about Asia: the governments, lenders, borrowers, investors and even some raters. With hindsight, it is easy to put the finger on the many shortcomings of Asia, very much like it has been easy to prove wise in post-mortem comments on the Savings & Loans debacle in the US, or the real estate disaster in France.

The following pages will demonstrate, with utmost modesty, the weaknesses of Asia's financial markets and what made them a major factor in Asia's downfall. In most road or air accidents, it is difficult to assign the blame to a single major cause, whether it is human or mechanical failure. More often than not, the major cause would not, on its own, have led to disaster, but the presence of other factors, themselves incapable of triggering major problems, combine with the major cause to create the mishap. Speeding cars are not in themselves seen dangerous until some other physical object of comparable or greater mass, a slower truck for example, presents them with a deadly obstacle.

It is no overstatement to say that financial markets in Asia were and are weak. Their weaknesses created opportunities for governments to go wrong in a string of decisions. Politicians are no technicians. In Asia, more often than not, they were elevated to their crucial position by a selection process very distant from democratic choice or selection on the basis of merit. It is not clear to democrats whether they should elect politicians on a specific platform, or to the contrary, on the basis that — once in place — they will exercise their judgment in the best interests of their constituents, in the assumption that they know better. Either way, the one discipline in which most politicians are weak is economics, and it is doubtful that they could know better than their flock. The most intelligent people make stupid decisions every day, and nothing, even being benevolent, educated and well-informed, will prevent it.

Greed and mischief compound the problems of incompetence. Asian values will be alluded to in this book. They include a quest for spirituality, away from materialistic values, that has long attracted the Western world to Asia. Yet behind the smiles, behind the Confucian ethics, sometimes lies the irrepressible urge for wealth. Not far behind, we shall uncover mischief. The extraordinary development of Asia in the past 35 years has created a contingent of profiteers, cheaters and swindlers at a faster rate than was ever witnessed in the West, except perhaps the Wild West. To be sure, the West has not been able to eliminate such people from public office or the inner circles of power and influence, and it is doubtful whether this noble end could ever be realized. What is certain is that Asia has not even attempted to address the issue.

The Crisis: What it is; What it is Not

Before progressing any further, we need a definition of the panic. We maintain the distinction between crisis and panic, but since everybody calls it a crisis, we shall do the same.

Is it a currency crisis? It is not. If it were, there would be a degree of justification of the currency adjustments that took place. Yet, the Asian currencies were generally not misaligned.[7] Most of them, on fundamentals, did not beg for any substantial adjustment. Clearly, their post-crisis levels are widely out of synch with fundamentals. If the adjustments were reasonable, the currencies of China, Taiwan, Hong Kong, India and some other countries would have also collapsed. We know that there are technical reasons behind this — capital accounts are not convertible and/or the countries hold vast reserves — but fundamentals cannot be ignored for too long.

Is it a stock market crisis? It is not. If it were, there would also be a degree of justification in the adjustments that took place. Yet, on fundamentals, it could be argued that many of the stock markets of the region were reasonably priced before the crisis. While the Hong Kong share prices went down in a reaction of asset deflation[8] to the rigidity of the currency, there was little justification, on fundamentals, for the collapse of other stock markets. This of course will not prevent the crisis from savaging earnings and from bringing *a posteriori* a justification for the stock price deflation.

Is it a political or a social crisis? Yes, to a degree, it is. It can be argued that the political and social equations have been shaken in Thailand, Korea and Indonesia, for example, and they certainly were begging for changes. Other countries may follow. It is difficult to generalize about similarities between any two countries in that respect, but the fact is that the crisis has been an opportunity to bring changes to the political scene.

Is it an investment crisis? No, it is not. Certainly the allocation of resources was imperfect, and the destination of the huge domestic savings and foreign investments was chaotic. Yet, the distressed countries share very few similarities.

To be sure, there were imbalances in currencies and stock market valuations, and there were political and social issues in each of the distressed countries. There was a misallocation of resources. But nobody can seriously argue that those dysfunctions could have resulted in a simultaneous crisis of confidence across the region.

The one common link between the countries was a long period of growth. The growth was largely financed with foreign money and was poorly managed domestically: the capital markets and financial intermediaries simply did not grow apace with the economies. To be more precise, the financial sectors did grow, but they never matured.

The Asian crisis is a crisis of growth. Everything else is ancillary. The currencies and the stock markets collapsed as a result of a panic, resulting from a change of perception in the minds of both domestic and foreign investors and lenders. These are the symptoms, not the malady itself.

Would the panic as we saw it unfold — an almost simultaneous collapse of currencies and asset values — have taken place if imbalances in currencies, investments or stock markets, or politico-social tensions had been, singly or jointly, decisive factors? Possibly not. Countries would have been jolted: Indonesia and the Philippines on the political or social side, Korea for its aging industrial structure, Thailand for its real estate craze, Malaysia for its grandiose projects. Yet they would have been hit at different periods and the ripple effect on other countries would have been limited.

Liberalization is also a contributing factor. With growth came wealth and with wealth came liberalization. The financial sector was not ready for liberalization. Greed, incompetence and cronyism conspired with a very poor credit culture to create financial intermediaries that were simply not up to the task. Countries like China, Pakistan, Vietnam and India, which exhibit similar weaknesses — with a variety of growth rates — but have yet to liberalize their economies, have not met the same fate.

The panic on currency and stock markets, which was only incident to the growth crisis, represents merely the transmission belt that carried the contagion from one country to the next. The panic resulted in an almost total simultaneity in the crises faced by the various countries.

Objectives

This book will first explore the consensus of many economists on the possible causes of the Asian crisis. It is perhaps appropriate to state what this book is not, before a reader with the proverbial encyclopedic curiosity starts looking for facts or figures which are not in these pages.

- This book is not the story, day by day, of the Asian crisis. Although there is a short history printed as an appendix, the purpose is not to regurgitate historical facts.
- This book is not a manual of bank technical analysis. There is a glossary of ratios as an appendix, but there are other excellent sources on this particular topic. The only technical points developed in the book to any substantial extent pertain to capital ratios, as they are central to the recovery of Asia's banking systems.
- This book is not an exhaustive analysis of each of the distressed countries from a macroeconomic point of view, beyond establishing the background against which the banking systems are struggling.

If this book is not what it is not, then what is it really about? It will try to impart the following views:

- The Asian crisis did not start in 1997 and did not finish in 1998. It started much earlier in the decade, and it will last for some time more. It will take anything from one to five years to resume normal growth.
- The banking systems of each of the five distressed countries (Korea, Thailand, Indonesia, Malaysia and the Philippines) would have met their fate at one point in time, regardless of the crisis that, by contagion, hit them at the same time in 1997.
- The majority of Asia's banking systems operate with abysmally low real capital ratios, so much so that a large proportion of the banks are theoretically bankrupt.
- Disclosure of financial information is below acceptable levels and, with very few exceptions, banks resort to creative accounting to mislead the world around them.

I shall endeavor to entertain readers by leading them through bank accounting principles and by explaining how creative Asian bankers have become over the years. In short, the disclosure of financial statements is limited, and the figures and ratios published by banks across Asia — with very few exceptions — are totally misleading. Crudely said, the banks have been cooking the books for years. Dozens of banks are bankrupt, but nobody knows about it.

Each of the five distressed countries (Thailand, Korea, Indonesia, Malaysia and the Philippines) receives a chapter, while another single chapter is devoted to a brief exploration of the countries not usually associated with the original victims: Japan, China, Hong Kong, Taiwan. The book will also explore two major sources of banking system weakness in Asia: the moral hazard and the disdain for proper corporate governance. Some space is devoted to the cure and the rehabilitation of banks. Included are comments on the IMF rescue packages and on the rating agencies. The conclusion will offer some views and suggestions on how each banking system can come out of the crisis.

Endnotes

1. Professor Miller made that remark several times, most recently in a public presentation in Hong Kong in October 1997.
2. This is a rough estimate. There are huge differences across countries according to the true ratio of bad loans to bank portfolios, the ratio of loans to total assets, the ratio of bank assets to total credit intermediation, and the ratio of credit intermediation to GDP.
3. China, India, Hong Kong, Taiwan and Singapore have, so far, only suffered indirectly from the crisis.
4. Citibank has long acted as an excellent school for commercial bank management, but Bank of America, Chase, American Express Bank and other names have also produced good local bankers. The British and European banks tend to keep their staff for longer terms, thereby depriving other institutions of talented staff.
5. It is impossible to be exhaustive in such a list. The reader will find some more names in the reference appendix. In addition, many excellent commentators have written for the *Wall Street Journal*, the *Far Eastern Economic Review*, *The Economist*, *Euromoney*, *Business Week*, the *Financial Times*, the *New York Times* etc.
6. We shall try here to avoid the usual cliché where the Chinese characters for "crisis" happen to be those for "danger" and "opportunity", implying for no good reason that finding the silver lining is exclusively a Chinese trait. Traduttore tradittore.
7. The currencies were not misaligned on a trade-weighted basis. They may have been misaligned on a purchasing power basis, though, and clearly it is difficult to accept that countries exhibiting such a variety of economic backgrounds could all maintain their currency closely linked to the US dollar. The reader will find more on that topic in Chapter 4 on Thailand.
8. In currency board situations and, to a large degree, when a currency is pegged, an overvaluation of the fixed currency almost always leads to asset deflation, and the reverse is true when the fixed currency is undervalued. Part of the unnatural explosion of asset values in Hong Kong in the 1990s is due to that phenomenon.

THE ASIA PANIC

Hundreds of them were lining up: young, old, some with young children. All were grasping those pieces of paper measuring what was owed to them. They all shared the same panicky look, constantly peering over the shoulders of those in front of them for a glimpse of their immediate fate. It had been a long day. From early morning, the family had debated hotly whether they should claim back their due, or if another day, another week perhaps would make no difference. The old question rebounded of saving or consuming. So did the question of whether one should ever trust someone else with one's possessions. If the government had licensed them to operate, why should anyone worry about them defaulting? Why would an honest person be penalized for having deferred the consumption of what is rightfully theirs? No ready answers. Only regrets. This should have been done yesterday. Accusations. The husband had long wanted to withdraw his due, the wife wanted to keep it all for a rainy day.

Often in such circumstances, impeccably dressed staff would walk down the queue, offering help and advice. At times, the manager himself would appear, distributing kind words to his many clients, some of whom he had never seen before and would likely never see again. At regular intervals, timed to attract attention, heavily protected delivery vans would park in front of the building and several staff members would carry huge boxes through the main entrance. The manager would comment that all customers would be served, that there was no reason for panic and that opening hours would be extended as needed.

This was a run, a real run. The place was Hong Kong. The target (or was it the victim?) was the St Honore bakery. Its crime? One of its minority shareholders was the Yaohan department store, which was about to be liquidated. St Honore had sold thousands of coupons valid indefinitely for the redemption of fat, fluffy, creamy cakes of all shapes and colors. Some people like them; they represent the most palatable gift of Western culinary tradition to Eastern palates. They are so popular that no wedding invitation card is sent without a cake coupon. People keep them in drawers until they need them for that special occasion, which never materializes. This creates a huge float of cake coupons that gives cake shop accountants a perpetual headache. Not that they fear a sudden wave of withdrawals, but it is always difficult to estimate how much should be accrued across the financial year-end.

In this instance, St Honore called in every available pastry chef in its group, and the bakeries worked overnight for several days to produce tons of those delicious cakes, whose shelf-life does not exceed a couple of days. Coupon holders each claimed possession of dozens of cakes, each of them capable of feeding a family of four or five for two days. St Honore staff wished them good luck and a good appetite. Hong Kong had gigantic indigestion.

Hong Kong likes a good run, whether justified or not. A few years ago, Standard Chartered Bank, not exactly a weak financial institution, suffered a short run. Nobody ever found out what started it, except for the tiny bit of suspicion that the bank may have had some minor shareholder whose nationality remotely associated him with the shareholders of a failed bank in another country. Rumors, Hong Kong thrives on rumors.

Hong Kong is a microcosm that encompasses everything good and bad about Asia, and the very same lunacies that drive amahs[1] and taxi drivers to bid up the price of an obscure firm operate everywhere in Asia with the same devastation. Markets, like people, are often manipulated. Asia is a huge gambling den where, among other minor aspirations to become happy, educated or caring, the central ambition is to get rich.

The end of the cake story? St Honore is still in business, but another company, Maria's Cakes, went bust. Irate cake-eaters joined thousands of coupon-holders of any denomination to urge the Hong Kong consumer council to request changes in the laws. It appears that hundreds of millions of dollar of coupons circulate in Hong Kong. People buy them as they come cheaper when bought in bulk for future consumption. People buy them as gifts for children. In a sense, this is akin to printing money, and some are taking the matter very seriously.

Perception, perception, perception. All runs have the same source. The symptoms of the Asian crisis were runs: depositors claimed their money back, foreigners wanted their funds back, lenders refused to renew loans, while millions of Malaysians, Indonesians, Koreans and Thais organized a run on their own currency, bidding up the dollar to unprecedented highs.

Thailand was hit first, and then the contagion affected the whole region. The transmission belt of the crisis was perception. Whatever happened to Thailand would happen to Indonesia or Korea, and international investors and lenders united with domestic players in a bashing of both the currencies and the stock markets. They wrongly perceived Asia as a single market. To this day, Asia remains that misty, distant, fascinating world to many Westerners. Asia must have done something right for its remarkable development, and the world recognizes that there are Asian values.

A superficial observation of Asia would reinforce the widely accepted idea that, once the weight of colonial oppression was discarded — only Japan and Thailand were never colonized — Asian countries could only prosper, in three or four decades closing the gap with Western industrial nations. After all, Japan had before the rest of Asia, alerted the world to the formidable capacity of a people to be frugal, industrious and creative. Japan rebuilt a devastated economy in no time and, for all its present problems, remains a phenomenon. It was as if the Western world, having won World War II, had banned the Japanese to their islands with instructions to work hard, eat little and supply the world with cheap products. It seemed as if they had been told to think of creative ways of putting to commercial use some of Europe's and North America's best post-war inventions or discoveries, such as the transistor, the integrated circuit or the small efficient car. Until the mid-1970s, Japan delivered, but the quality of the products remained low, outside some special lines like photographic equipment, a testimony to the country's natural penchant — touching on passion — for miniaturization. By the 1980s, Japan was producing better quality cars and computers, and was competing fiercely with the rest of the world for — among others — shipping and infrastructure projects. The quiet little man from Osaka or Kobe was teaching the world a lesson.

Soon enough, other countries in the region were following in Japan's footsteps. Taiwan and Korea, which had been previously occupied by Japan, were inclined to imitate their big neighbor's ways. They did so, however, with a substantial touch of local flavor, adding Chinese and Korean characteristics making their economies vastly different from that of Japan. The differentiation blossomed to the point where it would be insulting to assume, as some people do, that Taiwan and Korea have attempted to ape the Nippon model by simply reproducing what made Japan a success.

Hong Kong and Singapore are entirely different stories, both being former English colonies devoted largely to the promotion of the business interests of foreign firms. Relatively small cities,[2] they have long represented, by contrast to their immediate neighbors, islands of stability, wealth and relative comfort. They owe their success to the industriousness of their Chinese populations, who had little to learn from their masters. Little, indeed, except perhaps that a relatively fair legal system can attract offshore business, essentially in trade and financial services. A generous tax system and a dedicated, efficient and relatively clean civil service would also be required, but this was much easier to provide in city-states than it would have been in large multi-island countries.

The success story of the four Asian Tigers,[3] as they soon became known, is fascinating and would require several chapters. In short, however, it is important to notice that each of the four is unique and only shares some, but not all, of its strong points with the other Tigers. Various degrees of government interventionism, various shades of financial management, various types of industrial structures — all were combined in different cocktails to ensure the formidable success of the four economies. Whoever visited Seoul or Singapore 25 years ago will agree that this is nothing short of a miracle.

Situations change fast in Asia. In the early 1960s, two countries were outstanding examples of stability and growth. Ceylon (now Sri Lanka) was ahead of the pack in terms of stability and development, while the Philippines had the highest levels of education, good governance and remarkable growth indicators. Malaysia and Singapore at that time were sleepy backwaters. Back in the late 1950s, Rangoon (now Yangon), the capital of Burma (now Myanmar), had the busiest airport in South East Asia, essentially because Rangoon was the first substantial airport that could be reached, coming from Europe, after refueling stops in India. In the 1970s, Bangkok become more relevant as airplanes could fly longer, but it later started losing out to Hong Kong and Singapore as flight autonomy expanded. Asia was changing too fast for most of us.

Part of the success of Hong Kong and Singapore is due to the relative shortcomings of the other Asian countries, something to do with the fact that, in relative terms, they also were slightly ahead of the pack. The two city-states nurtured the very important service industries needed to manage the region's growth. Malaysia, Thailand, Indonesia and the Philippines — the main Association of South East Asian Nations (ASEAN) countries[4] — for various reasons, did not grow at the same speed. Thai shoe manufacturers, Malaysian shrimp farmers, Philippines breweries or Indonesian motorcycle distributors, all had difficulties in securing local financing and were turning to the financial know-how and resources of international banks located in the city-states. It is as if the two cities had been aircraft carriers in the midst of turbulent waters, offering Western firms the comfort and security they needed. In the early 1980s, foreign firms produced 85% of the goods manufactured in Singapore for export. Total assets of international banks in Hong Kong dwarfed that of local institutions.

Asians tend to be frugal, their savings rate being the highest in the world. They work hard, they believe in family values, Confucian respect for their elders and education. Those generalities are just that and the general view certainly conceals a vast spectrum of virtues. Obviously, in Asia as elsewhere, some people might be less industrious than others. It is just that they have different sets of values, mostly spiritual, which make them walk away from the over-materialistic environment found in some advanced Asian cities. Whatever the differences, there is no doubt that, by and large, Asia has, and is likely to maintain, a set of values now lost to — or perhaps never associated with — the Western world.

So What Went Wrong?

There were a combination of factors at play, but most people find it difficult to separate the factors leading up to the financial panic from those that are more fundamental. Let us make a clear distinction between the two sets. On the panic side, there were nervous lenders calling back their loans and nervous investors cutting down and then reversing the flow of funds. There were also Asian borrowers rushing to the exit, buying the dollar today because it was going to be cheaper than tomorrow, and a whole set of Asians betting against their own currencies. On the fundamental side, there was corruption, cronyism, malinvestment and rotten banking systems. The fundamental flaws deserved attention, and certainly each market was due for some correction. It is precisely the point made in this book: we are talking about a growth crisis. But I would suggest that it is the panic side that inflicted the heaviest damage. The transmission belts were the Asian currencies and the stock markets. Both fell beyond reason, in turn affecting the ability of borrowers to meet their obligations. This created a vicious circle of negative perception leading to further deterioration.

What made the crisis even worse was the poor handling of the matter by those in charge of the wide equilibrium, those with the big picture. This goes from stubborn bureaucracy in Thailand to a hesitant IMF stance, from poor political judgment in Malaysia to a state of denial in Korea and, in Indonesia, to a rush by first class passengers to save their wealth at the expense of the nation. Well thought of, well timed, limited and transparent remedies applied to each financial system would have spared Asia and the world the worst of the crisis, if not the whole crisis.

Why has Asia's set of values not protected the region from this crisis? What went wrong? What excesses, if any, associated with those values, have put an end to Asia's miracle? Is the miracle really over? A large number of commentators have made suggestions, and most of them are now largely shared.

So many comments have been made about the sources of the Asian crisis that it would perhaps be appropriate to enumerate and comment briefly on each of the perceived causes. Each reader will have his or her pick of which causes brought about which consequences. This book will lead the reader through that maze and suggest a possible thread.

Market Liberalization

The past 10 years have seen a global trend of internationalization based on the assumption that more trade will result in more wealth, and that the globalization of the economies will bring further economic efficiency. Such assumptions stem both from a resurgence of the relevance of Ricardo's Law and from the need to benefit from economies of scale. This essentially means that countries and economic agents must produce what they are naturally most capable of producing under the most attractive terms of trade (wine in Portugal, machine tools in Germany, shoes in China, etc.). Ideally, all markets are open in such a way that products are not restricted to markets too small for economic viability.

The liberalization of trade and the globalization of the economies would also imply a large degree of mobility for capital funds. In the name of efficiency, it is indeed preferable to allow investment and lending to find their most productive utilization, and that implies a reduction in barriers to the free circulation of funds.

Funds cannot find productive outlays unless fund providers are given the right to explore distant markets, and the liberalization of financial systems is a natural requirement. In short, countries that wanted to be part of the world's trade game became part of the world's financial scene. As a result, financial systems and, in particular, banking systems in many Asian countries started opening up to foreign funds. In a matter of 10 to 15 years, it has become easy for borrowers in most Asian countries to bypass the rigidities and limitations of domestic financial systems. The sheer size of money awaiting opportunities to partake in the phenomenal growth of Asia was vastly superior to what Asia could comfortably swallow. It is worth mentioning here that Asia's needs in terms of infrastructure would have been more than a match for such investment funds, but such funds were naturally chasing shorter-term and more rewarding opportunities, while Asian countries themselves mishandled their priorities. Think for a second what productive investment in infrastructure would have brought to Thailand if it had not been wasted on empty apartment buildings.

Asia was literally swamped with money. Here is a list (Table 1.1) of the exposure of Japan, Europe and the USA to the distressed Asian countries. Table 1.2 gives the exposure of individual banks. The amounts are so gigantic that it is little wonder some of them were directed at the wrong investment.

TABLE 1.1   EXPOSURE OF COUNTRIES TO SOUTH EAST ASIA (US$ BILLION) — DEC. 1997

Borrowers/lenders	France	Germany	Netherlands	UK	Japan	USA
Indonesia	4.8	5.6	2.8	4.3	23.2	4.6
Korea	10.1	10.8	2.8	6.0	23.7	10.0
Malaysia	2.9	5.7	1.0	2.0	10.5	2.4
Philippines	1.7	2.0	1.0	1.1	2.1	2.8
Thailand	5.1	7.6	1.6	2.8	37.7	4.0
Hong Kong	12.8	32.2	5.6	30.1	87.4	8.8
Singapore	15.4	38.4	8.7	25.2	65.0	5.2
Total — 7 countries	52.8	102.3	23.5	71.5	249.6	37.8

Source: IBRD

There have been suggestions that the major Western economies have forced financial liberalization on Asia with the aim of opening doors for their financial institutions. It would be ridiculous to talk about a conspiracy. One would be hard pressed to find signs of collusion. The British might want to hold on to their dominance in the field of colonial financial services. The Americans might believe that the undoubted benefits of open markets should apply indiscriminately to all countries, regardless of the maturity of their financial markets. The Europeans might have found investment opportunities in Asia comparatively better than what they have at home. But a vast conspiracy to pry open the Asian markets for the benefit of the West is a stretch. Such a claim smacks of cheap Third-worldism promoted by communist countries.

Malinvestment

The capital directed at Asia was never priced efficiently. This is a direct result of a number of rigidities and anomalies in capital and money markets. It was also the result of a huge oversupply of investment funds seeking to partake in Asia' s success. Capital was diverted from its most efficient uses. The foreign funds so easily obtained were directed at the wrong investments.

Markets in Asia are far from perfect. Many are still shallow and immature, with little correlation between risk and return. In a perfect market, the economic activities that are more rewarding than others for the same perceived risk would attract new entrepreneurs, introducing competitive pressures that would make those activities less rewarding. The adjustment would stop when the return is back to a normal level for that particular risk. This self-regulating model operates in mature economies, not in Asia.

Among the reasons why Asia is largely an imperfect market are the monopolies and oligopolies seen in most sectors. What comes immediately to mind is the cozy relationship between some politicians and their friends. But many other situations exist, where corruption is not necessarily a factor that limits competition and upsets the risk/reward balance. Hong Kong is supposedly Asia's most free market, but many important sectors like utilities, transportation and food supplies are oligopolistic.

Other factors are the lack of transparency, and inappropriate guidance by governments whose strategic or social ambitions are incompatible with market-led investment decisions. As explained below, access to cheap foreign currency funds has exacerbated the danger of directing funds to investments whose returns are not commensurate with domestic market expectations.

Foreign Currency Borrowing Under Managed Currencies

No one will deny that a relative stability in currency markets is beneficial. The whole concept of the European Union is largely based upon currency stability — the countries already are in a free-market zone — and European countries are preparing to give up some of their sovereignty in exchange for that stability. Asia is a dollar zone and Asian countries have tried to maintain their currencies around the American dollar. Some of Asia's problems would have been alleviated if currencies had been partly linked to the Japanese yen, the currency of a country that is both a substantial

TABLE 1.2   TOTAL EXPOSURE TO SOUTH EAST ASIA (US$ MILLIONS)

	Indonesia	Korea	Malaysia	Philippines	Thailand	Hong Kong	Singapore	Overall
France								
SocGen	936	3,185	325	304	1,613	5,710	3,800	17,189
CL	1,520	3,780	330	280	720	1,020	1,600	10,700
BNP	1,219	800	619	230	1,226	5,171	3,900	14,936
Indosuez	303	574	37	551	152	2,059	1,720	5,972
UE de CIC	429	(*)	204	144	243	158	980	2,176
CCF	18	(*)	(*)	(*)	(*)	216	(*)	234
United Kingdom								
Standard Chartered	1,683	1,386	3,357	(*)	972	(*)	(*)	(*)
RBS	969	325	60	239	500	305	208	2,662
NatWest	709	114	65	192	459	1,973	2,039	5,599
Barclays	360	190	140	(*)	204	1,071	1,271	3,576
HSBC Holdings	1,837	4,175	4,325	763	2,839	(*)	(*)	(*)
Schroders	131	(*)	37	(*)	331	499	2,039	3,038
Switzerland								
UBS	590	1,421	124	139	109	2,571	2,844	9,075
CSG	936	838	206	(*)	371	3,113	2,225	7,690
SBC	159	933	(*)	101	203	1,525	1,874	4,796
Italy								
BCI	104	228	115	(*)	194	1,639	(*)	2,279
Credito Italiano	7	(*)	(*)	(*)	(*)	287	(*)	318
Netherlands								
ING	907	748	109	671	671	812	1,859	5,995
ABN Amro	524	1,189	241	339	701	3,109	5,006	12,194
Rabobank	532	(*)	351	29	159	775	143	2,067

TABLE 1.2 Continued

	Indonesia	Korea	Malaysia	Philippines	Thailand	Hong Kong	Singapore	Overall
Germany								
Dresdner	980	1,993	276	618	872	2,706	3,072	10,764
Bay LB	204	1,775	805	72	2,045	2,519	6,039	13,628
Commerz	1,351	1,689	549	62	616	2,336	3,231	10,067
WestLB	708	2,185	114	199	735	6,062	2,145	13,081
Deutsche	1,192	731	295	359	641	4,830	6,781	15,988
Bay Vereins	560	541	54	77	542	995	1,934	4,703
NordLB	194	622	104	24	527	133	1,112	2,717
Bankgesellshaft	(*)	61	(*)	(*)	(*)	(*)	(*)	61
BHF	(*)	(*)	(*)	(*)	23	550	238	811
USA								
Chase Manhattan	2,500	5,400	900	800	1,900	(*)	(*)	(*)
JP Morgan	813	3,462	374	316	1,161	(*)	(*)	(*)
Bank of America	684	2,838	532	601	881	(*)	(*)	(*)
Citicorp	800	2,800	800	300	400	(*)	(*)	(*)
Singapore								
United Overseas Bank	654	109	5,082	63	244	(*)	(*)	(*)
Oversea-Chinese Bnkg Corp.	758	253	4,550	38	506	(*)	(*)	(*)
Japan								
Bank of Tokyo/Mitsubishi	3,683	3,836	2,537	520	5,902	(*)	(*)	(*)

(*) Data unavailable

Source: South China Morning Post *"Banks fear collapse in Indonesia", Barry Porter and Greg Torode, May 21, 1998.*
"European Banks and Asian Risk", Paribas, Nov. 12, 1997.

buyer of Asian products and a substantial supplier to the whole region. Even so, few transactions are expressed in yen, but this is another problem.

Asian countries attach their currencies to the dollar, while opening their doors to foreign exchange financing. This is the root of the devastating consequences of currency adjustments on domestic balance sheets. But more importantly perhaps, it has created opportunities for wrong investment decisions.

To understand why this happened, one should go back to the very basic nature of money lending. A money lender will lend money at, say, 10% interest[5] if the borrower can show that he will use the funds in whatever venture he or she is involved in, and obtain more than a 10% return while preserving the principal. Admittedly, this is an oversimplification, as often inflation may result in a capital gain on the principal, mitigating the need for a high return: for example property investors can come out winners even though rental returns are lower than funding costs, as long as property prices rise. But in a perfect inflation-free market, the money lender's basic stance must remain. Any other approach should be tagged as pawnshop lending, whereby the lender does not pay attention to the destination of the funds he is parting with, as long as he is keeping enough security or collateral to meet both principal and interest.

In normal circumstances there is a complex relationship between inflation, interest rates and expected return on investment. In such circumstances,[6] when interest rates are in the vicinity of say, 15% — the hurdle rate — any investment yielding less than the hurdle rate would be rejected as economically unreasonable: it would be tantamount to wealth destruction. In any country, assuming a borrower can normally obtain a local currency loan at an interest rate of 15%, it would be economically unreasonable to allow him to apply for a loan expressed in US dollars. The borrower would pay only 10% for his loan and would use the funds locally after changing the dollars for the local currency. It is unreasonable because the temptation would be to invest in local projects yielding between 10% and 15%, that is below the hurdle rate. Such projects should normally be rejected. They do not pass the hurdle rate test. In theory, they are destroying wealth.

This is exactly what had been happening for years in several Asian countries, especially in Thailand and Indonesia. Borrowers should have factored in a devaluation risk premium when selecting investments. The investment yield should have been higher in order to meet the hurdle rate. Roughly speaking, the devaluation risk premium is equal to the interest rate differential between the two currencies. The relationship is more complicated than that,[7] but, as an indication, the difference of 5% between interest rates should be put aside as a provision against the expected or potential devaluation of the currency. There are all sorts of variations around the same theme. Intuitively, one should sense that, by playing with yield curves, with the availability of funds and with the actual pricing of various types of loans, it is possible for a borrower to minimize his costs by surfing on the many options open to him. In perfect markets, though, there is little to gain or lose. What the borrower saves in interest costs is lost in currency devaluation adjustments.

In reality, the markets are not perfect, and this imperfection has endured in

Positive or Negative Carry
Under Fixed Currency Rates

Under a quasi-fixed currency regime, the currency is either closely pegged to the dollar, or it is managed, meaning it is maintained within a close distance of a fixed rate, like in Thailand taken here as an example. With some adjustments, one can analyze in a similar way the currencies managed within a controlled descending or ascending pattern. The assumption here is that the currency does not fluctuate and that the interest rate on the currency is higher than the dollar interest rate. Since there is no danger of the local currency devaluing against the dollar, it would be a safe bet to borrow dollars and exchange them for the local currency. The local currency is placed or invested until maturity, when the proceeds are exchanged back to dollars at the same exchange rate. As long as the interest received on the placement is higher than the interest paid on the funding, it is an attractive transaction. The investor enjoys a "positive carry": as long as he carries his foreign exchange position, he will receive more interest than he would if he did not hold that position, while he runs almost no foreign exchange risk.

If the currency is not fixed, but moves in a predictable, deteriorating pattern, like in Indonesia, the same reasoning holds true, except that some of the positive carry is lost to the devaluation of the currency during the period. If the deterioration is predictable, such a loss can be factored in and the transaction can still be attractive.

This is largely a zero-sum game, and the investor's positive carry is mirrored by someone else's "negative carry". In this particular case, the negative carry is a loss to the central bank. Indeed, the dollars sold by the investor eventually end up in the books of the central bank, which will deliver bahts against them. It prints a fresh supply of bahts. The bahts can be invested in securities or deposits, or sunk into local projects. In any event, this inflates the money supply which, one way or another, must be mopped up if inflation is to be contained. Another reason why it must be mopped up is that a baht surplus will lower local interest rates, rendering investment in Thailand less attractive. Therefore the central bank issues bonds or similar instruments to absorb the baht, and this is called "sterilization". The bonds carry the baht interest rate, paid by the central bank. The dollars are placed by the central bank in dollar capital markets. At the end of the line, the central bank has liabilities in baht at a high interest rate and corresponding assets in dollars at a lower interest rate. This is a negative carry, which is paid for by the Thai taxpayer.

Incidentally, the negative carry suffered by a central bank is the price to pay for trying to control both the exchange rate and the interest rate.

Macroeconomic theories show that the price can indeed be very high. It is wiser to attempt to control either the exchange rate or the interest rate, but not both. If the exchange rate is fixed or controlled, the central bank must accept that the interest rate will fluctuate according to market forces and, predominantly, as a function of monetary policies followed by the country whose currency serves as an anchor. This is typical of pegs and currency boards. If, to the contrary, a central bank wishes to have full control on interest rates, money supply and other monetary policy matters, it must not attempt to control the value of the currency. These are two extremes and many countries will find themselves settling in between.

When the currency is controlled and domestic firms borrow foreign currency for unhedged local investment, wealth is transferred from taxpayers to arbitrageurs. Why would central banks wish to maintain such a situation? Basically to maintain a steady flow of funds into the country. If an investment in Thailand brings a 15% return in baht, with no danger of a currency adjustment for the holder of dollars who otherwise would be looking at a return of 10% elsewhere, the investor will be tempted to bring his dollars to Thailand. Developing countries need capital and they need liquidity. With the kind of growth seen in Thailand in the past 10 years, local capital markets have not been able to supply the high levels of funds needed for expansion. Foreign funds have been welcome. Here is another reason: the system as described appears to increase the foreign reserves of the country. Granted, total debt also increases, but the increment is sterilized and buried in the books of the central bank, ready for use, should the need arise.

Who were those arbitrageurs who benefited from the positive carry? They were primarily the investors, both foreign and domestic. Statistics show that mostly local investors have benefited from the system. Other beneficiaries were the banks, both foreign and domestic. If domestic Thai borrowers get dollars instead of baht, their interest savings are huge. There is a natural temptation for the banks to ask the borrowers to let them share the spoils with them, and spreads are wider. This gives banks a better return on their assets in dollars. It could be argued that they were running higher risks as the crisis eventually demonstrated, but the banks usually would not perceive the risk to be higher on account of the currency switch. They were just enjoying the windfall.

some Asian countries for quite some time. There is a vicious circle linked to managed currencies when there is little or no control on capital flows across the borders. As a result, central banks end up subsidizing the wrong kind of investment. There are numerous differences between currency boards, pegs and managed currencies, but they all bring about similar imperfections when domestic borrowers are allowed to access foreign funding.

Market Rigidities

Government Intervention

With the exception of Hong Kong, to a degree, all Asian countries suffer from too much government. Taxes are not necessarily high, nor are they imposed on a broad spectrum of potential contributors. Governments remain frugal, even in military expenses, but the state has its word to say in many industrial, commercial and financial decisions. Banking systems are largely in the hands of state-owned or state-controlled institutions. The Hong Kong case is special, but not very different conceptually. HongKongBank has long controlled almost 50% of all deposits placed in locally incorporated banks. Prior to July 1997, HongKongBank was actually running Hong Kong. Forget about the Queen and her Governor: they had little say in running the colony. Even the Jockey Club had more influence than the Governor in what made Hong Kong tick. Hong Kong was in the hands of HongKongBank, and so was the banking system, which therefore was hardly free from the interference of that particular brand of government. In Taiwan, Indonesia, China and Korea, many of the major banks are controlled by the state, while some of the major names in Malaysia, the Philippines and Thailand also fall into that category.

Governments are in a position to dictate their terms to the financial institutions and to direct — or more often than not, to misdirect — investments to the wrong beneficiaries. This misallocation of funds finds its sources in corruption, nepotism, cronyism or, often, in simple mismanagement. For the same reasons, Asia is suffering from a sickness still only partly eradicated in the West: if a firm is not doing well, creative ways will be found to keep it alive. The notion of cutting off a finger to save an arm is totally at odds with the Asian mentality. Witness the convoluted company structure typically found in Malaysia or in Korea. Cross-guarantees, cross-shareholdings, mergers: there is a heavy arsenal of tools that make it possible to avoid liquidating an ailing venture.

When Failure Hits

Not surprisingly, few Asian countries have elaborate bankruptcy laws and in countries that do have them, there are so many obstacles in enforcing them that they are simply not used. In the whole of Indonesia, it looks like only a total of 13 cases[8] went to court in the four years prior to the crisis. It is simply not feasible, nor worth the time and money. Cases drag for years. The taxis and buses bought by Steady Safe, the Indonesian firm that allegedly brought down Peregrine, will be rusting after years on the road when the Peregrine liquidators — or more likely their descendants — eventually get the case to local courts. The chairman of an Indian bank once cut short a meeting with Thomson BankWatch analysts, as he had to rush off to court to testify in a case involving a delinquent loan of a relatively modest few million rupees. Asked why such a senior person had to appear in court on such a modest matter, he replied that he was the officer-in-charge when the loan was granted and when it went sour. How long ago did that take place? Twenty-three years before!

Lenders prefer to negotiate with borrowers. At the end of the day, it saves time, money and, more importantly, face. Saving face is one of the most important rules in Asia, widely misunderstood by non-Asians. Once a failed ice-cream manufacturer was chauffeured to the Hong Kong airport in the Jaguar of a European bank manager: an elegant exile to Taiwan was the only hope the bank had to see the delinquent borrower come up with part of the amount he owed. In another famous case, the Abalone King who fled Singapore for Taiwan leaving millions in debt behind him, had the elegance of writing to his many creditors — none of them knew that their ranks were swelled — to apologize for the inconvenience. By now, he may very well be back in business with the same banks.

People

Labor markets are relatively free in some countries like Hong Kong, much too free perhaps, as that freedom brings with it a lack of social protection. At the other extreme, labor laws were so rigid in Korea that, until very recently, companies had absolutely no flexibility in managing their labor needs. Korea had indeed copied from Japan, pushing the concept to extremes and effectively preventing the country from making any adjustment.

Asians rightly perceive education to be a very important factor of development: families are prepare to devote a high proportion of their income to ensure their children are educated. This has produced some of the highest literacy ratios in emerging economies, even before the various countries had reached a level of wealth generally associated with high levels of education. Yet the general view obscures the fact that there are huge disparities in the region, and that the allocation of resources has often been inefficient. Education is sometimes highly elitist, like in Japan. It is at times skewed in favor of universities, at the expense of a broad based education of the masses, like in Thailand. Asians tend to favor learning by rote, as opposed to — if one can accept this oversimplification — the Western-style thorough research and critical thinking. Worse yet, higher education in a place like Hong Kong is more expensive — in this particular case to the taxpayer, not the student — than in the best US universities, as a result of a number of inefficiencies.

The Business/Bank/Politicians Triangle

Collusion between big business and politics is a fact of life. In Asia, the equation is more elaborate in that banks, when they do not belong outright to governments, are usually in the hands of either big businesses or politicians or both. In most cases, any idea that banks operate at arm's length in Asia should be shelved, as it would be very naïve and contrary to what we know about Asian credit culture.

Money lenders in Asia do not lend on the strength of a project or a balance sheet, but rather on the basis of who the borrower is and what collateral is offered. Keeping that in mind, it is not surprising to see the close relationship between banks, state and the major companies.

In some countries, banks, the government and major companies also happen to be in the hands of the same people. This fact is usually not disclosed in financial statements in Asia, because most people use nominees to register ownership and because the typical family group is not structured as a holding company. It is generally structured as a complicated web of affiliates and associated companies. In the few situations where groups do publish detailed company structures, the result is a spaghetti-like magma; it is often impossible to figure out who is behind which company in what consolidated proportion.

One of former Indonesian president Suharto's sons received a license to operate a regional airline. He no doubt benefited from the deal, but so did some distant cities in the archipelago. Phone companies, toll roads, power generation firms and generally every economic activity that involves massive investment and long-term operating deals is beyond the reach of the average citizen. Asian governments cannot afford the expense and are happy to offer the deal to others. It is inevitable that those other people happen to be close to the regime. The terms of the deals are invariably too generous to them: how else would they agree to the terms? From deal to deal, the divide widens between the prosperous few and the masses.

Is collusion a bad thing? It is conceptually undignified. It leads to excesses, it produces the likes of Mobutu and Marcos. But at the same time, when collusion remains within decent bounds, the system hastens development and, on the whole, economies prosper. A huge transfer of wealth passes from the many to the few, but the system promotes development and creates wealth at such a pace that the whole nation benefits. In those matters, the difficulty is for governments to maintain a decent balance between good and evil. Stretching this a bit, one would conclude that countries where there is a respect for rules and consensus — countries where people sit and think — are doing poorly compared with countries where people bend the rules to get things done. India versus China, perhaps. This is probably going too far, but the reader will sense that, as horrendous as collusion might look, it is often just skimming away the cream, leaving in its stride more development than if it did not take place.

Size and Structure of Financial Systems

Asian firms borrow too much. Financial intermediation is too high in Asia. Asia built its economies on shifting sand and growth was too high. In the world of construction, we know that the lower layers must dry before we can add higher layers. Asia did not allow the consolidation — the digestion perhaps — of its first stages of development without rushing to further expansion.

Asia is a world of high debt for corporations, as they have not been able to mobilize equity or quasi-equity funds in sufficient amounts to sustain their growth. Gearing ratios, the measure of debt against equity, are extraordinarily high, particularly in Korea and Thailand. Overall, they are much higher than in more mature Western economies.

Not enough of the huge savings generated in Asia end up as captive investments in the economies. Most of those savings have sought the relatively safe protection of bank deposits, while companies struggle to mobilize stable equity funds. Most stock markets in the region have acquired the reputation of casinos, essentially because companies operate with limited transparency, because the markets are relatively small and therefore subject to unnatural amplitudes, and because they are manipulated. Not surprisingly, such stock markets have at once attracted investors not averse to risk — Asians love gambling — and repelled the majority of households seeking safe investments. Social protection in the shape of retirement funds, whether private or state-run, is still pretty basic, forcing households to sterilize a great proportion of their savings in plain-vanilla investments. In most circumstances, this means bank deposits. Table 1.3 illustrates the high deposit growth of recent years.

TABLE 1.3 TOTAL DEPOSIT GROWTH RATE: AVERAGE OF DOMESTIC COMMERCIAL BANKS

	1991	1992	1993	1994	1995	1996
Indonesia — State Banks	1.40	5.62	8.75	5.01	6.41	15.76
Indonesia — Private Banks	23.74	21.74	24.43	29.05	30.88	35.32
Malaysia	27.47	14.88	25.61	19.09	29.51	25.70
Philippines	15.26	16.55	34.34	23.32	19.96	23.32
Thailand	19.53	16.16	19.44	16.18	15.00	12.74
South Korea — Nationwide Banks	N/A	8.79	25.29	27.18	21.29	10.04
South Korea — Specialized Banks	31.74	12.30	79.76	26.53	33.99	10.84
South Korea — Provincial Banks	N/A	8.47	68.80	22.60	28.06	15.13
South Korea — Old Merchant Banks	N/A	N/A	37.71	31.23	37.31	39.98

Source: Annual Reports

Banks are increasingly flush with deposits that they must use in the most efficient way. Companies are begging for funds to sustain their growth, and gearing ratios increase. Asian governments run a tight ship and they seldom borrow from their citizens. They may do so in subtle ways: for example, India commandeers large "reserve funds" from banks and China finances subsidies to state-owned enterprises with huge bad loans funded by small depositors. But, by and large, there are very few safe outlets for savings outside of the banking systems.[9]

Bank loans are, by definition, much less stable than any other kind of financing. Highly geared corporations are extremely vulnerable to changes in the cost and availability of funds. Whether the shock is external, like a change of the risk perception in the eyes of foreign lenders, or internal, like a credit crunch brought about by economic uncertainties or a change in the interest rate structure, corporations are squeezed. The sudden lack of liquidity in the market or the excessive cost of funding can destroy a balance sheet in no time. In fact, the lack of liquidity has been a major factor in Asia's corporate failures in recent months, ahead of strict insolvency problems. Too many economic agents have become dependent on the maintenance of a flow of cash that they did not control: the uninterrupted availability of bank loans and the liquidity of commercial counterparts.

High savings fed into a deficient financial structure make that structure eminently unstable. Any attempt at liberalizing the structure is likely to exacerbate that instability. In the case of Asia, it is not at all established that the benefits of liberalization in terms of efficiency would outweigh the increased instability.

Many Asian banking systems are very small, so small in fact as to be too fragile yet to sustain external shocks. One of the major problems for external observers is the lack of a clear perception of what Asia looks like, its geography, the diversity of its culture and, more technically, what constitutes the banking systems. We all accept that it is difficult to figure out the geography of Asia, with such a large number of nations and the unusual shape of some countries. Some people in the West still think that Hong Kong is in Japan and Singapore is in China. Who knows that China shares a border with Afghanistan, but that Thailand and Vietnam have no common border? Who knows that Jakarta, clearly located some distance to the south-east of Kuala Lumpur, sets its clocks one hour behind of it instead of one hour ahead? Who knows that, from many buildings in Singapore, one can see both Indonesia and Malaysia and that, from downtown Macau, one can wave a hand to a friend in China? Who knows that, at some points, Myanmar and Thailand are less than 30 kilometers wide? Who knows that, for each Singapore citizen, there are 44 Pakistanis, 20 Thais or 15 South Koreans? Who knows what is the relative size of the various Asian economies (Table 1.4)?

The size of the banking systems is usually not very clearly perceived. Admittedly, it is difficult to compare sizes when, in some countries, most of the banking functions lie in the hands of commercial banks, while in other countries there are numerous, if small, non-bank financial institutions. There are about 45,000 finance companies in India,[10] but the largest 100 account for 85% of that category's assets. The average size varies considerably across the region. The 15 Thai commercial banks have together as much in total assets as the more than 200 commercial banks in Indonesia.

TABLE 1.4   1996 GDP (US$ BILLIONS)

	GDP
Japan	4,337.9
China	797.6
South Korea	480.2
India	334.5
Taiwan	273.3
Indonesia	227.3
Thailand	185.0
Hong Kong	157.8
Malaysia	94.4
Singapore	92.8
Philippines	83.8

Source: Capital Information Services

Inside the countries, the distribution of assets among the commercial banks varies widely. In Hong Kong, Malaysia and the private sector of Indonesia, just a few banks — sometimes only one — cover over 25% of total assets. In Korea, Thailand and Singapore, the top is less heavy. Using more sophisticated tools would give better results, for example the Gini coefficient or the tools developed by Herfindhal. But a simple table with the proportion of commercial banks needed to command respectively 25%, 50% and 75% of total assets or total equity gives a pretty good idea about the distribution.

Looking at the commercial banking sector in Table 1.5, and concentrating on local banks only, one would be surprised at some figures[11]. The figures discussed here were those posted at the end of 1996, and not the end of 1997, as the year 1997 saw a number of changes — in particular, in exchange rates — that have yet to stabilize.

Roughly speaking, the local commercial banking systems stacked up in a surprising way for the uninitiated. In terms of commercial bank assets, India, Thailand and Indonesia were each of roughly similar sizes, slightly ahead of Malaysia and Singapore. The entire banking system of the Philippines was not bigger than the single DBS Bank of Singapore. Yet Singapore is tiny, and one would have to add up Singapore and Malaysia to reach the size of Hong Kong. In turn, Taiwan is as big as Hong Kong, Singapore and Malaysia together. All four of their commercial banking assets together were barely larger than Korea alone, which was only about 70% of the size of China. And the Chinese commercial banking system, in the vicinity of US$1,300 billion, had about the combined size of the world's largest two banks.[12]

This is a small pond, and it is easy to understand how financial liberalization and the opening up of local financial systems to the world was likely to bring about waves that were disproportionate to Asia's market size. This is at least one fact that the world should not dispute Dr Mahathir, Malaysia's Prime Minister who has expressed strong views on this topic (see Chapter 7).

TABLE 1.5 COMMERCIAL BANKS SIZE DISTRIBUTION

	Total assets			Total equity		
	25%	50%	75%	25%	50%	75%
Taiwan	8	21	46	8	24	48
Indonesia — State Banks	29	43	71	14	43	71
Indonesia — Private Banks	6	13	32	6	16	35
South Korea — Nationwide Banks	13	33	47	13	33	47
South Korea — Specialized Banks	13	25	50	13	38	50
South Korea — Provincial Banks	20	30	60	20	40	60
Malaysia	5	14	36	9	18	45
Philippines	8	19	38	12	23	42
Thailand	13	20	40	7	20	40
Hong Kong	4	14	39	4	11	36
Singapore	18	36	45	9	27	36

Note: Table shows what proportion of total number of banks is controlling a minimum of 25%, 50% or 75% of total assets or equity. Banks with less than 0.5% of the system's total assets are disregarded.
Source: Annual Reports

   Foreign banks play an important role in several countries and they are treated in a variety of ways, for reasons linked to history, nationalistic ideas and trade pattern. Both Hong Kong and Singapore harbor countless international names, albeit with some restrictions, legal or practical, in respect of domestic banking. As a result of its colonial past, Malaysia has long suffered from the overwhelming presence of foreign banks and, in 1994, took the drastic decision of forcing them to incorporate locally. For years, the Philippines froze the development of its handful of foreign banks, until 1996 when it invited foreign names to take up to 60% in local institutions, while also opening up the market to foreign bank branches. Alongside nationalized local banks, the sub-continent has always tolerated some private banks and some foreign banks, but their role is pretty limited. In Indonesia, foreign banks are restricted to small branches or representative offices, and to small joint ventures with local names. Thailand kept its doors close for years, until 1996 when foreign banks, especially those which had established offshore units,[13] were invited to apply for a local license. China strictly restricts the scope of activities of foreign banks, as befits a country operating under socialist standards. Korea and Japan, for cultural reasons, will always make it difficult for foreigners to operate domestically, even under circumstances where the markets become ostensibly open.

Which Cause is Relevant?

We have an Asian crisis and an Asian panic. These are two different stories. The crisis was inevitable and probably beneficial. The panic was an epiphenomenon that we should have avoided.

Currency and equity markets reacted wildly. Unmatched supply and demand act on prices, pushing them up or down to a point of equilibrium. There is no strict relationship between the depth of imbalance and the resulting price adjustment. Sometimes relatively small gaps between supply and demand result in substantial price adjustments. The erratic behavior of some market participants has made it much worse.

Aristotle was the first philosopher to study the various types of causes and the relationship with their supposed consequences.[14] While his suggestions have been reshaped over the years by, among others, Leconte and Malebranche, he certainly established some basis for the distinction between the various sources of events. He made a distinction between four types of causes. Although more modern approaches have improved on his thoughts, he is there to remind us about a few principles of causality.

In the contemporary tale of a woman run over by a bus, we might say that, had the poor woman stayed in bed that morning, she would not be dead by now. But if that bus had been slightly behind schedule, she might equally still be alive. We all agree that those two pre-existing conditions — getting up in the morning and the bus not running late — had to be established for the woman's death. Yet it would be difficult to blame the accident on either of the two conditions, even as a contributing factor. After all, the poor woman could have died of a heart attack on that same day or been run over by a truck. This simple example illustrates the difficulty of apportioning the blame between the various pre-existing conditions. The matter is made more complicated by the realization that, usually, several causes contribute to a single result, and that one fact can induce a combination of different results.

The Asian crisis and the Asian panic would not have taken place had not a string of concomitant circumstances been present at the right time. It is hard to state that a single cause could have been at the same time necessary (it should be there) and sufficient (no other cause is needed). The only conclusive test for a possible contributive cause should perhaps be the following: would the crisis and the panic have taken place had that cause not pre-existed? And was there any other cause needed? One should submit all the causes to those two tests.

There is no doubt that market liberalization was a contributing factor to the Asian situation. The flow of financial funds in search of lending opportunities has grown over the years. Those Asian countries where the flows could easily enter and as easily disappear opened themselves to difficulties. But this cause was not necessary. For example, the Korean and Indonesian banking systems needed no such help to go wrong. Banks simply lent too much to the wrong borrowers.

Malinvestment was certainly a contributing factor in most countries, less so perhaps in the Philippines and in Indonesia. Surely, without it, non-performing loans would have been modest. Yet, malinvestment did not take place in Indonesia and the Philippines beyond dangerous limits.

Over-borrowing in foreign currencies was a decisive factor, at least in Korea, Thailand and Indonesia. Thailand clearly suffered the most because the rigidity of its currency management encouraged malinvestment. This was certainly a sufficient factor for Thailand's crisis, and definitely a necessary factor in the regional panic. But there is nothing fundamentally wrong in complementing high savings ratios with foreign borrowing when financing growth.

Collusion, corruption, cronyism, nepotism and favoritism: all contribute to divert some of the fruits of development from the masses to the privileged. Used with moderation, those can hardly lead to a crisis or a panic.

Market rigidities and deficiencies in the structure of the financial systems are a strong factor in the crisis, less so in the panic. We said that greed and incompetence created weak banking systems. But they received help from directed lending, poor commercial laws and an appalling regulatory environment. Without such shortcomings, greed and incompetence would only have hurt individual lenders, not a whole region.

What are we left with? The panic that started in Bangkok on July 2, 1997 had more to do with sentiment than with fundamentals. It fed on itself to engulf the whole region. It triggered a number of investment decisions, both from the region and from the rest of the world, which resulted in a credit crunch. The fire fed on weak financial systems that were about to face a crisis, very serious in Korea and Thailand, less so in Malaysia and Indonesia, and probably mild in the Philippines.

In short, we should blame the crisis on some factors, essentially the weak financial systems, and the panic on other factors – mostly the over-borrowing in US dollars. There is nothing wrong with Asian values. The miracle is not over yet.

Endnotes

1. An amah is the traditional word for a Chinese maid. The word was extended to maids of any nationality. Amahs and taxi drivers usually, but not always, enter the market when it is close to its peak.
2. Asia has a large number of very large cities. There are cities in Asia, bigger than Sydney, Berlin or Washington, whose names are unknown to most Westerners. With 6 million residents in its entire territory, Hong Kong only has half the population of Jakarta or Shanghai.
3. The four Asian Tigers are Korea, Taiwan, Hong Kong and Singapore, Asia's more advanced countries outside of Japan. They are also called "newly industrialized countries" or NICs, but that definition can apply to several other Asian countries.

4. The original group of South East Asian countries only included Thailand, the Philippines, Indonesia, Singapore, Brunei and Malaysia. The recent inclusion of Vietnam and the discussion in respect of other countries might very well result in a diluted version of the association, very much like the European Union, if left unchecked would soon include Afghanistan, Sudan and Uruguay.

5. For the sake of simplicity, we shall assume interest rates to be the three-month rates, as many corporate loans are granted on that basis. Naturally, if another period were selected, since each currency exhibits a specific –and changing- yield curve, slightly different comparisons would result, but this would not affect the reasoning.

6. In each market and each currency, there is an established range of market return expectations that is influenced by factors such as inflation, risk perception, the interest rate structure, government borrowing needs etc… It is only a coincidence if the hurdle rate is the same in two different currencies, unless the currencies or the economies are linked in some way.

7. The comparison between interest rates will point to different conclusions according to the time horizon selected.

8. This relates to bankruptcy cases stricto sensu.

9. Small depositors in fact have very few options to park their funds, simply because commercial banks and finance companies are, literally, the only game in town.

10. Many Indian finance companies collapsed and disappeared in 1997 and 1998.

11. Cutting off the very small names eliminates freak ratios when the number of observations in the sample is a factor.

12. It should be clarified again that we are talking about domestic commercial banks, as opposed to foreign banks or domestic non-commercial banks like merchant banks, leasing companies or finance companies.

13. See the chapter on Thailand for an explanation on the Bangkok International Banking Facilities.

14. In his "Metaphysics".

CRIME AND PUNISHMENT

To many in France, cheating the state by escaping payment for a ride on a state-owned subway is as natural as walking freely in a public park. Before class distinctions in the Paris Metro were abolished by the socialists after 1981, fines for those caught without a ticket were almost the same whether they were caught travelling in first class or in second class cars. As a result, first class cars were often full of cheaters while fare-paying passengers had to ride in second class. As long as the risk remains the same, why not increase the reward? Why not travel in style?

In an ideal world, ethics and morality expressed through the conscience of each individual intervenes. But in the world of economic humans, each actor weighs his or her risks and rewards. Human nature seldom changes, and not all are righteous. "Moral hazard" in the original sense of the words refers to the risk that when an individual is insured against outside risks, or perceives himself to be insured, constraints of morality, ethics or self-preservation that would otherwise restrain him from increasing that risk, are paradoxically eroded by the assurance of return without risk. Unsurprisingly, this phenomenon first had to be addressed in the context of the insurance business, although as a result of the increasing importance of deposit insurance, both express and implicit, the concept has become closely associated with the banking industry.

Moral Hazard

To understand how moral hazard affects banks, it helps to understand its effects in the property or casualty insurance contest. Traditional insurance arose to cover accidental hazards where loss is both unanticipated and unintended. Although random and catastrophic to anyone insured, such losses are predictable in the aggregate. The number of automobile accidents, fires, deaths, and other catastrophic events that will occur on average in large populations over a period of time is predictable. From the insurer's perspective, such losses are both expected and calculable within specified parameters. Usually insurers avoid insuring against events which are more likely to occur at the same time. Since fires spread easily, it would not be good practice for an insurer to provide coverage against all the houses in a single neighborhood.

Prior to the establishment of central banks as lenders of last resort, deposit insurance was essentially non-existent. Rather than keeping their savings under the mattress, potential depositors had to be persuaded of the strength and security of banking institutions. Since in the early days of banking, disclosure hardly existed and more small savers would not have been in a position to assess an institution's strength even if it had, banks built imposing edifices and cultivated a reputation for frugality and respectability.

But as the financial crises of the late 19th and early 20th centuries demonstrated, within a fractional reserve banking system, even a well-capitalized and relatively liquid bank could not withstand a run engendered by a financial panic. The Great Depression of the 1930s brought home the need for a high-level of bank regulation and insurance in many industrialized nations, and many governments during this period initiated deposit insurance.

The rationale for the government facilitating deposit insurance was that confidence in the banking regime was essential to economic growth, and that in a well-supervised financial system bank failures are infrequent, predictable and largely preventable events. Social equity also came into play. Protecting small savers against the irresponsibility of the bankers in whom they had put their trust came to be seen as only fair and just. With the central bank functioning as the lender of last resort, providing liquidity when needed, bank runs were ostensibly banished to the history books. In such an environment, banks could operate consistently and reliably to supply appropriate amounts of credit to a healthy economy.

Unfortunately, in practice, the prerequisites for a smoothly functioning deposit insurance system are rarely present. The banking and business cycles have not been banished. Consequently, bank failures are usually not random, but linked closely to the prevailing economic climate. Rather like houses in the same neighborhood, banks are vulnerable to the effects of contagion, with liquidity shortages affecting many financial institutions at the same time, as the recent Asian crisis has so clearly demonstrated.

The dangers are exacerbated by moral hazard. In the ordinary insurance context, moral hazard covers a multitude of sins, ranging from the criminal to the merely unethical. At one extreme is the automobile driver who fakes or even causes an accident to recover from an insurer; at the other, the vehicle owner, who fails to lock her car or maintain it, secure in the knowledge that in the event of theft or collision, she will recover her loss, or most of it. Indeed, the deductible limits common in many insurance policies reflect an attempt to reduce moral hazard.

Moral hazard includes, but does not imply, insurance fraud. The building owner who fails to install fire prevention equipment, the insured who employs an arsonist to torch an unprofitable business, the homeowner who negligently smokes in bed represent various facets of moral hazard. While the resulting consequences may not always be entirely under their control, the thread running through all these illustrations is that the insured's behavior will have an impact on loss and recovery upon the insurance contract.

In the banking context, the risk and impact of moral hazard is particularly pronounced. In the case of an explicit deposit insurance scheme, such as applied to United States savings and loans until the 1980s, the danger was not fraudulent behavior on the part of depositors and bankers (although significant amounts of fraud did occur), but instead a stimulation of the appetite for risk. As Gary Stern, President of the Federal Reserve Bank of Minneapolis succinctly put it, "once a person or institution is insured, the insured has an incentive to take on more risk than otherwise." Since in the financial industry, more risk usually equates with greater return, the incentive is all the greater. Exacerbating the tendency even further is the fact that traditionally, deposit insurance schemes provided 100% coverage, without deductibles, up to a certain limit. The US$100 billion bailout that the savings and loan debacle of the 1980s necessitated is apt testimony to the dangers of moral hazard.

Of course, it is not only depositors who are subject to moral hazard. Indeed, in Asia, deposit insurance is the exception rather than the rule, and a more insidious form of moral hazard has arisen. This is the moral hazard to which a bank's shareholders are given, when they are implicitly insured against bad credit decisions. Such implicit insurance typically comes in the form of express or unspoken government support for local banks — or in the case of the IMF for international institutions — that pose the threat to prudent bank management. It is not necessary for banks to cheat by circumventing laws and regulations, like the freeriding Paris Metro passengers, though in Asia such behavior has not been uncommon. The Korean banks who bought Indonesian junk bonds or lent to insolvent Chaebol[1] in the belief that the government would always be there to back them up are the more typical and tragic manifestation of the phenomenon.

It was generally accepted before the crisis that most banks would be rescued if they ran into trouble. Banks "too big to fail" or "too small to fail" have been the beneficiaries of this free insurance plan. The bank that is too big to fail is one whose demise is likely to create social and economic chaos. Arguably, Thailand, where a relatively small number of banking institutions exist (in contrast to their weaker brethren, the finance companies), had a fair number of banks in this category. But even in countries where the number of institutions is larger, there are usually a few dominant institutions safe in the knowledge that their existence is believed to be essential to the economic health of the countries in which they are situated; or perhaps more accurately, that their demise would bring economic disaster.

The bank that is too small to fail is less well-known but nonetheless real. This is the institution whose failure would cause a loss of face even though it may not create a disaster. Since the cost of rehabilitation is minimal, when such small institutions are threatened, regulators often prefer to bail them out than have to explain any defects in the banking system that may have contributed to their exiting from the scene. In short, a bank is deemed too small to fail if a rescue package is likely to cost so little that it would be seen as a small price to pay to maintain stability.

Whether too large or too small, armed with the knowledge that, in the balance of probabilities, they will be rescued, bank shareholders know that increasing the risk of their activities will substantially increase the potential for profits, while the downside risk remains the same. Hence a propensity to take unreasonable risks. Where some or all of the shareholders exercise a dominant role in the day-to-day running of the bank, as opposed to a situation where the bank lists a large number of small shareholders, the temptation is magnified. Most Asian banks fall into the former category.

Moral hazard also applies to international lenders and investors who have poured money into Asia with abandon over the past five years. Many banks, most infrastructure projects and a large chunk of favored companies in Asia can claim close ties with governments. Their success, or their survival, depending on the circumstances, hinges on those ties and they all feed on the perception that, should the need arise, government support will be made available. Such a perception gives comfort to international lenders and investors who are happy to obtain high rewards for taking low risks. Such imbalances attracted them in hordes and they now feign surprise and indignation when government support is withdrawn, either under IMF pressure or because government coffers are empty. The moral hazards that contributed to the Asian crisis will cast a shadow over the region's banking sector for some time to come, but an immediate task is at hand. Governments, trade partners and the IMF must find solutions to rehabilitate the banking sectors of the most distressed Asian countries. Whatever the solutions, an important lesson would be lost if errant shareholders do not see their investments marked to their true market value.

Bank Equity Funds

Within a capitalist system, such as prevails to a greater or lesser degree throughout the region, with the exception of China, Vietnam and Laos, banks are limited liability companies run for the benefit of their shareholders. When ordinary manufacturing or service firms become insolvent, if an arrangement cannot be worked out with creditors, the companies are liquidated and their equity is used to satisfy existing obligations according to the priority of creditors.

By virtue of the fact that banks play a special role in financing economic development, they tend to be accorded somewhat better treatment. To be sure, the economic costs of a bank collapse go beyond the loss of their equity. In many cases, it does make sense for the government to bail out a failed bank. The same rationale does not extend, however, to the bank's shareholders. They should be the first to pay for their mistakes.

The currency turmoil and the collapse of the region's stock markets certainly have made the shareholders' position weaker than they bargained for, but they only have themselves and their regulators to blame. A lethal combination of mandated policy lending, uncontrolled growth and weak governance has resulted in huge loan defaults. But they found a fertile ground in poor credit controls and the sheer greed of many bank shareholders. Lenient rules on the classification of non-performing loans have allowed banks to conceal the extent of their difficulties.

A clear understanding of such difficulties would have dampened the enthusiasm of depositors and creditors and would have put a lid on the wild asset expansion that compounded the problem. Many Asian financial institutions were already exhibiting poor asset quality well before the present problems erupted. In fact, many banks were virtually or potentially bankrupt before the end of 1996. It would be unthinkable to justify a degree of leniency towards bank shareholders on the grounds that some of the blame could be apportioned to the crisis. Not only are the banks largely to blame for what happened, but also their shortcomings will inevitably delay the resolution of the crisis.

Shareholders funds are meant to provide a cushion so that, at all times, the assessed value of a bank's assets remains above that of its liabilities to creditors and to depositors. For this reason, regulatory authorities impose minimum capital adequacy rules to ensure that shareholders' equity is in adequate proportion to the volume of a financial institution's loans and other assets. International norms established by the Bank of International Settlements (BIS) recommend a net level of equity equal to at least 8% of assets at risk.[2] (Several pages are devoted to capital ratios in Chapter 3.) On a regular basis, shareholders' equity is technically adjusted for profits, losses, dividends and fresh injections of capital and it is usually easy to track the adjustments in published financial statements. However, in those countries still making the transition to a market system, such as China and Vietnam, mysterious entries affect shareholders funds that cannot be justified by generally accepted accounting practices.

A number of adjustments are needed to ensure that the assets are kept in the accounts for what they are worth. The actual realizable value of the assets should be the only guide to the determination of such adjustments. Likewise, fluctuations in the value of positions in foreign exchange, money markets and any derivative product should be measured as accurately as possible. Any surplus must be counted as a transient windfall, while any deficit must be deducted from capital funds until the end of the next adjustment period.

Naturally, regulators tend to be less than zealous in ensuring that such adjustments take place, as they know very well that too stringent a scrutiny would reveal to the world the sorry state of their country's banks. Should regulators be reasonably strict, a large number of banks under their supervision would exhibit poor capital ratios and dozens of them would be technically bankrupt. This would affect most of the large banks in Japan, China, Korea, Indonesia, Vietnam, Pakistan, Bangladesh, Sri Lanka, and many smaller banks in those and other countries. Only banks in Hong Kong, Singapore and the Philippines would, with extremely few exceptions, be above the international suggestions for a capital ratio of 8% of risk-weighted assets.

Of course, banks can and do operate with negative equity, which is technically possible if liquidity is maintained. More than half of the largest Asian banks are bankrupt and have been so for quite a while. It is true that, when the beans are counted, a bankrupt company cannot normally survive. But, in the world of Asia's financial institutions, the beans are often not counted, so that the fiction of solvency can be maintained. As long as the authorities, depositors and creditors carry on offering ammunition in the shape of advances and deposits, the institution will survive. In many cases, the sole perception that, should the need arise, funds will be made available to the institution is enough to ensure its viability.

If history is any indication, however, regulators tend not to react promptly or correctly to avert potentially serious problems down the road. This can be seen after the fact when circumstances eventually lead regulators to put an end to the artificial survival of a moribund institution. By the time this occurs, full scrutiny is inevitable. Typically, when the bank's books are explored, its equity is found to be largely negative. In fact, it is often found so strongly negative that, unless fresh funds are pumped into the institution, there will not be enough in the till to reimburse depositors. It becomes a politically sensitive and delicate balancing act to apportion the burden of the losses among the various parties involved: depositors, shareholders, creditors, regulators and the taxpayers they serve. Europe and the USA have longstanding rules dealing with such matters. In Asia, shareholders, taxpayers, depositors and other creditors end up sharing the cost of a bank failure in proportions which are often an insult to common sense.

Who Should Pay For a Bank Failure?

Small depositors should never suffer. They are ordinary people who are in no position to judge whether a bank is safe. If this is a difficult call for educated creditors, it is an impossible task for ordinary depositors. They must rely on the regulatory authorities that license financial institutions and are supposed to monitor their health constantly. Such depositors should not suffer from mistakes made by regulators. In Western countries, this approach is usually supported by a system, formal or informal, of deposit insurance. Although such systems distort competition as they tinker with the balance between risk and reward, the moral hazard they engender is usually outweighed by the increased public confidence they bring to an imperfect market. Few Asian countries offer a protection of that nature, in any case. In practice though, there is often enough leeway in bankruptcy laws for governments to bend the rules in favor of small depositors. This is a small price to pay for social peace, and other creditors are often coaxed into paying such a price if they want to see any support for their own claims.

Large depositors and other creditors are sophisticated operators who should be able to make their own choices, provided sufficient information is available to them as to the financial health of the institutions with which they transact business. This is wishful thinking. In Asia, unfortunately, disclosure of credit information is fairly limited (see Chapter 3 for comments on disclosure) and often downright misleading. In many countries there are serious doubts as to the accuracy of the limited information that is disclosed. Nevertheless, the lack of transparency is discounted in the risk appraisal and in the pricing, and at least large depositors and creditors are in a position to understand the risks they face. It is therefore not unreasonable to ask large depositors and commercial creditors to suffer the consequences of their choices.

Taxpayers should, in theory, be left out of the picture, except to the extent that they bear responsibility for misguided policies perpetrated by the politicians they elect or tolerate. Fiscal wastage is by no means limited to governments' support of financial institutions. In Asia, more money is routinely wasted on military equipment and corruption than on failed financial institutions. As discussed elsewhere (see Chapter 3 on state-owned banking institutions), Asian banks are often used as a conduit for government intervention in the economy. Western nations keep reliable tabs on their citizens and their economic activities, and they do influence economic decisions through a comprehensive arsenal of loans, subsidies and tax rebates. This, however, would not be practical in Asia owing to the fact that economic agents are often physically distant from central governments and that no serious control can be exercised on financial incentives.

Using government-controlled financial institutions is a reasonable substitute for a welfare system, and it is an expedient way of distributing subsidies. There is no doubt that such a system is not immune from the ravages of corruption, but in some environments it may be the most efficient way of influencing economic decisions. Lending is directed at state-controlled corporations and some non-government borrowers with no illusion as to their ability to service the loans. Periodically, governments divert funds from the state budget to make up for such loan losses. Arguably, they do not do so in a very coherent manner, leaving at times the situation to deteriorate beyond reasonable bounds. China and India are clear examples of such situations. It would appear that losses found in such banks are entirely the result of mismanagement, but it is not the case. Loan losses are disguised subsidies and it is only natural for taxpayers to carry the burden, as they would in situations where outright subsidies are distributed.[3] Just as imperfections exist in markets, so do they also exist within political systems.

As suggested before, shareholders are, with very few exceptions, the most culpable parties. They may be unknowingly guilty, but this makes no difference. They own the bank, they select its management, and they collect their reward in dividends and retained earnings. The whole concept of equity investment revolves around the notion that all other liabilities must be met before equity holders are rewarded. It is morally unacceptable that shareholders should not be the first to pay for their mistakes. This is all the more so because banks are typically limited liability corporations: the actual exposure of shareholders is usually limited to the capital funds.

If the seed capital funds themselves are safe, the system is permeated with moral hazard. In some countries, like Indonesia, some bank shareholders are known to flout the rules and to borrow from their own banks in amounts vastly superior to their equity, contributed and earned. Such arrangements render them at virtually no risk of losing much, should the bank collapse. This attitude makes a mockery of equity investment principles and should not be tolerated. It is unacceptable even when related party lending is limited to the official, but often disregarded, level of 10% or 15% of shareholders funds. In many cases, an amount of 15% of official shareholders funds is in fact larger than the actual equity left in the bank, since posted equity is often artificially inflated by creative accounting methods.

Rehabilitation

For a variety of reasons, many of them political, regulators often do not have the strength to act decisively when a bank is weakening. In crony capitalistic regimes, linkages between bank shareholders and political authorities enable the regulated to circumvent the regulators. Ideally, regulators should identify the problems before shareholders funds are exhausted and when appropriate, they should insist on an immediate recapitalization of the bank. But the political environment in which they operate often precludes determined action. Nonetheless, crises often bring opportunities and a climate of reform that facilitates new policies.

The most relevant indicator of when authorities should intervene is the bank's recovery indicator (RI) (see Chapter 3 on capital ratios). The RI measures the number of years needed for a bank, should its capital funds be exhausted, to generate enough net cash flow to restore its capital ratio to the minimum level required in its country. This postulates that future circumstances will not differ materially from historic circumstances and that the problems that have led the bank to its predicament will not impair its ability to operate in the future. If there is a reasonable expectation that the institution will be able to generate the cash flow implied by its RI within the confidence interval set by the authorities, then it should be rehabilitated[4] under close surveillance. No dividend should be paid and the owners should not borrow from the bank. All profits should be diverted to retained earnings and converted to capital in order to offset previous losses.

If rehabilitation through future earnings is impossible, then the only solution is a call for a fresh injection of capital funds by existing or new shareholders. Often the shareholders are not able to top up the bank's equity — a not uncommon situation if the bank is listed and widely held — or are unwilling to do so. In that case, the authorities should impose a reduction of capital to a face-saving level of a fraction of the original equity, and force the institution to seek fresh equity funds, under pain of immediate liquidation. Malaysia went that route with some institutions in the aftermath of the mid-1980s crisis. It is exactly the kind of strong medicine that Thailand adopted in January 1998 and that Indonesia had in mind when creating IBRA, its government bank rehabilitation body.[5]

A bank always has a residual value even when its book value has fallen to zero. For one thing, it operates as a going concern and its franchise is worth something. In many countries, a bank license can have a substantial value. Therefore a negative book value does not necessarily indicate that the bank is irretrievably bankrupt. In some cases, however — in fact in too many cases — regulators intervene too late: equity is so negative that no adjustment for intangibles will bring it back to an acceptable level. Shareholders would first have to restore it to positive territory prior to rehabilitating it to the level prescribed by local regulations. This, for many shareholders, would be throwing good money after bad, and the temptation is to walk away from the institution. In such a case, it becomes difficult, if not downright impossible, to rescue the bank through a reduction of capital followed by an injection of fresh funds, since the new shareholders would be paying more than the bank is worth, even including intangibles. If a car is destroyed in a road accident, and it takes more money to repair it than it would be to buy a new one, the car will not be repaired. Yet, its owners can still elect to fix it, and pay more for the privilege. It is their choice. But nobody will buy the crashed car from them. The same goes for banks. Liquidation or straight nationalization become the only solutions when they fall beyond repair.

As noted, time is of the essence. Regulators should be able to intervene as soon as there are signs of possible insolvency. Delays in the investigation of ailing institutions often permit more of the net asset value to be eaten away subsequent to the initiation of an investigation than was lost before the problem was acknowledged. To be sure, the liquidation process in itself is costly — liquidators and lawyers are expensive — and this is yet another reason why intervention is necessary well before equity has disappeared completely.

Rehabilitation through future earnings is the only solution that would spare the shareholders. In all other situations where solvency cannot be restored with rehabilitation measures, shareholders must theoretically suffer, either through dilution or through liquidation. Creditors and depositors also must lose something. Unfortunately things are not as simple as that. Obfuscation becomes the order of the day as the apparent complexity of the banking and financial system enables vested interests to mystify the general public. The taxpayer becomes the ultimate saviour.

What is too often disguised is that greed is still the main cause of many bank failures. This has been the case with regard to the so-called "merchant banks" in Korea. In 1997, some of these institutions have been found to be exposed to the single Kia Group to the tune of over 120% of their own equity.[6] Similarly, for many years, some major private sector banks in Indonesia have indirectly lent to their major shareholders over twice their equity investment in the banks. Likewise, many Thai banks have borrowed huge amounts in foreign currencies to feed unproductive domestic investments at wider margins. Most rescue operations involving banks translate into a transfer of wealth between taxpayers and the creditors, depositors and shareholders of ailing banks.

In Korea, for example, the taxpayers are poised to carry the losses of many financial institutions. To be sure, in some instances, this would be justified on the grounds that banks were directed on national policy grounds to lend to weak borrowers or, as is mostly the case, simply on the grounds that the regulators failed to stop the banks from making deadly mistakes. After all, governments made such mistakes on behalf of voters and taxpayers.

Why has the problem of terminally ill banks and financial institutions been allowed to fester? One reason is to save face in the fond but unrealistic hope that conditions would return to those that prevailed in the bubble economy years that preceded this and previous economic busts. Another is the prevailing notion in Asia that the stability of the country and the reputation of its financial system are more relevant than an orthodox regulation of its money lenders. Generally in Asia, regulators are apparently not willing to allow the shareholders of some banks to face their just punishment. Instead, these shareholders are permitted to hold on as they continue to ask unconscionable amounts for shares that are worth very little, thus delaying the process of recovery.

The regrettable consequence is that owners of banks at both ends of the spectrum are virtually assured to be salvaged in case of problems, and therefore they cast caution to the winds. There is no downside risk for them. If they are tempted to abuse the system, as many are, they do so on a large scale. They start gambling with their depositors' money. As things stand at present, chances are that some of those bank owners will be allowed to escape punishment, all in the name of stability, or in a bid to spare any embarrassment to the authorities.

The international financial community's perception of incompetence on the part of Asian bank regulatory authorities has played an important role in the crisis and its slow resolution. For example, it could be argued that, had the shareholders of weak Thai finance companies been less greedy and the authorities more alert to their problems, many of them could have been liquidated at the expense of their shareholders well before the crisis reached the terminal phase. Their indecisiveness became a catalyst of the present turmoil. In turn, Asia's currency turmoil and stock market crisis have exacerbated the problems faced by the region's banks and finance companies. They, however, only have themselves to blame. To a large degree, the avarice of bank owners and the complacency of regulators have rendered the present turmoil in Asia more painful than it had to be.

Winners and Losers

The world's economies are not in a zero-sum game, whereby the losses of an economic agent are a gain to another economic agent. The wealth of the nations generally grows over time, but wealth can be destroyed. The Asian crisis has created hardship for many, without a corresponding benefit to anyone else, if it were possible to measure such things. Yet, not everything has been lost.

The Asia crisis has created bad loans and investment losses in the books of financial intermediaries, investment houses, individual investors and other economic agents in amounts that cannot be ascertained. More relevant is the question of whether or to what extent wealth was destroyed. There is no doubt about it having taken place, but the amount of wealth destruction is much more modest than it appears. When some commentators claim (Kadir Jasin in *New Sunday Times,* May 10, 1998) that Malaysia saw its national wealth destroyed to the tune of US$250 billion "as a result of the attack on the ringgit and the stock market nine months [earlier]", they are widely off the mark. The reality is that whoever is to blame for the "attack" did not destroy wealth in that amount, not any more than anybody should be thanked for "creating" wealth by bidding up the ringgit and the stock market in the years prior to the crisis.

When a bank lends money to a borrower who eventually fails to pay it back, what is the overall loss to the economy, meaning the difference between the gains and the losses of all economic agents, in this case the bank and the borrower? The answer will depend on what the funds were used for. If the money was used to buy an office tower whose value subsequently fell by half, was there wealth destruction? Not necessarily. There was a transfer of wealth from the bank, and perhaps partly from the borrower, to the seller of the office tower, seeping down largely to the original land owner. Similarly, if the funds were used to speculate on the stock market, with negative results, the bad loan created in the books of the bank does not represent a net loss to the community. Rather, it is a transfer from the shareholders of the bank to one or more punters who did make a profit mirroring the bank borrower's loss. Alternatively, the funds might have been borrowed for investment in a manufacturing plant whose only production ends up having no ready market, and the project is a total loss. In this case, wealth was destroyed, and there is an obvious net loss to the community.

The crisis may have resulted in a deterioration of the terms of trade for Asian products. This is a sensitive subject and it is of relevance to some countries. But in the case of the five Asian countries that saw their currencies plummet, there is little evidence of any significant wealth destruction resulting from an alteration of the terms of trade. Some politicians have been whining about the increased cost to their citizens of acquiring goods and services from abroad. A prominent politician publicly claimed that the 60% devaluation of his currency effectively robbed his people of 60% of the value of all imports, in this case 60% of US$80 billion per year, or US$48 billion. If a country was importing such goods and services for the equivalent of US$80 billion per year before the crisis, the same transactions will indeed cost 60% more in local currency after the crisis, if the dollar has gone up that much. If the terms of trade are not altered — that is if local products are exported at the same international price as before — the US$80 billion of exports, normally balancing the imports, will bring in 60% more in local currency after the crisis. Adjustments in pricing will alter the picture, since currency adjustments do affect competitiveness, but there is no indication that they will lead to an impoverishment of Asian populations, at least directly.

The one factor that irks politicians most is the negative adjustments to GDP per capita brought about by the devaluation. This is very much a matter of national pride. Indeed some Asian countries have now reached a GDP per capita equivalent or superior to that of the poorest Western European countries. By the time Hong Kong was liberated in July 1997, it was as wealthy as its colonial masters were, and had long had nothing to learn from them.

It is true that a currency devaluation has the immediate effect of adjusting downward the all-important gauge of per-capita GDP. Yet politicians should pause and reflect on the endless currency fluctuations among Western nations. The dollar went up against the currencies of most European countries in the past few years, making European per-capita GDP seemingly shrink in US$ terms. Since the currencies of most Asian countries were closely linked to the dollar, their per-capital GDP, when compared to that of European countries, received a mechanical boost. Asian politicians should learn about symmetry: none of them told their constituents about such artificial adjustments to their relative position in international comparisons, when they were in favor of East Asia.

Now that the reverse is taking place, why should they suddenly complain? Why scream about the fact that fresh adjustments to their national currencies are taking place, sudden perhaps but largely justified? This is as childish and short-sighted as the megalomaniac declarations of the Shah of Iran in the early 1970s when he was telling his people that Iran was soon to become the world's fifth largest economic power.

Liquidations, Mergers and Nationalizations

At one point in the near future, it will be possible to estimate the extent of the damage inflicted by the crisis on each of the region's banks. By and large, it should be assumed that the losses of many banks in the most affected countries (Korea, Indonesia, Thailand, and Malaysia) will exceed their capital funds by a wide margin. Short of letting private sector banks operate with negative equity, the likely decision of regulatory authorities will be to insist on a recapitalization exercise.
Judicial liquidation is usually not an option, for several reasons. It is costly, it carries a social stigma, and most Asian countries are ill equipped to handle bankruptcy procedures, let alone when thousands of small creditors are involved. There seem to be three possible ways of solving the problem: fresh capital from domestic sources, foreign investment and nationalization.

In most cases, there is abundant capital available from local sources, but it will be difficult to attract it to rehabilitate the banks. So far, Thailand is the only one of the distressed countries that has recorded any success in that direction. Foreign investors are waiting in the wings and will seize opportunities everywhere, as they already have in Thailand in a limited way. But some banks for sale are not exactly offering the kind of return on equity foreign buyers would expect. This problem can be reflected in the acquisition price, but, as things stand, many banks would have to carry a negative sale price to attract a buyer. It would be conceptually difficult to ask the seller to pay the buyer for him to complete the acquisition, and we come back to liquidation or nationalization.

In spite of its socialist connotations, nationalization looks more likely in most cases, at least as a stopgap measure pending a stabilization of the economies. The beauty of nationalization is that governments can make full use of their penchant for cooking the books. Once a bank is nationalized, the deposits are virtually guaranteed and the bank is protected against any liquidity problem. It can call on the Ministry of Finance at any time for liquidity support. New state shareholders can use creative accounting so that the banks are seen posting internationally-accepted capital ratios. The recognition of bad loans becomes an arbitrary exercise. Nationalized banks can be used to support ailing corporate borrowers selected by the governments. Above all, the nationalized banks can be made to swallow weak financial institutions in arranged mergers.

In crises, regulatory authorities often use mergers as magical tricks. Putting together two weak companies to create a strong one is seen as a panacea. This flies in the face of arithmetic and basic accounting principles, but many people fall for the trick. It buys time, but solves little. The only case where a weak institution can successfully be rescued in a merger is when the acquirer is larger and stronger, while the weak bank is small. Unfortunately, Asia is for now littered with the opposite: many large weak banks for a few small strong banks.

The other side of the coin is that nationalized banks suffer all over the world from the same malady: a bureaucratic style feeding complacency. Worse yet, cronyism seeps in. In Indonesia, it is well known that a borrower who intends to repay the loans would borrow from private sector banks, while if the intention is not to repay, it is best to approach a state bank.

The IMF has attached certain strings to its financial assistance. In particular, its funds should not be used to bail out rotten firms. The nationalization exercise in IMF-supported countries must therefore be approached with caution. Generally speaking, it is not sufficient to punish the shareholders in the process: if lenders and creditors — outside of small innocent depositors — remain unscathed, the IMF funds will have been deployed against the principles. Therefore, governments are careful to disguise their support so that the flouting of the IMF recommendations is not too obvious. The issue of bonds in exchange for dud loans is a good example. The creation of a special vehicle to park non-performing loans is also a good trick. The IMF knows, the whole world knows, but faces are saved. This is deplorable. Moral hazard will never be eradicated if shareholders, lenders and creditors do not suffer. The compromise seen in some countries is a mistake, such as Korea, where some commercial banks are clearly beyond repair and are nevertheless permitted to carry on operating. It would have been much better to see some commercial banks fail altogether. The lesson was not learned. The punishment does not fit the crime.

Endnotes

1. A Chaebol is a Korean conglomerate where the various firms are loosely linked through their shareholders. There is generally no real holding structure, at least for the group as a whole. See the Chapter 5 on Korea for further details.
2. The risk associated with each of the assets is the basis of the BIS suggested classification. The BIS classification is described in Appendix 2 of this book.
3. In fact, distributing subsidies through bad loans can prove more efficient than other methods in some countries. On a regular basis, banks can reach many more people than any other government body. The analyst should think twice before blaming state-controlled banks for all their bad loans.
4. Assuming a bank has lost all of its original 8 capital dollars per 100 dollars of risk assets (its risk-weighted capital ratio has fallen from 8% to 0%), it must generate 8 dollars in retained earnings to restore its capital adequacy ratio. The return on risk-weighted assets is never equal to the return on assets, and it is generally not disclosed, but the analyst can calculate a rough estimate. If a bank can be expected to retain such earnings to the tune of, say, 2% per year, it will need 4 years to recover and its RI is equal to 4. At 1.5% per year, the RI will be 5.33. The number of years actually necessary will of course depend on the proportion of capital that was destroyed. Each bank has a separate RI that will change over time, but it is an important ingredient in the decision to allow a bank a slow rehabilitation, as opposed to a violent merger, liquidation or nationalization.
5. At the time of writing (June 1998), Indonesia had yet to implement the all-important rehabilitation step of forcing out the shareholders of failed institutions. The IBRA supervision has meant very little so far.
6. There is no fast rule about how many eggs should be put in the same basket, but any exposure to a single name above 10% to 15% of a bank's own unimpaired equity should be a maximum.

BANK ACCOUNTING IN ASIA 3

I f accounting is a science, bank accounting is more of an art. There are established rules in bank accounting, by nature different from general accounting. Going around those rules, especially in Asia, has been perfected into an art form that deserves several volumes. A thorough inquisition would go beyond the purpose of this book, but it is worthwhile exploring in a few short pages this fascinating world. After all, if we agree that the weaknesses of the banking systems is at the root of the Asian crisis, it should be interesting to understand how the banks have succeeded in concealing the true state of their affairs. Readers who are familiar with bank accounting may elect to skip this chapter, but some comments and anecdotal examples will entertain them. Those readers interested in technical definitions of bank ratio will find a glossary as an appendix.

Governments and bank regulators are evidently aware of the tricks used by banks to project a good image of themselves to the public and to foreign creditors. There is a sort of national pride attached to offering a seemingly strong rendition of the health of domestic banks. Every trick imaginable is used, and many are in fact more than tolerated by the authorities: they get their blessing. Overall, at least until the crisis erupted, almost all of the Asian banks appeared to be solvent. The reality is vastly different; even before the crisis, many of them were in fact bankrupt.

We shall explore bank accounts and how they are publicized from several angles: firstly, the accounts themselves, then the tricks used to embellish them. We shall explore how poor public disclosure of such accounts appears to be in Asia. Eventually, we shall try to understand why this situation is allowed to linger and what should be done about it.

Disclosure

It is a generally accepted principle that if people wish to be entrusted with someone else's money, they should provide sufficient evidence of their ability to restitute the funds at a later stage. This principle is valid in most circumstances, and it should be especially so with banking operations where the recipient is usually highly geared. An industrial company may borrow twice its equity, while a bank routinely borrows, or accepts deposits for, 15 to 20 times its shareholders funds. Banks have a duty to disclose how strong or weak they are, and they have to do so according to certain accounting rules. The disclosure of bank financial statements in Western countries is generally comprehensive. Disclosure is excellent in North America and rather good in Western Europe and Australia. In emerging markets, with a few exceptions, this is not the case. In Asia, the degree of disclosure is simply abysmal. In 1993, Capital Information Services, Asia's largest bank rating firm and the predecessor of Thomson BankWatch Asia, developed a model to measure to what extent banks were disclosing relevant information in their annual reports. The model was a scoring sheet giving a subjective weighting to every aspect of bank accounting disclosure, including non-quantitative information. Table 3.1 was the result (Singapore is not on the list).[1]

TABLE 3.1   DISCLOSURE OF INFORMATION IN ASIAN BANKS (1993)

	Extent of details[2] on					
	P & L	Liabilities	Assets	Other figures	Non-figures	Total
Thailand	94	93	144	96	15	442
Malaysia	87	90	110	96	40	423
Indonesia	75	118	107	72	29	401
Taiwan	90	100	84	80	45	399
Philippines	67	74	77	96	21	335
South Korea	54	101	94	24	56	329
Hong Kong	9	19	27	8	31	94
China	13	18	7	0	0	38
Max. Possible Score	200	210	350	120	120	1000

Source: Capital Information Services

The results were utterly embarrassing for Hong Kong. In spite of its status as an international financial center, Hong Kong was ranking barely above China and considerably below most East Asian countries. In China, the average bank — not Bank of China, which was better than that — would print a grand total of 17 significant amounts on a 50-gram document. In Malaysia, Public Bank's annual report weighted in at 620 grams.[3] In both countries, annual reports were bilingual. In Hong Kong, a bank had only one line talking about deposits: the total. No indication as to whether deposits were from banks or small depositors, or as to the proportion of savings deposits or similar information. It was impossible to attempt an analysis of a bank's liquidity. The same went for profit: one line only in net profits. Even that information was useless, since banks were routinely squirreling away in inner reserves the funds they thought they might need in leaner times. For the same reason, the capital ratios were all wrong. It is only in 1995 that the Hong Kong government insisted on more disclosure by banks. One of that government's most respectable representatives once publicly acknowledged that the improvement resulted from the pressure of Capital Information Services.

The analyst is not interested in the quantity of the information unless it is reliable. Many countries in Asia that do provide more details than others in fact provide dubious information. As a rule, the nicer the pictures and the longer the chairman's message, the lousier the real information.

Something Out of Nothing

There is no limit to creative accounting. In March 1993, Bank of Ceylon embarked in a remarkable quest for respectability by cooking its books in a spectacular way. The bank is the largest financial institution in Sri Lanka, with about US$2.4 billion in total assets, representing about one-third of the banking system. It belongs wholly to the government and employs over 10,000 staff. The bank has been largely bankrupt for many years, a fact that does not attract any blame from the analyst, as it is perfectly acceptable owing to Bank of Ceylon's social role in the country. As it is a government bank, it has a number of social duties, for example supporting certain categories of farmers, or lending to government employees at preferential rates, and the obligation to finance sectors of the economy targeted by the state. As a result, the bank is not very profitable and it carries substantial amounts of bad loans. That its employees have few of the incentives found in the private sector makes the matter of efficiency a compounding problem, to say the least.

In 1993, the government-shareholder wished to embellish some ratios and offered the bank what is called on the sub-continent "restructuring bonds". The matter is clearly documented and there is no suggestion that the authorities wanted to conceal the transaction. Those bonds are essentially long-term government borrowings — Bank of Ceylon's bonds carry a 30-year maturity — that cannot be sold down by the purchaser. The amount issued to the bank was Rs 13.5 billion (about US$300 million) and was meant to clean away some bad loans[4] (for Rs 9.6 billion or about 20% of total loans) and recapitalize the bank (for the remaining Rs 3.9 billion). To have an idea of the magnitude of the government's gift, one should realize that, at the end of 1994 — the funds had by then been properly digested — the equity of the bank was a mere Rs 7.5 billion. The government essentially borrowed money from Bank of Ceylon in order to inject capital funds back into the bank. This was brilliant. Thanks to the arrangement, the bank had suddenly become one of the most highly capitalized banks in the region, with a BIS ratio of no less than 10.6%.

But the story does not stop there. No money changed hands, but the government bonds carry an interest of 12% annually, which comes in handy in shaping the bank's profits. In fact, in 1994, no less than 78% of Bank of Ceylon profits came from that miraculous source, propelling the bank's return on average assets (ROA) to a dizzying 2.29%. This places the bank ahead of everyone else in Sri Lanka, and this ROA is definitely among the best in the region. The Thomson BankWatch analysts had only one question for the government: why on earth did they stop at US$300 million?

Why would Asian banks be so secretive about their operations? It is true that should a bank look weak, rumor-happy Asians would immediately think of removing their deposits. In a distant past, there was indeed little protection for depositors and creditors, but times have now changed. Other reasons usually invoked include the danger of giving away information to competitors, the control exercised on them by auditors, tax inspectors and regulatory authorities, and the fact that those who should know do know. How convenient!

Banks are happy to mislead their competitors, while the word "cheating" is more appropriate for what they do to regulators, investors and depositors. There is little that competitors need to know about banks that they cannot obtain discreetly, or make guesses about. Anything else is either not worth knowing, or so dangerously relevant that everybody should know.

The problem is both quantitative and qualitative. When published, the figures seldom describe the banks with a reasonable degree of truthfulness. While it is relatively difficult to tamper with figures describing deposits or cash flow, banks tend to be very creative when it comes to capital funds. Many still operate under the assumption that depositors and creditors focus on capital ratios to gauge the creditworthiness of the institution. The assumption, alas, is correct, and in normal circumstances would be acceptable. But a lot of creativity goes into the valuation of assets, in particular loan assets, and in turn this affects the amount of provisions put aside against non-performing loans. Commercial banks are in the business of taking calculated risks. A proportion of their gross income must routinely be put aside to offset the occasional bad loan. Since provisions represent a sizable chunk of recurrent expenses, any miscalculation — whether inadvertent or voluntary — has a direct influence on recurrent profits, which in turn will affect retained earnings. This is how mistakes eventually reach capital adequacy ratios.

In most Asian countries, auditors do not have the responsibility to check that accounts are correct, beyond ensuring that transactions are entered in the right account on the right line of the balance sheet. They are routinely prevented from making any meaningful comment on bad loan provisioning or off balance sheet entries. Dozens of financial institutions failed in Asia in recent years. Prior to their demise, their auditors had never identified their problems, or more accurately had never revealed them. For many technical and practical reasons, the auditors simply are not in a position to react to the atrocities they uncover. Sometimes they wouldn't. The fact that they may be affiliated to the best international names makes no difference. This is definitely not a regular occurence, but I once heard a bank manager in Hong Kong confess that, to ensure leniency, he was routinely bribing some senior staff of one of the big international firms, one of those names charging millions for their work.

Banks usually cheat by trying to look better than they really are. There are counter-examples, where banks would cheat by looking worse than they are. This they would do for tax reasons or in order to improve their negotiating position with unions. Perhaps they would want to save profits for a rainy day. But whichever way they go, they deploy considerable energy and imagination in trying to mislead external observers.

CAMEL

There are four major sub-sections in bank accounting: Capital, Asset quality, Earnings and Liquidity. The analysis of the four sections, together with that of a middle section covering Management, is usually referred to as the CAMEL analysis. It is not clear, beyond being an easy acronym, why that noble animal was at all selected for this task, but there certainly is at least one analogy: bank accounts can be left without attention for quite a while and nobody will complain. Depending on the observer's angle, the various sections will have more or less relevance. Equity analysts will focus on earnings, regulators will look at capital and liquidity, and raters will watch asset quality.[5] Most will succumb to the mystification.

Capital

Capital ratios measure solvency. This is the theory. In practice, solvency is not measured only by what is in the accounts, it is most importantly measured by what could potentially affect the accounts. The first set of measures is based on objective factors, while the second set of measures is partly based on management's judgment.

Capital ratios are a theoretical measure of the gap between a company's liabilities — not including its equity funds — and its assets. In cases when liabilities threaten to exceed assets and trigger a state of bankruptcy, it is important to ensure that losses are met by the shareholders and not by the company's suppliers and lenders. Financial institutions are highly geared, much more so than commercial or industrial companies. The deposits they take and the money they borrow vastly exceed the funds committed by the shareholders. It would be socially irresponsible to allow financial institutions, through mismanagement, bad luck or fraud, to renege on their obligation to repay depositors in full. This gives capital ratios an important role in monitoring the health of such institutions, even though, for a variety of reasons, the ratios usually do not give a true enough picture of the situation.

Various types of capital ratios are in use. Not a single one gives a perfect picture of a bank's solvency, even when there is no doubt about the truthfulness of the accounts. The reason for this imperfection lies in the fact that a bank's exposure to losses changes daily. A good ratio would, by nature, measure a bank's own equity funds against those potentially changing losses. Both the large variety of transactions and the diversity of borrowers and counter-parties make every line of the balance sheet a different story. A perfect capital ratio would measure the statistical likelihood of assets keeping a sufficient value against liabilities, together with the statistical likelihood that other transaction losses would not eat away the equity.

The various ratios in use in the past were comparing total equity to some or all types of deposits, or total equity to total assets, whether directly or through a reciprocal ratio called leverage. The old ratios are like the abacus: they still work, but they are technologically outdated. Such ratios tell the analyst something about the bank, but they are more useful as comparative ratios when all banks exhibit approximately the same asset mix, as they vary considerably from country to country. Another crude attempt at measuring capital against the most dangerous activities was the ratio of total equity to total lending. This is now largely obsolete because banks take huge risks outside of their loan portfolio, although the lack of disclosure often forces the analyst to rely on those archaic instruments.

In short, the banks have long followed a set of rules in relation to capital funds that do not apprehend the real risk they are exposed to. For what they are worth, the general guidelines suggest that, for each 100 units of risk assets, a bank should carry eight units in unencumbered equity or quasi-equity.

Enter the Basle Committee of the BIS. In 1988, it made some recommendations for an improvement in the calculation of solvency ratios. The main change was that the value of each asset was to be adjusted to take into account the risk it represented for the institution. There are many flaws in that approach, but it is already an improvement over the crude leverage ratios, like the equity-to-loans ratio or the equity-to-deposits ratio.

On the denominator side (the assets), the new ratio was giving various weights to assets according to the perceived risk of potential delinquency. For example, mortgage loans are typically less risky than commercial loans, and it is natural for banks to earmark less capital in support of mortgage loans than they would in support of other lending activities. Each of the sub-groups of assets is similarly assessed for its risk. The denominator also received a contribution from non-lending risk.[6]

On the numerator side (the equity), a new differentiation was introduced to separate permanent equity funds (the so-called "Tier 1" components) from those funds which, by nature, were not necessarily destined to remain in the books, like subordinated loans (the "Tier 2" components). This Tier 1/Tier 2 differentiation allowed more quasi-equity in the formula as well as offered a ready measure to ensure that minimum amounts of Tier 1 capital were present.

The main purpose of the 1988 capital ratio reform was to treat all banks similarly, regardless of domicile and of local accounting conventions, in order to create a level playing field in international banking. The formula was going to be almost the same in all OECD countries, and banks were going to need consistent levels of supporting capital. At the same time, the measurement of the actual risk to bank equity was refined, and it included off balance sheet items as well as the items traditionally found on the balance sheet proper. The required minimum for the new equity-to-risk ratio was set at 8%. Nobody today seems to recall why that particular figure was selected. The most plausible explanation is that the major Western countries had figured out that their banks would be able to abide by the new rule. Had the reform taken place at a time when most Western banks were likely to reach only a ratio of 5%, it would be a safe bet to assume that 5% would have become the norm.

The original reform of 1988 (a fresh reform is under study), leading to what is commonly called the "BIS ratio" or the "Cooke ratio", was a welcome first step in the right direction. Yet the BIS ratio approach was lacking for several reasons. It was allocating the risk by type of product, rather than by quality. It was also suffering from different definitions across countries and, more importantly, it was blind to non-credit risks, even though off balance sheet items were taken into consideration. The reader will find in an appendix the composition of Cooke ratios.

Value-at-risk

More recent research has introduced the notion of value-at-risk (VAR). This notion looks at each type of asset or transaction with the view of determining how much damage it could potentially inflict on the bank's equity. The value at risk is equal to the potential changes in underlying factors, multiplied by the sensitivity of the value of each asset to such changes. Underlying factors such as market prices, historical default rates, collateral, duration of the transaction and credit ratings determine, within a reasonable confidence interval, how much capital really is at risk. By taking that approach, regulators can refine their analysis and intervene on the strength of indicators that, in the past, would not have triggered intervention. At the same time, banks can optimize the allocation of equity by directing scarce resources to those activities that will improve the risk/reward relationship. In the most refined VAR models, banks know how much of their equity is at risk in each activity and how much income each activity produces. The best banks would eliminate all risks whose rewards are deemed insufficient. They would concentrate on obtaining the best return for each dollar invested in the capital funds theoretically needed for each activity. Note that the VAR approach looks at the worst-case scenario pertaining to credit risk, while the statistical approach[7] to market risk assumes that a bank can either gain or lose from voluntary or involuntary market positions. Earnings-at-risk computations are seldom used in Asia, except in their basic form of profit sensitivity to interest rates movements. Since most of the assets and liabilities in Asia carry floating interest rates, the sensitivity analysis is very rudimentary.

With the power developed today by computers, it has become relatively easy to build and operate a VAR model or an earnings-at-risk model, but the model will not operate properly if the assumptions are incorrect. Bank managers are the final arbiters of what risk the bank is perceived to be taking in each activity, and they can easily feed the model with overoptimistic assumptions. This is particularly true in Asia where even the more basic capital-at-risk models in use are being manipulated.

Minimum capital adequacy ratios are justified on prudential grounds. The higher the level, the least likely a bank will reach a point where it will be tempted or forced to meet losses with its depositors' money. But there are a number of questions that remain unanswered. Where should the lower limit be? What technical factor did the BIS consider when it set the standard capital ratio at 8%? Why was it not set at 6% or at 10%? And is there not something inherently wrong with imposing the same capital ratios to all banks in all countries?

Uniformity in Capital Ratios

There are strong arguments why, from a prudential point of view, capital ratios should not be uniformly imposed on all banks in all countries. Furthermore, it can be argued that market circumstances should, in many instances, dictate the adequate level of capital ratios. The purpose of these next two pages is to demonstrate that there is nothing inherently wrong with suggesting that Asian banks, presently deprived of capital, could do quite well without it — to a point. To be more precise, one should consider a range of factors before taking a regulatory decision in this matter.

Capital Funds as a Cushion

Capital funds are used as a cushion to absorb fluctuations in the value of assets. Liabilities remain predictable: creditors and depositors cannot claim more than their due, while if they neglect to claim, the banks benefit from the mistake. Assets can fluctuate in value. If they lose some of their value, capital funds are substituted in order for the institution to meet its liabilities. If a capital ratio must be high enough to allow a bank to go wrong without going bankrupt, then the ratio should represent the maximum proportion of risk assets an institution could possibly lose before regulators can take corrective action or can reasonably declare it unfit to operate. One year seems a reasonable period, during which banks are not normally expected to lose more than 8% of their assets, barring fraud or dissimulation by their managers. One might argue that, on that basis, authorities in countries where reporting and auditing are more frequent, corrective action can be and is taken earlier, and therefore the limit could be lowered. However, this differentiation would imply a judgment on the quality of the regulatory framework in each of the countries, which could be both painful and politically sensitive. If such an attempt was made in Asia, it is probably the banks operating in Hong Kong, Singapore, the Philippines and Malaysia that would come out with the lowest need for capital funds. Barring such a differentiation, there should be consensus around a minimum level for capital ratios, to be applied across the board. By consensus, this level was fixed at 8%. It was probably dictated, more than by anything else, by what governments of many OECD countries thought their banks could achieve. What relevance does that factor have in the Asia situation?

Restoration of Capital Funds

Nothing is either black or white in the assessment of asset quality. A loan that looks shaky may end up being reimbursed fully, while other loans might turn sour without warning. This usually is the major factor in the sudden deterioration of capital ratios, but it does not necessarily indicate a trend. In other words, a bank could possibly have lost considerable amounts of money to bad loans or bad investments while keeping intact its capacity to generate its usual stream of cash flow. This is the reason why regulators will in most cases allow a bank that has lost part of its equity to make an attempt at rehabilitation, on the grounds that the operating capacity of the institution has not been impaired. Assuming its BIS ratio has fallen from

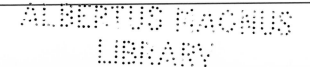

8% to 4%, how many years will a bank need to restore itself to 8% on the strength of internally generated reserves? Recent pre-crisis ratios suggest that, after such an incident, it would, for example, take the average Malaysian bank less than three years (this is the RI) to restore its capital ratio to 8%, while the average Taiwanese bank would need five years. Generally, banks in the countries where it is possible to generate strong profits, like the Philippines or Hong Kong, as opposed to those with weaker prospects, as in Taiwan and Korea, stand a better chance of rehabilitating themselves. From that angle, it appears that BIS guidelines should be more lenient in Malaysia or the Philippines than in Korea or Singapore.

Capital Ratios Dictated by Market Forces

Capital adequacy ratios can also be dictated by the capital markets. This has to do with the rigidities of each market. There is an arithmetic link between the three ratios: the ROA, the Return on Equity ratio (ROE) and capital ratios. A bank whose assets are equivalent to 12 times its equity will have a ROE equivalent to 12 times its ROA. This arithmetic relationship also translates into a capital ratio of 12 times[8] (other types of capital ratios are in fact in use, but this simple leverage ratio clearly illustrates the case). The three ratios are very rigorously linked together by mathematical relations. It is impossible to fix all three ratios unless they follow strictly such relations. If two of the ratios are fixed either by the markets, as is the ROA, or by the regulators, as is the leverage (or any such capital ratio), then the third one, the ROE, will have to remain within narrow limits. Such limits may not be compatible with market expectations. It is impossible to impose a leverage that turns out to be incompatible with the market-driven ROA and the market-driven ROE.

The ROA is largely fixed by the markets. By and large, most commercial banks in a given country exhibit profit and loss accounts consistent with the tax regime, general administrative costs and interest rate structure they are operating under. To be sure, there are ample deviations around the average, reflecting business franchise, management skills and asset mix, but the ROA of most banks is largely pre-determined by the domestic market circumstances they share. A market-driven ROA and a leverage imposed by regulators will mathematically produce a resulting ROE.

Is that resulting ROE in line with the realities of the markets? Generally, it is not. The resulting ROE is often at odds with return expectations of market participants. It might be argued that stock markets would adjust bank share prices to eliminate the discrepancy. By and large, they do, but in a very inefficient way. Price/earnings ratios for Asian

financial institutions vary from about 5 to well over and that vast amplitude cannot be explained only by risk perceptions and by market return expectations. In addition, stock markets have a life of their own and often they will price bank shares at a level which is at odds with the resulting ROE.

For example a leverage of 12 times (often associated with a BIS ratio of 11% — the reader will be spared the detailed calculation)[9] and a ROA of 0.6% will result in a ROE of approximately 7.2% which may very well fall short of market expectations. Had the leverage been higher at 20 times (often associated with a BIS ratio of 6.5%), the resulting ROE would have been 12%. The resulting ROE is not always too low, but often it is, and banks will endeavor to improve it. It is true that they would do so even without market pressure, as yield maximization is a natural objective, if not always a high priority. But if the resulting ROE is too low, as is often the case in Asia, pushing up the ROE has to be a priority. Economic growth is strong, and stronger yet is the growth of bank assets: this situation translates into frequent calls on bank shareholders for additional capital funds, which will only be forthcoming if the ROE is attractive.

To jack up their income in order to meet market expectations in terms of ROE, the banks usually resort to one or more of three methods, all of which are potentially dangerous: increasing the risk of some assets, generating speculative non-lending profits or concealing non-performing assets.

Too Diverse For a Single Rule

In short, there are three approaches to capital adequacy: capital as a cushion pending intervention, restoration of capital funds by rehabilitation or capital dictated by markets forces. Which one will best meet the legitimate needs of regulators, depositors and creditors? In emerging markets, it seems obvious that a little of each will be necessary. From a creditworthiness point of view, more is always better than less, but, as explained in the market approach, this may bring about undesirable effects. The one conclusion that comes to mind is that the Asian banking markets are too diverse for a single rule.

Whether one looks at the problem from the prudential point of view or from the market point of view, it looks conceptually difficult to conclude that capital ratios can be uniformly imposed on all Asian banks. In any event, at the present level of 8%, very few of them would qualify if the ratio calculations and adjustments[10] were strictly applied to them the way they are in the most advanced of the OECD markets. By and large, most banks in Asia, with the exception of those in Hong Kong, Singapore and the Philippines, and the best banks in some of the other countries, would exhibit very poor capital ratios.

The matter of capital ratios is under review in the West. The most significant changes are likely to pertain to the assessment of the actual risk each financial activity entails. The various value-at-risk models and the earnings-at-risk models look increasingly valuable.

Asset Quality

Asset quality is the most important factor in determining a bank's creditworthiness. Asset quality directly affects the provisioning decisions, which largely determine the level of profits. In turn, the profit stream will affect capital ratios and the solvency or otherwise of each bank. Banks can still survive with negative equity if it is known that government support is explicit or implicit. This explains why, in Asia, despite appalling asset quality in many banks, weak banks have survived for years when objective asset quality indicators would point to theoretical insolvency.

The main factors affecting asset quality are the degree of diversification of assets, exposure to troubled industries or troubled markets, the size and duration of loans, the growth of the loan portfolios, the presence of directed or policy lending and related party lending. A bank endowed with a good credit culture, operating in a mature market, protected by safe commercial and bankruptcy laws, will normally enjoy the safest possible asset quality. Needless to repeat at this juncture, most Asian banks lack one or more of those basic conditions to qualify for a remotely acceptable asset quality label.

Name lending and relationship lending are so prevalent in Asia that the very notion of lending on the basis of the borrower's ability to generate cash flow is foreign to most credit officers. The external observer can only rely on the passive protection of a relative diversification of the loans across a large spectrum of industrial, commercial and individual borrowers. Any attempt at analyzing the possible concentration of loans on certain names meets with the inescapable reality that borrowers use dozens of different legal entities to book their loans. This incidentally explains how related party lending can so easily escape scrutiny.

Danger flags like sudden switches in strategies, or substantial growth of loan portfolios, would alert the rater to potential problems. It is generally a good idea to compare a financial institution to its immediate competitors, although all of them have often been found equally and feverishly involved in asset growth.

The rater will assess a bank's grasp of its asset quality by checking the internal approval and control procedures and the loan review system. She will inquire whether a risk rating system is in place, if there is a watch list, and what the bank's attitude would be in the presence of problem loans. Asian banks will swear that such procedures are in place, and perhaps they are. At the end of the day, asset quality will largely depend on the credit culture and strategy of the institution.

The terminology employed to study the quality of assets can vary considerably. The notion of non-accrual loan is seldom used in Asia. All delinquent loans are lumped into the non-performing loan category, whether they no longer accrue interest or they no longer meet reimbursement schedules. The only consistency across Asia, with some exceptions, of course, can be found in the rough division of non-performing loans (NPLs) into three broad categories: substandard, doubtful and bad loans. But the definition of each of the sub-categories varies widely. In almost all cases, the definitions are much more lenient than in Western countries, at the extreme with bad loans maintained in the current category up to one year after they became delinquent.

Many weakening loans are restructured. The original terms are altered, with the maturity extended or the interest lowered. Most restructured loans are disguised. Delinquent borrowers receive fresh loans, often indirectly through associated companies, so they can be seen as servicing their original loan. By definition, the aggregate amount of restructured loans is difficult to assess, but they often represent as much or twice as much as the NPLs officially admitted to. In 1996, when the best among Japanese banks started telling the world that they had restructured loans in their books (surprise, surprise!) such loans were found to be as large as those already labeled delinquent.

In short, the recognition of NPL in Asia is a very artistic notion and rules, when they exist, are much too lenient. In any event, they do not contribute as they normally should to a fair determination of the state of affairs of financial institutions. If weak assets are not identified, nothing can be done about nurturing them back to health or, as the case may be, to put aside partial or full provisions against them.

The loan loss reserve methodology also varies from country to country and from bank to bank. In Asia, whenever the embarrassing situation cannot be dissimulated any longer in the recognition process, liberties taken in the handling of the problem act as a softener: provisions are seldom taken to the full extent of the damage. This is most obvious in the case of government-owned banks, or when the state directs private sector banks' lending activities, but the neglect affects almost all of the financial institutions.

Theoretically, banks should be able to examine regularly each one of their assets — most of them loans — and decide whether there is a statistical or specific risk for the asset to lose some value. A provision is made accordingly, in such a way that, should the worst scenario take place, the bank suffers no further loss. Historical experience, present conditions and expectations for the future all contribute to the decision, which relies on the management's judgment. A great deal of discretion is attached to such decisions, which explains why it is so easy to err on the side of dissimulation.

Statistical provisions are made in response to the perception that a given percentage of like loans will fail, for example typically 3.5% of all credit card advances. Many countries insist on an across-the-board statistical provision of 1% of total lending. This is akin to equity or reserves and is no different from a rule that would set the capital adequacy ratio at 9% instead of 8%[11]. "This particular rule creates a mathematical quirk in the ratios of high growth lending institutions and many Asian banks fall into that category. Each new loan in the books at the end of the year imposes the diverting of a provision of 1% from that year's profits. Some types of loans will be sufficiently rewarding for the accountant to divert the 1% provision without much damage to the profits. For many new loans, however, after the provision is diverted, the contribution to the net interest income in that particular year does not approach the average contribution of the existing portfolio, and profitability ratios stand diluted. Since banks need to look profitable, the temptation will always be to grow through more rewarding, and therefore more risky, loans. The need for specific provisions is easier to grasp but, as explained earlier, bank managers in Asia lean towards dissimulating their institution's need for them. The external analyst is at a loss to understand what decisions were actually taken, because banks in Asia tend to be very secretive in such matters.

In the best situations, banks disclose two figures: the net cumulative provisions and the amount put aside in that particular year. No details are given about specific provisions and, worse of all, little indication as to write-offs and recoveries. Write-offs are the actual transfer of provisions to cover a loss, and recoveries are made up of — often unexpected — repayments or the proceeds of a borrower's liquidation. With so little disclosure, it is often impossible to use financial ratios to gauge a bank's asset quality. In North America and some European countries, provisions are a serious matter and banks tend to take them whenever they are needed, even at the cost of posting losses in a given quarter. Nothing like that exists in Asia where such a candid approach would be a loss of face.

What factors make the provisioning process so imperfect in Asian countries? There are a number of reasons, found in most emerging markets. They are worth mentioning as most observers of bank accounts in OECD markets would expect banks to come clean on such matters. The single most important reason why Asian banks fail to provide enough against bad loans is that they do not generate enough operating profits. As things stand presently in Asia, provisions often swallow over three-quarters of the operating profits generated, leaving little room for additional efforts. But assuming banks were willing and able to provide adequately for their asset losses, the authorities may prevent them from doing so. The tax authorities, which find a ready source of tax income in the country's banks, are often reluctant to let them put aside provisions. They often put an arbitrary cap to provisions, for example 2% of total lending, regardless of the banks' actual needs. When there is priority or directed lending, many loans are still considered as current until authorities decide otherwise. The legal process of executing a collateral or taking a borrower to court is difficult. Lenders cannot simply foreclose on a collateral, sell it out and reimburse themselves on the proceeds. They often need a court approval that could take several years to come. Meanwhile, the delinquent loan must remain in the books. Generally, the value itself of any collateral is difficult to assess, making it impossible to gauge the level of provisions needed against a delinquent collaterized loan. In Asia, banks often do not have the required skills to examine their own books and to determine the level of provisions needed.

Another important factor preventing Asian banks from doing the right thing in terms of provisioning is the fact that they are growing much faster than in OECD countries. Consequently, they are always short of capital funds. Low profits resulting from high provisions would be detrimental to a bank's good showing on stock markets. High growth means frequent calls on fresh equity, which will not be forthcoming if the bank is perceived as less profitable than the average. The reality is that Asian banks, partly due to their high growth rate, must put aside substantial provisions every year and it is a big drain on recurrent profits, reflecting badly in the eyes of untrained observers. As a result, Asian banks tend to vastly underestimate their needs for provisions. If they were doing the right thing in that respect, many would simply go bankrupt.

Earnings

There is a debate among rating agencies covering Asia. Some say that the level of earnings is one of the major criteria in their judgment. If a bank is profitable, they claim, everything else is likely to be positive: asset quality will be high, provisions put aside and capital ratios maintained. Thomson BankWatch offers a different view by saying that asset quality is more relevant than anything else,

---

Read the Fine Print

One of the largest private sector banks in Indonesia was publishing splendid earnings ratios every year. The bank was not a likely candidate for such results. How it sustained its earnings remained a mystery until an analyst found out what was happening. The owners of the bank would simply conduct large foreign exchange and treasury transactions through the bank, sometimes holding mirroring positions — meaning if one was losing, the other one was automatically winning by the same amount. As the transactions unfolded, the winning part was entered in the bank's account and the losing part in the owners' company account. This trick would, at no cost to the owners — not even in respect of profit taxes — create an endless flow of profits from the owners to their bank, making the bank look unusually profitable. With those results in hand, the bank managers could tour the world and secure substantial interbank facilities. In turn, this funding source allowed the bank an increase in its related party lending for the direct benefit of its owners.

Dirty Hong Kong

At the Hong Kong subsidiary of a major European bank in the 1970s, the chief accountant would routinely request instructions as to the amount of profits the bank was to record. Within reason, the managers could instruct the accountant to record almost any figure they wanted. Their aim was, ostensibly, to smooth out the profit history of the bank. The reality was more sinister: when in their view too much profit was available, rather than risking being asked to repeat the performance and in the process perhaps embarrass the local staff, they would pocket the money themselves. How generous, how thoughtful! Nobody ever noticed until a story appeared in a couple of minor Hong Kong newspapers claiming that the managers were milking the bank. Someone from inside had talked.

The expatriate managers of the bank had milked the banks for years. When auditors and supervisors visited Hong Kong, they were wined, dined and entertained, sent out on junk trips and generally made to find it difficult to discover anything. The managers made arrangements to maintain several sets of accounts — anything was possible in Hong Kong — and the bank subsidiary ended up being one of the least profitable of the colony. Any dog with a hat and a banking license could make considerable money in Hong Kong, but that particular bank couldn't. Nobody, however, questioned the poor performance. Apparently, since the subsidiary's original capital funds were carried at their long-depreciated value in the books of the parent, the poor return on assets in Hong Kong translated into a high return on equity for the parent's investment. How convenient! Greed fosters greed and the managers started deploying considerable creativity in their cheating. A mishap almost unmasked them when a manager sought, by mistake, to enter into the accounts a small sum that did not belong there. The sum represented the proceeds of the sale of an expensive car which was part of the loot and whose purchase under his name was never recorded. One can imagine the embarrassment if it had happened with the sale of one of the many flats received as "presents" from borrowers. In a refreshing twist of poetic justice, all but one of the managers lost all they had — and more — in the collapse of the market in the early 1970s. The manager who escaped was much brighter, much wealthier and much luckier than the others. He was forced by the circumstances to bail out almost all his accomplices, who had substantial borrowings in the bank's books and could not face them. For unknown reasons, one of them was left with his losses. For six long years, the books had to be cooked month after month so that this manager's loan would never appear. He had, the story goes, an interest in one of his female employees, whose charms also appealed to the department's deputy manager, a local Chinese. One thing leading to another, the deputy was sacked. However, unfortunately for the wicked gang, he had a journalist friend. Hence the denunciation.

At that time, Hong Kong journalists, when treated properly, could turn a blind eye on embarrassing information, and the matter could have been laid to rest. It would have been if the sacked deputy manager had not written to several high-ranking officials in the bank's home country. The head office brass could no longer ignore the problem. They dispatched a young manager to Hong Kong without telling him that something was amiss. To their Board of Directors, they said he was sent there to sort out the problem. To the local staff in Hong Kong, they said he was coming with the mission of computerizing the bank's accounts, some of which were still kept by hand. The reality was that the only part of the accounts that was kept by hand was the Profit & Loss Accounts, and the hand keeping those particular accounts was that of one of the crooked managers. Reality was also that, once he arrived in Hong Kong, the young manager was to be kept from looking at the accounts until he got tired of asking for them.

The young man never gave up and he eventually found out that the expatriate managers had milked hundreds of millions out of the bank for years. They did it in several ways: bad loans to friendly borrowers — huge loans were granted against barely floating ships on their way to scrap yards; special commissions — bearer's checks received with loan applications were common; special arrangements with developers — with several flats for the managers and their friends; special arrangements with other financial institutions for the return to the managers of certain commissions, parallel cash banking. The list was seemingly endless.

The story does not stop there, with threats and maneuvers to expel the young man, followed by his dismissal on spurious grounds. He had not realized that his own boss at the head office was involved, and this cost him his job. He was lucky, in a way. Another young man, dispatched by a Malaysian bank for a similar mission in Hong Kong was found murdered in a back alley. If you insist on knowing the end of the story, here it is. The young man never gave up. He went to the president of his bank, who listened to him and sent a team of investigators to Hong Kong. They found out he was right. The president terminated the expatriate managers and the bank regained its prosperity. What the young man never told the president is that his inspectors did not see half of it. When he left Hong Kong, he took away hundreds of documents incriminating several senior managers of the parent bank, whose names he has kept secret ever since. As a vengeance, he decided to let the rogue managers spread the rot at the head office, and spread the rot they did. But that is another story.

as long as it can be ascertained. It is true that a bank can hardly fake its profitability for a sustained period, while it can do so with asset quality. But the reality is that, in Asia, owner-managers of banks can and do manipulate the accounts in order to look more profitable. They rely on analysts being simplistic in their approach. Long-run profitability is a good sign, but short-term profitability can be a mirage.

Several factors beyond operating cash flow influence profitability ratios: taxes, accounting rules, restructuring costs, among others. In most, but not all, Western countries, those factors would have an impact on the bottom line in the precise period when they were created. In Asia, as in many emerging markets, banks enjoy considerable freedom in transferring profits and losses from one period to another.

Commercial bank profits in Asia derive mainly from lending activities. Authorities happily manipulate the net interest margin, which is the most important contributing factor to those profits. Economic efficiency in intermediation would dictate that the spread between deposit and lending interest rates be as small as possible. The gap between those rates varies widely across Asia. Wide in Indonesia and the Philippines, it is rather narrow in Taiwan. It would be interesting to explore the potential correlation between the intermediation gap and the general health of the economies of the region. A wide gap does not necessarily lead to an enrichment of bank owners at the expense of the public. Indonesian bank owners lose much of the gap to high inefficiency, and so do bank owners in the Philippines. But the gap is so wide in the Philippines that the transfer of wealth from the public to the banks is as visible as it is in Hong Kong, where banks do deserve their fat earnings, thanks to a high efficiency. The efficiency ratios are featured in Chapter 6 (Indonesia) and Chapter 8 (The Philippines).

Asians who gamble in stock exchanges are so focused on the notions of profit growth and profit per share that they miss out entirely on the real meaning of bank profitability ratios. A bank can create more income out of more total assets. Anybody can do that. It is very simple: just run up the assets. The ROA will tell the analyst whether the profitability has actually improved. Even that test is not sufficient, as the ROA may have improved simply on the strength of a modification of the asset mix. Moving assets towards the high-risk zone will almost always create more profits, even where total assets remain unchanged. Such basic remarks hold for any bank in any country, but they are more relevant to Asia. This is because Asia has witnessed such a sustained growth in lending and assets: the growth has offered many more possibilities to modify the asset mix than in a typical lower-growth Western market. From the investor's point of view, better earnings will derive from a relative depletion of the bank's capital in relation to total assets. If a bank can expand its assets while adding equity in a smaller proportion, the ROE will improve. This fact will be missed by the punter focused on profit growth. The analyst, for his part, will make a note of the potential deterioration of the bank's capital strength, and possibly, but not necessarily, draw the conclusion that the increased earnings are of dubious quality.

The quality of earnings also rests on the recurrent nature of the income stream. Again Asian banks distinguish themselves from those in the rest of the world in that they tend not to disclose enough details about the source of their earnings. Until the mid-1990s, in terms of income, banks in Hong Kong did not have to disclose more than their total net profits. Not a word on how they were achieved. And even that single figure was incorrect, as the banks were indulging in transfers to and from hidden reserves. It was therefore impossible for analysts to reach an opinion on the quality of the earnings. But even if more details were supplied, for example the total of the interest income separately from that of the non-interest income, the information would remain misleading. This is because the nature of commercial banking induces frequent transfers between the two main streams of income. Without being too technical, let us mention a couple of examples. Many banks carry currency swaps in their books, often involving currencies whose interest rates are vastly distant. A swap or a forward will create a profit or a loss — depending on the direction of the transaction — while creating a reverse entry in foreign exchange profits.[12] An American bank would rectify the accounting blip by creating an internal reverse entry, something the Asian bank will ignore. On a different front, Asian banks often charge loan administration fees in lieu of interest whenever government rules put a cap on interest rates. No adjustment takes place, making it difficult to judge whether the bank actually receives an interest income commensurate with the risk profile of its portfolio.

The poor treatment accorded by Asian banks to their provisions makes it very difficult to accept income statements at face value. Many countries permit the accrual of interest on delinquent loans for several months before they are — correctly — diverted to interest-in-suspense which is not a profit; it is a provision. Naturally, if a delinquent loan must appear current for political or other reasons, interest is capitalized and the banks must recognize it as a profit. As detailed earlier in the section dealing with asset quality, banks neglect to put aside enough provisions to meet their NPLs. This inflates their profits, as any observer will guess. But considering the high proportion of gross cash flow that banks eventually divert to provisions, a small adjustment in the amount put aside every year creates a wonderful opportunity to cook the books. Let us take an example. Even though they do not provide enough for their bad loans, many banks in Asia must divert as much as 80% of their gross cash flow to provisions every year, leaving only 20% to the taxman, dividends and retained profits. By reducing provisions by only 10%, down to 72% of gross cash flow, a bank can expand its pre-tax profit from 20% to 28% of gross cash flow, an improvement of 40%. The board of directors takes all the decisions in the matter of provisions. The directors have a large degree of discretion in their decisions. Each country has rules on the recognition of NPLs, but there are many ways to accommodate them. Most loans are protected by some collateral, whose value is an important factor in the determination of the provision needed. The value of the collateral is often estimated very generously and the real impact of the trick only hits when the collateral is liquidated.

And the Winner is...

India is a great country: trains run slowly but according to the schedule. Banks do the same. No document is ever lost in an Indian bank, even if it takes 25 years to retrieve it. The reader will forgive me for being very technical here, but the story is worth a ton of chicken curry. This is a promise.

Indian banks are huge and they cover an immense territory, a situation that wisely calls for the subdivision of accounts along regional lines. The reader familiar with the inevitable loose ends created by millions of transactions will appreciate that, at the end of any accounting period, a number of transactions between regional branches cannot immediately be reconciled. India exemplifies this to the extreme, essentially because Indian banks are not highly computerized. Indian bank staff are justifiably worried that computerization would jeopardize their double status as civil servants - most banks are state-owned — and bankers. Accordingly they have resisted any change for years. In short, Indian banks carry huge amounts of unapplied funds in their accounts under the headings "other assets" and "other liabilities". This distinction is the source of an interesting new page in accounting books.

India is still very much a socialist country where banks have social responsibilities, including that of losing money to borrowers who can't or won't pay. As a result, the banks have carried huge quantities of non-performing loans in their books since for time immemorial. In the early 1990s, the government decided to sanitize the accounts. Nationalized banks were divided into the good, the bad and the ugly. The good ones were supposed to clean away their bad loans on their own and, suddenly, even though government-appointed auditors had declared the accounts very clean and the provisions very sufficient the year before, the good banks started announcing huge losses. The bad banks did more or less the same, with the difference that the government had to inject fresh equity cash to prevent them from declaring bankruptcy. This the authorities did over two or three years, depending on the condition of the patient.

For the very sick among the bad ones, there was no way to find enough equity funds so they received permission to enter the loss in deduction of "other liabilities" instead of "shareholders funds",[13] pending better times. This is where having massive "other liabilities" becomes useful. Good accountants will remember that a profit is a liability, while a loss must be deducted from equity or shareholders funds, which is also a liability. The whole affair was highly unorthodox, but the banks came very clean about it. Nothing was concealed. The ugly banks, clearly beyond repair, did not have enough "other liabilities" to shelter their colossal losses. They had to find another solution. They found it. It is the most ingenious, the most extraordinary idea. Nothing seen, or unseen, in China, Vietnam or Pakistan can beat this one: instead of deducting the losses from "other liabilities", they simply added them to "other assets"!

Commercial banks and finance companies in Asia would not be profitable if they were money lenders only. Over the past few years, they have sought to create cash flow from a large spectrum of peripheral activities as well as distant pursuits. To traditional service charges on both deposits and loans, they have added mortgage fees and credit card fees. To their letter-of-credit and transfer fees, they have added asset management fees and income related to securities, trust and investment activities.

Banks also enjoy endless opportunities for position-taking in a variety of financial pursuits, like foreign exchange and derivatives trading, money market transactions. They also trade in financial instruments like commercial paper, certificates of deposits and generally all types of securities. There are many rules preventing them from taking unreasonable positions. They are meant to limit any damage to the banks' viability should the markets turn against them. The problem here is two-fold. In some countries, the rules are too lenient. For example, in Taiwan, Korea and Japan, banks are permitted to invest huge amounts in equities, and this has proven disastrous in recent years. The analyst will try to estimate what risks the bank is taking and whether its traders know what they are doing. The opportunities for going wrong are endless.

Liquidity

The liquidity of a bank's balance sheet is extremely difficult to gauge. Unlike capital ratios, which are a snapshot, and profit ratios, which cover a specific period, liquidity ratios only give an approximate measure of a bank's strength. A good definition of liquidity is the capacity of a financial institution, at any time in the future, to satisfy potential claims on its cash flow. Such claims are evaluated against potential sources of cash flow. Potential claims on cash flow include, besides the withdrawal of deposits, events like maturing debt or the default of a counterparty. Banks can source cash flow from the following: interbank deposits and interbank borrowing capacity, central bank borrowing, and generally marketable, pledgeable or securitizable investments and loans.

A bank should submit its balance sheet to all kinds of stress tests to determine the impact on its accounts of any modification of the yield curve. A change could affect profits but, more importantly, it could affect the bank's ability to secure funding for its operations or to make profitable use of any surplus. Tests also measure the estimated gaps between assets and liabilities for each future period, and their likely impact on liquidity.

The problem with static liquidity ratios like the loans-to-deposits ratio is that they fail to apprehend the liquidity position at all future maturities. Such ratios should satisfy prudential norms at any point of time in the future. This creates serious conceptual problems. Each liability has a maturity, but substantial amounts have very short maturities, as in fact they are demand deposits. Savings accounts holders do not withdraw their savings frequently, in spite of the short-term nature of such deposits. Therefore a proportion of short-term deposits can safely be considered as carrying longer maturities.[14] But in the case of a crisis, as in the recent Asian turmoil, liquidity dries up and such assumptions cease to be correct. As a result, it is important to examine the real nature of the funds listed on both sides of the balance sheet. There is nothing wrong in a bank relying on purchased funds — funds that it asked for, rather that was offered; or being aggressively invested — exhibiting a high-risk or non-liquid asset mix, but the bank should not indulge in both. Needless to say, many Asian banks, in particular in Indonesia and in Thailand, have no idea how to measure that risk. They do not even have a contingency plan should liquidity dwindle.

Off-balance Sheet Items

Contingent accounts or contra-accounts constitute off-balance sheet items that are basically a reminder to the bank that a guarantee is in force or an agreed transaction falls due some time in the future. Any commitment a bank might have in respect of a transaction or guarantee must be recorded as an off-balance sheet entry. As one can imagine, the fact that those entries pertain to transactions that have not yet reached maturity or completion opens the door to cheating opportunities.

Banks may sign deals and commitments that go unrecorded. They also can sign deals with counterparties that are not necessarily creditworthy. When the deals mature, such counterparties may walk away from their obligations, leaving the bank with a loss. More than any other type of transactions, the derivatives would fall into that dangerous category. As a matter of fact, many Indonesian banks signed derivative deals that went wrong in the wake of the financial panic. Derivatives can be used *inter alia* to alter interest rate risk sensitivity, to close asset/liability gaps or to balance exchange rate positions. They are definitely too dangerous for many Asian banks.

It is difficult to decide what is a safe level of off-balance sheet volume, as it would depend on the type of business banks are involved in. In countries like Hong Kong, many banks carry huge amounts of such items, simply because they swap HK dollar deposits for US dollar deposits at the request of their clients, but those are safe transactions.[15] In countries where trade finance is a major activity, substantial amounts represent trade related business. Keeping this in mind, Table 3.2 lists the average level of off-balance sheet items in proportion of total assets.

The average conceals large differences among banks. Table 3.3 lists some of the Asian banks that exceed a level of 40% of off-balance sheet items, compared to total assets.

Banks in Table 3.3 do not necessarily represent a danger in terms of creditworthiness, but the list certainly includes some potential victims of mishaps.

TABLE 3.2 TOTAL CONTINGENT ACCOUNTS (% OF TOTAL ASSETS)

	1994	1995	1996
Pakistan	77.9	103.7	116.3
Indonesia	43.3	42.8	63.3
Malaysia	45.9	54.8	56.4
Taiwan	45.4	49.1	53.4
Nepal	48.7	45.5	45.5
Hong Kong	54.1	61.9	42.5
Sri Lanka	37.3	33.5	38.7
Bangladesh	28.8	31.7	31.7
India	30.7	32.8	29.9
Singapore	33.8	28.0	28.5
Korea	38.9	26.5	26.2
Thailand	21.8	20.3	25.1
China	28.0	25.1	24.9
Vietnam	7.1	10.6	5.7
Macau	6.6	5.0	4.3

Source: Annual Reports

TABLE 3.3 TOTAL CONTINGENT ACCOUNTS
(% OF TOTAL ASSETS, ASIAN BANKS EXCEEDING 40% IN 1996)

Sri Lanka	1994	1995	1996
Union Bank of Colombo Ltd	N/A	23.38	55.71
Commercial Bank of Ceylon	75.18	57.84	41.51
Hatton National Bank	48.52	42.32	51.51
Sampath Bank	33.08	35.52	46.64
Singapore	1994	1995	1996
Development Bank of Singapore	49.22	48.27	61.04
United Overseas Bank	63.80	56.70	52.01
Pakistan	1994	1995	1996
Allied Bank of Pakistan	50.09	65.37	55.65
Askari Commercial Bank	113.86	119.27	114.28
Bank Al Habib	101.43	88.28	108.49
Faysal Bank	N/A	119.06	148.76
Habib Bank	57.10	63.00	63.00
Habib Credit & Exchange Bank	61.93	62.47	N/A
Metropplitan Bank	145.98	113.38	111.76
National Bank of Pakistan	34.67	41.03	41.03

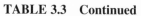

TABLE 3.3   Continued

Platinum Commercial Bank	N/A	483.12	694.69
Prime Commercial Bank	61.97	104.95	150.20
Prudential Commercial Bank	N/A	119.10	119.10
Soneri Bank	80.79	80.05	68.76
Union Bank	169.85	151.48	115.04
United Bank	56.73	56.48	N/A
Bangladesh	**1994**	**1995**	**1996**
Agrani Bank	35.96	40.40	40.40
Arab Bangladesh Bank	41.65	46.12	46.12
National Bank	47.34	60.61	60.61
Taiwan — Established banks	**1994**	**1995**	**1996**
Bank of Kaohsiung	50.23	50.28	45.07
Central Trust of China	196.14	197.76	206.29
Chang Hwa Commercial Bank	53.42	53.62	52.67
Chiao Tung Bank	93.44	121.20	123.78
Chinatrust Commercial Bank	48.89	42.00	49.57
First Commercial Bank	25.30	30.50	59.86
Hua Nan Commercial Bank	62.61	68.83	65.19
International Commercial Bank of China	135.22	115.22	126.48
Overseas Chinese Bank	71.87	77.46	72.81
Shanghai Commercial & Savings Bank	44.46	40.03	52.00
Taipei Bank	50.02	46.28	46.86
Taiwan — New banks	**1994**	**1995**	**1996**
Chinese Bank, The	34.68	35.07	41.55
Chung Shing Commercial Bank	31.72	100.89	107.83
Cosmos Bank	42.21	52.36	97.20
Dah An Commercial Bank	100.68	62.03	56.22
E.Sun Bank	65.52	61.76	73.25
Fubon Commercial Bank	90.93	102.24	116.95
Grand Commercial Bank	43.65	74.63	100.29
Pan Asia Bank	46.64	N/A	44.39
Ta Chong Bank	24.24	44.64	56.62
Taishin International Bank	48.53	59.64	48.42
Thailand	**1994**	**1995**	**1996**
Bangkok Bank	56.54	49.27	63.89
Bank of Asia	20.33	54.41	164.31
First Bangkok City Bank	32.31	31.81	40.79
Nakornthon Bank	79.64	53.90	66.47
Siam City Bank	33.78	42.79	41.47
Siam Commercial Bank	35.55	42.75	52.38
Thai Danu Bank	31.62	34.98	48.55
Indonesia — State banks	**1994**	**1995**	**1996**
Bank Dagang Negara	33.72	42.00	38.57
Bank Ekspor Impor Indonesia	68.67	67.29	357.54
Bapindo	46.52	46.52	N/A

TABLE 3.3 Continued

Indonesia — Private banks	1994	1995	1996
Bank Bali	34.11	40.01	65.19
Bank Buana Indonesia	60.83	44.13	54.76
Bank Central Dagang	35.00	53.09	N/A
Bank Dagang Nasional Indonesia	58.75	63.00	74.15
Bank Duta	49.43	82.92	70.89
Bank Internasional Indonesia	114.23	102.71	54.65
Bank Jaya	32.60	45.62	N/A
Bank Mashill	38.33	64.83	56.50
Bank Niaga	78.58	97.54	120.94
Bank Nusa International	45.86	55.09	77.97
Bank Tiara	48.41	39.29	176.32
Bank Umum Nasional	55.63	83.45	69.91
Bank Universal	118.10	134.37	103.27
Panin Bank (Pan Indonesia Bank)	43.59	63.98	49.68
Prima Express Bank	54.68	79.69	54.59
Tamara Bank	63.89	55.46	77.97
Unibank	91.31	64.81	N/A

Korea	1994	1995	1996
Korea Development Bank	108.19	50.34	69.99
Asian Banking Corp.	97.19	100.47	65.73
Hyundai International Merchant Bank	96.84	65.31	62.13
Korea International Merchant Bank	113.89	48.56	67.76
Korea Merchant Banking Corp.	96.93	75.43	67.95
Korean French Banking Corp.	128.98	87.74	82.69

India	1994/95	1995/96	1996/97
Bank of India	31.94	44.55	47.95
Global Trust Bank	92.08	67.83	107.48
HDFC Bank	4.66	202.61	292.07
ICICI Bank	110.25	69.26	44.98
IndusInd Bank	75.92	70.84	55.33
Times Bank	N/A	59.15	86.29
Uti Bank	24.06	249.04	152.73

China — Mainland	1994	1995	1996
China and South Sea Bank	62.54	54.30	58.44
China State Bank	50.67	53.17	56.74
Kincheng Banking Corporation	54.91	47.19	43.88
Sin Hua Bank	44.12	36.82	43.53

Malaysia	1994	1995	1996
Arab-Malaysian Bank Berhad	93.73	101.70	99.13
Arab-Malaysian Merchant Bank	22.78	73.32	88.27
Ban Hin Lee Bank	59.13	54.93	52.28
Bank Bumiputra Malaysia	39.77	43.46	49.48

TABLE 3.3 Continued

Bank Islam Malaysia	28.88	47.16	50.99
Bank of Commerce	73.35	76.71	80.40
DCB Bank	81.90	97.72	94.86
Eon Bank	26.41	50.49	46.95
Malayan Bank	40.69	51.58	53.43
Multi Purpose Bank	83.53	77.89	71.18
Pacific Bank	62.36	59.04	46.29
Perwira Affin Bank	138.51	120.35	109.32
Public Bank	28.58	32.59	46.26
Sime Bank (United Malaysia Bkg Corp.)	48.04	52.72	58.60
Southern Bank	44.66	67.78	68.36
Hong Kong	**1995**	**1996**	**1997**
Bank of America (Asia)	63.39	53.61	56.30
Bank of East Asia & United Chinese Bank	23.57	37.87	53.24
Dah Sing Bank	48.87	47.54	74.76
Hang Seng Bank	50.87	61.55	51.15
HSBC Investment Bank Asia	163.64	131.69	81.36
International Bank of Asia	48.08	40.61	56.12
Jardine Fleming Bank	466.15	226.32	290.73
Ka Wah Bank	178.89	104.06	70.22
Po Sang Bank	85.17	45.10	47.09
Shanghai Commercial Bank	63.72	51.84	60.35

Source: Annual Reports

Bank Analysis in Asia

How does the theory translate into a serious analysis of Asian banks? The problem is immensely difficult for the analyst.

Asian banks are in dire need of fresh capital funds, following the financial crisis of 1997. It would be wrong, however, to blame the crisis for too high a share of the problem, as Asian banks have in fact long been operating under weak capital ratios. One could in fact argue that Asian banking systems were short billions of dollars in capital funds at the end of 1996, prior to the crisis.

In Asia, three major factors affect the validity of using bank capital ratios as indicators, without considerable adjustments.

Insufficient provisions.   Banks often carry assets whose quality is questionable and for which insufficient provisions have been put aside. Such assets could be loans or investments in securities. This is often the result of years of neglect and, in a high number of cases, proper provisioning would eat away most or all of the institutions' shareholders funds. The matter is sometimes made worse by

Related Party Lending

In mature markets, banks have often reached a large size, both in terms of total assets and shareholders funds. The large size precludes control by a small number of shareholders and, when it is still the case, such shareholders are often themselves controlled in an atomistic way. A large number of independent shareholders, not acting in concert, is both a bad sign and a good sign. It is a bad sign because it is likely that the financial institution will lack a clear sense of direction, absent a well-defined strategy. In addition, the management will report to a board of directors not necessarily representing the voices of myriads of shareholders. Such a board will perpetuate itself over the years for want of an organized alternative.

It is also a good sign in that there should be no temptation to use the deposits entrusted with the bank to promote the businesses of a privileged section of the shareholders group.

In non-Japan Asia in contrast, as the banks remain relatively small, they are often in the controlling hands of just a few shareholders. In many cases, it is easy to imagine that some individual or families have enough wealth to control, directly or through holding companies, entire financial institutions.

Some banks are so small that any wealthy individual with no banking experience could acquire them using pocket money, signing a check on a Saturday afternoon. In fact, many non-Japan banks in Asia are controlled by families, not companies. To make matters more complicated, such banking families in Malaysia, Indonesia, Thailand and the Philippines are overwhelmingly of Chinese origin. This fact introduces yet another dimension to the question of stability and survival, in the broader context of racial tensions.

The temptation is always there to use the banks as piggy banks for the family, drawing from the deposits to finance the family's other ventures. This is done in many subtle ways, so as not to contravene the rules governing such related party lending. Among the favorite ways around the rules are the following:

- Lending to a seemingly independent company or individual, who will on-lend the funds to a related company.
- Asking another financial institution to lend to a related company, against a guarantee not entered in the books.
- Lending to a company related to another bank, against a similar cross-lending from the other bank.

Central banks are very much aware of what is going on, but they are helpless if the transactions do not appear to break any rule. In a celebrated case in Indonesia in 1996, the owners of a bank milked the bank under the very eyes of the central bank, which happened itself to be a large minority shareholder in the bank.

Is related-party lending objectionable? To answer that question, one must first make up one's mind as to the relevance of capital ratios. If capital funds are indeed meant to ensure that, should some of the bank's assets lose value, such funds will be sufficient to cover the losses before depositors and creditors are affected, then the capital funds should always remain positive. Related party loans constitute a negative capital entry, and they should always be deducted from capital funds prior to the computation of capital ratios.

unprovided liabilities under off-balance sheet entries. The adjustments to capital ratios on account of the lack of provisions against non-performing assets would generally inflict considerable damage to a bank's standing.

Related party lending. This practice involves lending directly or indirectly to borrowers associated with the shareholders and it is endemic in Asia. It may not be visible, but shareholders often borrow more funds from their banks than they commit in shareholders funds, thereby rendering useless the notion of capital adequacy rules. This questionable practice affects public sector banks as well as private sector banks.

It is not entirely relevant, though, to assimilate the related party-lending perpetrated by governments to that of private sector institutions. In the case of state-owned banks, the notion of capital ratio, whether properly adjusted or not, is totally irrelevant. But for the private sector, proper adjustments on account of related party lending would, in quite a large number of cases in Asia, result in banks posting negative capital ratios. Exactly why the regulatory authorities are blind to that problem is one of the great mysteries of the Asian financial world.

State-controlled banks. There are many state-owned or state-controlled banks in Asia, most notably in China, Korea, Taiwan, Indonesia, South Asia and Indochina. Many of them, but thankfully not all of them, are in fact bankrupt and survive only on the strength of the guaranteed or implied support of their state shareholders. Capital ratios are therefore irrelevant to them. They carry loans that would not have been extended, but for their status as government banks. If proper adjustments were made to the capital ratios posted by state-owned and state-controlled Asian banks, in respect of non-performing loans, a large number of them, accounting for the majority of all banking assets in Asia, would post BIS ratios substantially short of the 8% benchmark.

State-controlled Banks

Many Asian commercial banks fall into the category of state-controlled institutions. This extraordinary situation affects almost all banking systems. There are several categories of state control. State ownership can be direct (Bank Negara Indonesia), partial (Krung Thai Bank) or indirect (Keppel Bank). The ownership can be in the hands of entities close to the state (Thai Military Bank). Private banks are often instruments of the state, even though they belong to the private sector (Cho Hung Bank). All told, most countries in Asia have banks in one or more of those categories. Even Hong Kong before 1997 had a major bank with a close connection with the state: after all, HongKongBank (formerly known as the Hong Kong and Shanghai Bank) was running the colony, with the Jockey Club and the colonial government, in that order, distant runners-up.

Controlled or not, banks suffer from state directives restricting their commercial autonomy, ranging from interest rate fixing to lending directed at favored borrowers. As a result, the usual performance ratios carry little meaning. Net interest margins are artificially inflated or deflated by interest rate policies. Fees and commissions are skewed due to services performed for the government. More importantly, a bad loan is not a bad loan until the government says so, and provisioning for bad debts may not represent anything. Liquidity ratios are of no relevance, as such banks can count on state support in case of need. In any event, the government may require assets to be distributed in a pre-determined way and state-owned banks are used as channels for government funds, or for example, as vehicles for tax collection. Asset quality is generally very poor since most lending is directed at state-controlled corporations. Non-government borrowers who would otherwise not deserve any attention obtain funds as a substitute for government subsidies, a vehicle for government policy or, worse of all, a form of political patronage. Who cares whether a state-controlled bank is solvent? Capital adequacy ratios have absolutely no meaning. They are strongly influenced by inadequate measurements of profitability and asset quality.

Governments routinely "borrow" substantial funds from state banks, giving rise to a new concept of related party lending. It does not really matter, but technically state-owned banks are the worst offenders in this category, as they lend to the state or to state-owned companies in amounts that vastly exceed their capital funds. Direct lending to the state usually takes the shape of liquidity reserves frozen with the central bank, a legitimate move that also affects private sector banks. Often finance ministries achieve monetary targets by acting on the availability of credit through additional reserve requirements. In addition, in some Asian countries, the capital markets are not sufficiently developed for governments to finance their deficits through direct issues, and confiscating deposits from financial institutions is an easy option.

Despite the obvious flaws in financial ratios, the analysis of state-controlled banks can be performed on the basis of comparison between similar institutions in the same country. The creditworthiness of state-controlled banks has always been highly dependent on the link between the state and its banks. Traditionally, it was anticipated that the state would come to the rescue of a troubled institution it controlled, but recently, the assumption that the creditworthiness of government and of state institutions are the same has become questionable. State-controlled banks cannot have the same rating as the state whenever the link with the state looks tenuous. Furthermore, a credit rating always encompasses not only the likelihood of the commitment being honored per se, but also the likelihood of a timely payment. State banks usually end up paying their debts, but delays are possible. Clearly the relationship between a government and a state financial institution is constantly evolving. Such banks now venture into new and more risky product lines and this relationship will increasingly be tested, making the rating a very difficult exercise.

The Elusive Capital Adequacy Ratio

Capital ratios have lost their meaning. Even if a single rule was to apply to all countries, as at present the 8% rule, it could be argued that the hurdle is too high. With the exception of Hong Kong, Singapore and the Philippines, the Asian banking systems are on average below 8%, sometimes well below that level, often in negative territory. The difference between restoring bank capital to 8% and restoring it to, say, 5% is equal to 3% of risk-weighted assets. To realize the magnitude of the difference, one should use a rule of thumb as follows: in non-Japan Asia, on average, 1% of risk-weighted assets is roughly equal to 1% of GDP. All the distressed countries of Asia will have to devote in the vicinity of 20% of GDP to restore their banking systems to health. Is the last 3% that necessary?

Market realities give regulators a compelling reason to become flexible in imposing capital ratios. What is the point in forcing unrealistic capital ratios onto banks when natural market forces or other reasons prevent them from reaching those minimum levels in the normal course of their business? Unless they have access to fresh equity, they have three courses of action.

To move to riskier assets. One of the weaknesses of the BIS ratio is that it is blind to the actual degree of risk of various assets within wide categories. A loan to IBM requires the same supporting capital that a car loan to a taxi company in Jakarta requires. By moving loans within the same category to higher risk levels, banks generate higher interest income without affecting their capital ratios. This increases their risk profile in a seemingly painless way and produces immediate results in terms of profitability, which in turn creates an immediate upwards adjustment to capital ratios. Naturally this move can result in painful experiences in terms of non-performing assets, but that secondary effect will not materialize immediately.

To seek fresh sources of non-interest income. Alternatively, or concurrently, banks can seek additional income over and above the safe and recurrent level of non-lending profits coming from transactions associated with plain-vanilla money lender activities. Commercial foreign exchange trading gains, trade finance fees, credit card charges or loan administration fees are examples of fee generating activities that are relatively safe and always make stable contributions to the bottom line. Additional income would be generated by speculative activities in foreign exchange, money market, securities or derivatives trading. This is an entirely different field, a minefield in fact, that even the best equipped Western banks approach with caution. For most commercial banks in Asia, it is difficult to take that route without exposing the bottom line to the vagaries of the markets. This is not necessarily dangerous, but do the banks know how to control the risk? The sorry state of several major Korean banks, which have in recent periods lost up to 20% of their equity in securities trading, is a strong reminder of such dangers.

To resort to creative accounting. The ultimate method in achieving ratios acceptable to the regulators and to the markets has been used in all but a few Asian countries. It consists in embellishing the bottom line by reducing the amounts diverted to loan loss reserves. The classification of loans into the various non-performing categories is less than scientific, and all sorts of tricks can be used, including loan restructuring, to give external analysts the mistaken impression that the matter is under control. In many cases, this deception conceals weak net asset values behind seemingly acceptable profitability ratios. Untrained or uninformed observers are in no position to know the truth.

In the past few years, banks in Asian countries where capital ratios are weak have largely resorted to all three tricks, with creative accounting a definite winner. Unrealistic expectations in terms of capital ratios lead banks to take unwise decisions. By imposing minimum capital adequacy ratios above those dictated by market realities, regulatory authorities in Asia have in fact precipitated their charges into a vicious circle. Gambling activities and riskier loans lead to more non-performing assets and the capital ratios get weaker. Since it is deemed unwise to recognize that weakness, banks have to resort to creative accounting.

Is creative accounting not the ultimate form of corporate artistry?

Endnotes

1. Singapore banks have started becoming a little less secretive in recent times but, not long ago, their disclosure standards were barely better than in Hong Kong. Since the model involves the subjective weighting of various ingredients, it would not be wise to leave the door open to criticism by Singapore banks. In a theatrical gesture bordering paranoia, a senior banker in Singapore, holding his bank's annual report in hand, once told me that anything I needed to know was in the report and that I should not even think of asking any incidental or additional question.

2. A model was built giving various weighting to each and every financial detail expected from annual reports. Each column of Table 3.1 gives scores to banks against a maximum possible score in respect of one major disclosure category. The model adjusts for the absence of information on types of transactions some banks do not enter into. It gives subjective weighting according to the relevance of each type of information. Applied to North American banks, the model usually gives scores in a range of 900 to 970 out of a perfect 1000.

3. No one would seriously compare the quantity of financial information on the basis of the weight of annual reports, but this simple comparison gives a serious hint that indeed there are substantial differences across Asia.

4. The distinction is purely cosmetic. In reality, there should be no distinction between fresh funds meant to clean away bad loans and fresh funds meant to recapitalize the institution. Bad loans are written off against profits. Negative profits eat away at capital funds, which must be replaced the same way they are replaced when other types of losses have depleted them.

5. As incredible as it might look, some analysts, even in rating agencies, still believe that profitability is an indication of good health in Asia. This absurdity has led some rating agencies to rate private sector Indonesian banks at inappropriate levels. In a famous example, back in 1995, two large such banks received the same rating from a major rating agency when one of them was safe while the other bank was an accident waiting to happen — and it did happen.

6. For example, a guarantee issued by a bank can result in a loss as devastating as a bad loan.

7. The statistical approach is the old fashioned concept whereby, within a given confidence interval, some measurable maximum gain or loss can possibly result from holding a position.

8. The definition of Leverage is slightly different in that equity is deducted from the numerator of the ratio, but the conclusion remains roughly the same. See the definition of all the ratios in an appendix at the back of this book.

9. The Leverage takes all assets at 100% of their value. The BIS ratio takes assets at their risk-weighted value. It reduces the conceptual value of assets to take into account the risk they represent. The difference between total assets and total risk-weighted assets is not the same for every bank, and it changes

constantly. This is because no two banks exhibit the same asset mix. Among others, a major visible difference lies in the proportion of quasi-liquid assets to total assets.

10. Major adjustments to capital ratios are the result of underprovisioning and of related party lending.

11. This of course is not totally correct in that total lending is not equal to total weighted assets, but this does not detract from the argument.

12. A US$/DM swap, for example, would result in the interest income being boosted by the interest rate differential. On a one-year basis, swapping DM for US$ would result in an artificial interest income increment of about 2% to 3%. But an almost equivalent amount would be lost in foreign exchange trading, creating an accounting quid pro quo that needs adjusting.

13. Net profits of the year, after deduction of dividends, if any, must be entered in the balance sheet as retained earnings or reserves. Such reserves are added to the existing capital funds on the liability side of the balance sheet. Conversely, losses are deducted from existing capital funds. If such funds are too thin, deducting the losses will bankrupt the institution. Hence the need to park the losses in "other liabilities".

14. In a mature and stable market, it is possible to observe the stability of savings accounts and to decide that on aggregate 80% of such accounts, for example, behave like one-year term deposits, while the remaining 20% are volatile. Considerable research in that field has been done over the years in North America and Europe.

15. It is therefore too simplistic to infer from the volume of contingent accounts that a bank is doing something dangerous. If only Asian banks disclosed more information about themselves, and were to show the legitimacy of most of their off-balance sheet transactions, it would be possible to exonerate many of them. In the absence of acceptable disclosure of such transactions, the external observers can only look at rough ratios that may not do justice to some banks.

THAILAND

T hailand is the cradle of the Asian crisis. It was from Bangkok that the panic first spread to the rest of the region. Nowhere else can the blame be more surely laid on stubborn bureaucracy and self-interest. The Thai crisis was probably inevitable, but Thailand is squarely responsible for the panic that it created. The authorities handled the problems very poorly. The first cracks in the financial system appeared in 1994, but the Thai politicians kept their heads in the sand until July 1997. Of all the Asian countries affected by the financial panic, Thailand is the one that most deserves the comment that this crisis was largely self-inflicted.

The Banking System

Thailand was badly hit, along with other South East Asian nations, by a financial crisis in the mid-1980s, mainly driven by uncertainties in commodity prices. The country went through a string of golden years between 1986 and 1995, in what will soon be seen as the best development period of its economy.

Yet, Thailand's financial markets in the 1980s could best be described as fairly shallow. Equity markets were modest, there was little in the way of long-term financing opportunities, and the banking sector was basically limited to a short list of banks and a small but growing number of finance companies. Other types of non-bank financial institutions existed, with some of them going through difficult times, but the bulk of the business was in the hands of 15 banks and the major finance companies. When the 1997 crisis erupted, Finance One, the largest finance company, had assets in the vicinity of US$4 billion, roughly equivalent to the size of the 12th largest bank.

Bank of Thailand (BOT) was seen as a competent and benevolent regulator. It would protect its charges, arbitrate difficulties amid bank shareholders and keep them out of trouble. There were occasional difficulties among non-banks, but the last serious problem among commercial banks was the collapse of Sayam Bank in the early 1980s, with government-owned Krung Thai Bank promptly swallowing the ailing bank.

Most of the Thai banks had been seriously affected by the mid-1980s' crisis, although perhaps not as severely as their southern neighbors in Malaysia. There was a big difference, however, in the way the problems were disclosed. Truthfulness in financial accounting was, and still is, pretty limited in both countries, but at least the central bank in Malaysia came public with the level of NPLs in the books of its charges, while little was admitted in Thailand. In both countries, individual banks were allowed to camouflage their non-performing assets and to rehabilitate themselves over the years. The remarkable growth of the region in the late 1980s and early 1990s miraculously turned that strategy into a success.

In the case of Thai banks, the rehabilitation resulted in a very visible improvement in profitability ratios. The remarkably steady growth of their return on average assets (ROAA) (from under 1% in 1989 to just above 1.7% in 1995) is unprecedented elsewhere. The smoothness of the curve also indicates that there must have been an invisible hand guiding the figures towards politically correct levels, within the loose constraints of accounting realities. As discussed in Chapter 3 devoted to bank accounting, there are many ways to cook bank books, but profitability ratios are probably a bit harder to massage than other ratios. Yet, to do so is still possible. In the past, a number of banks would bypass the Profit & Loss statements and deduct provisions straight from equity. BOT used to permit this practice, even though it would justifiably attract qualifications by the bank auditors.

As can be seen in Table 4.1, in 1994 and 1995, profitability stabilized at a relatively high level. To the extent that rehabilitation can be measured by the banks' capacity to generate profits, those years mark the end of the recovery period. By 1996, the banks had fallen back to the lower profitability levels of the late 1980s, a sign, if it was needed, that things were not as brilliant as the rest of the world thought they were. If nothing else, the weakening performance of most Thai banks in 1995 and 1996 was a clear sign that problems were looming.

TABLE 4.1 COMMERCIAL BANKS RETURN ON AVERAGE ASSETS (%)

	1988	1989	1990	1991	1992	1993	1994	1995	1996
ROAA	0.90	0.64	0.94	0.96	1.29	1.52	1.63	1.73	1.06

Source: Annual Reports

Totaling close to US$50 billion by the end of 1996, BIBF loans contributed significantly to the entire external private sector debt of Thailand. It would be wrong, however, to attribute the demise of a chunk of the Thai banking system to that BIBF misallocation, as Thai domestic borrowers already had almost unlimited

The Bangkok International Banking Facilities

Foreign financial institutions were not exactly welcome in the 1970s and 1980s, except as minority partners in non-banks, a proposition that was not very attractive and was also fraught with danger. This situation changed abruptly in the early 1990s when the Bangkok International Banking Facilities (BIBF) were created. With the end of colonialism signalled by the impending return of Hong Kong to China, there was a general feeling in Asia that no single financial center was going to emerge as a credible substitute for Hong Kong. However, a number of countries figured that, with the appropriate legal framework and more importantly a soft tax regime, it would not be difficult to attract international financial institutions to conduct some offshore business in unlikely places like Labuan, Manila or Bangkok.[1]

As foreign banks had long been frustrated in their quest for an entry to Thailand's retail banking market, the authorities promised them or let them hope that, after a suitable stint under the BIBF pavilion, they would be allowed a slice of the growing local market. More recently, Thailand has also announced that foreign banks will be allowed more access to the local market, under certain conditions, and that new domestic banks would be given a license to start operating.

The BIBF status was also offered to domestic banks, and it was supposed to promote purely offshore transactions whereby banks borrow from overseas and lend overseas, without any interaction with domestic activities. As we shall see, this was not to happen, and the BIBF will go down in history books as a Trojan Horse invading the banking sector: a gift it should have refused.

Since the 1970s, it had been possible for Thai borrowers to turn to international lenders to obtain loans and facilities in various currencies other than the baht. This was by no means a situation limited to Thailand, as thousands of borrowers in countries like Korea, Indonesia, the Philippines and Malaysia were, over the years, attracted by the huge amounts of ready funds from rich countries in search of lending opportunities in Asia. There was no restriction to the geographic distribution of assets in the books of BIBF banks, both Thai and foreign-owned. They could select assets both inside and outside of Thailand. Domestic lending is typically called "OUT-IN" since the liability side is offshore while the asset side is onshore, as opposed to the "OUT-OUT" situation where both the liability and the asset sides are offshore. The temptation was strong for the international banks to opt for OUT-IN transactions, that is to divert part of their OUT-OUT offshore business to domestic lending. After all, this was no different from booking those domestic dollar loans in Hong Kong or

Singapore. All other things being equal, it is easy to imagine that the Thai authorities welcomed a situation where business was relocated from other Asian cities. In their zeal, they neglected to realize the danger of having the Thai domestic banks do the same: they were also using their BIBF division to lend offshore dollars to local borrowers. In early 1997, it is estimated that a staggering 65% of all BIBF assets were of the OUT-IN variety, a deviation that was probably not intended by the authorities.

opportunities to borrow from offshore sources. Yet, BIBF's additional OUT-IN loans were definitely the straw that broke the camel's back.

Thailand was obviously the best candidate to join the long-established club of the Asian Tigers (Korea, Taiwan, Hong Kong and Singapore), and its staggering growth could not be entirely financed from within. It was with the encouragement of the IMF and the World Bank that the country embarked in the early 1990s on substantial financial liberalization. Externally, it meant the dismantling of almost all foreign exchange controls and the transfer of a sizable portion of the external borrowing of the private sector to BIBF. Internally, it meant deregulation of the financial industry, giving more freedom to banks in matters like asset mix and interest rates. With it came the loosening of rules in respect of the two major quantitative controls a central bank can exercise on banks: liquidity and capital ratios, or more precisely the way they were measured. By any measure, Thai banks ended up being the least liquid of any banking system in Asia. Capital ratios looked reasonably good, but they were achieved on the back of lenient rules on NPL classification.

A Deluge of Funds

Most people would agree that a stable exchange rate against the currencies of major trading partners is generally beneficial. In such a case, there is little uncertainty about the amount of local currency that will flow in or out from an export or import contract expressed in foreign currency. The risk of maintaining open positions in foreign currencies is limited, and therefore little is wasted in hedging costs. The currency is seen as stable and therefore is not prone to exaggerated fluctuations on account of little bouts of good or bad news. Inflation can be contained. It is easy for the central bank to manipulate and stabilize the local currency, but this comes at a price in terms of control over interest rates, especially in the extreme situation where the currency stability is maintained through a currency board.

The other side of the coin is that, if there is partial or full convertibility, it becomes difficult for the currency to swallow the sometimes large fluctuations in funds flowing in and out of the country. Countries that have substantial foreign currency reserves can handle the fluctuations easily, and in the few years preceding 1996, Thailand was comfortable in that respect. But as stable as this might appear, maintaining near-fixed currencies still carries a risk. All other things being equal, it will always seem less risky to hold the foreign currency, even for residents, who by nature are or should be holders of the local near-fixed currency. Things are therefore not equal and the near-fixed currency must carry a premium in the shape of a higher interest rate. The premium will be determined by the perceived risk that the fixed rate will not be maintained, by government money market interventions, and by the actual volume of local investment sought from non-residents. In Thailand, the baht has long carried interest rate premiums, and so has the Hong Kong dollar.

Thailand had incompatible targets. The country was faced with the difficult task of balancing the various objectives that its government had set for development: financial liberalization was necessary, a stable baht was preferable (Table 4.2), and foreign investment was needed if the country was to become the fifth Asian Tiger. It is not impossible to accommodate all three objectives, but it is extremely difficult. One cannot forcibly control both interest rates and exchange rates, and wise politicians trusting wise economists would recognize that fact. But in the case of Thailand this was ignoring the weakness of human nature. The temptation was there and the Thai government thought it could succeed. Everyday, it seems, produces new sorcerer's apprentices.

TABLE 4.2   CURRENCY TABLE

	Dec. 91	Dec. 92	Dec. 93	Dec. 94	Dec. 95	Dec. 96	Dec. 97	15 Jun. 98
US$ per baht	0.03956	0.03918	0.03915	0.03986	0.03970	0.03905	0.02116	0.02285
Base Dec. 1991 = 100	100	99.04	98.96	100.76	100.35	98.71	53.49	57.76
Baht per US$	25.28	25.52	25.54	25.09	25.19	25.61	47.25	43.76
Base Dec. 1991 = 100	100	100.95	101.03	99.25	99.64	101.31	186.91	173.10

Source: Capital Information Services

Undeniably, more foreign funds were made available to Thailand than were actually needed or could safely be swallowed. Several reasons can be advanced to try and explain that unusual situation. The country was rightly seen as one of the most promising emerging markets in the region, and it can be argued that it still is promising today. Interest rates and investment yields were generally falling in Europe and North America in the early 1990s, while Asia had demonstrated its extraordinary potential in the production of superior returns on investment. Not surprisingly, not only did financial institutions rush to lend to Asia, but also pension funds and investment houses started developing a growing interest in Asia. Given the relatively small size of the economy of a country like Thailand and the

TABLE 4.3   ECONOMIC INDICATORS

	1991	1992	1993	1994	1995	1996	1997	1998p
Currency								
Baht/US$ (end period)	25.28	25.52	25.54	25.09	25.19	25.61	47.25	40.00
Real Exchange Rate, % change	−5.7	−3.2	−4.5	−6.9	−6.6	−3.1	76.5	−24.3
Real Economy								
Real GDP, % change	7.0	7.1	8.2	8.6	8.7	6.7	−0.4	−3.0
Fixed Investment as % of GDP	38.0	39.5	39.9	40.1	42.8	39.8	39.1	34.5
Official Unemployment Rate (%)	3.5	3.6	3.4	3.2	3.0	3.3	3.7	7.0
Money and Prices								
Consumer Price Inflation (end period) (%)	5.7	4.1	4.6	5.1	5.8	4.8	8.0	9.0
Lending Rate (%)	19.00	17.54	15.60	14.38	15.50	15.00	18.00	N/A
Reserves (US$ billions)	17.52	20.36	24.47	29.33	35.98	37.73	26.18	28.50
Domestic Savings Rate (%)	31.1	31.3	32.5	33.6	34.2	38.4	37.0	38.0
Balance of Payments								
Exports (US$ billions)	28.23	32.10	36.41	44.48	55.45	54.41	58.00	74.00
Imports (US$ billions)	34.22	36.26	40.70	48.20	63.42	63.90	67.00	65.00
Trade Balance (US$ billions)	(5.99)	(4.16)	(4.29)	(3.72)	(7.97)	(9.49)	(9.00)	9.00
Current Account Balance (US$ billions)	(7.57)	(6.30)	(6.36)	(8.09)	(13.56)	(14.69)	(3.40)	7.00
Current Account Balance, % GDP	−7.7	−5.7	−5.6	−5.9	−8.2	−7.9	−2.1	3.5
Foreign Debt (US$ billions)	35.99	39.61	45.84	60.99	65.00	89.00	97.00	105.80
as % of GDP	36.9	36.2	37.1	43.1	42.4	54.0	61.0	85.5
Debt Service Ratio (%)	13.0	13.7	18.5	15.6	13.9	14.7	27.7	31.3
Governmant Finance								
Gov. Surplus/Deficit as % of GDP	4.7	2.8	2.1	1.8	3.0	1.6	−0.6	−2.0

Source: Thomson BankWatch Inc.

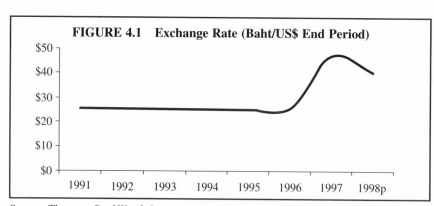

Source: Thomson BankWatch Inc.

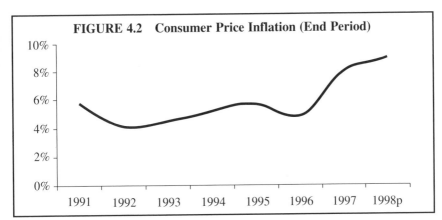

FIGURE 4.2   Consumer Price Inflation (End Period)

Source: Thomson BankWatch Inc.

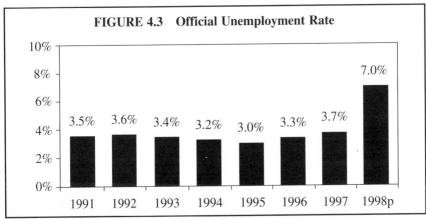

FIGURE 4.3   Official Unemployment Rate

Source: Thomson BankWatch Inc.

FIGURE 4.4   Foreign Debt (US$ billions)

Source: Thomson BankWatch Inc.

huge investment capacity of the rich countries, a small shift in fund allocation from a major US investment house could easily submerge the capital markets of such a relatively small Asian economy. A seemingly innocuous decision to reallocate funds, taken in a New York boardroom, could move small markets in Asia.

A good confirmation of this theory can be found in the seemingly endless list of foreign financial institutions that bought into floating rate certificates of deposit (FRCDs) issued by Thai banks in the past few years. Almost all 15 banks resorted to that sort of financing, and not one of them deemed a long-term rating for the debt at all necessary: the buyers did not bother to insist on a neutral examination of the banks' ability to meet their obligations. International financial intermediaries always had drawers full of potential buyers. Even the weakest names, among them some desperate cases, could access the market. As a result of this blind approach on the part of lenders, the pricing of the issues, which would normally show a gap between good and bad names, was both relatively indiscriminate — weak names did not pay much more than good names — and generally much too low for the risk.

The banks were paying relatively little for their US dollar borrowings, simply because too many dollars were chasing too few opportunities. Not that there were no other investment opportunities in Thailand, far from it, but there was a wide category of investors who were only interested in what they perceived to be the safe world of local banks. In their innocence, they believed that perhaps the watchful eye of the regulators made banks better risks than corporates. While disclosure is minimal and truthfulness abysmally low in the books of local banks, they are much better in that respect than domestic corporate borrowers. As such, banks became a good proxy for Thai risk.

Unfortunately, the foreign funds so gathered were directed at the wrong investments, owing to the artificial "positive carry" created by the fixed exchange rate (the mechanism is explained in Chapter 1). A large chunk of excess foreign lending and investment went to property: Bangkok is lined with half-finished buildings, while many of those that were built in recent years lay empty. In the best of times, it would take at least five years for Thailand to absorb the excess capacity. If the present circumstances prevail, close to 10 years will be needed.

The Defense of the Baht in 1997: Accounting Tricks

By early 1997, it was becoming clear to some external observers that it would become increasingly difficult to defend the parity of the baht. It is a sad fact that some Thai officials, among them Bank of Thailand officials, did not share such views. They embarked on wasting the country's reserves in order to maintain an artificially high level for the baht. This turned out to be the trigger for the Asian currency crisis.

Was the baht overvalued? Back in the mid-1980s, the baht was devalued, like other regional currencies, and more or less pegged to a weak dollar. When the dollar started climbing back again, in recent years, increasing in value against most European currencies, the Australian dollar, Eastern European currencies and many more, most currencies in East Asia went up with the dollar. Closer to home, the Chinese yuan was devalued in 1994, and the yen was knocked down substantially from its high levels. According to BOT statistics, the baht, on an effective exchange rate basis — that is against the currencies of its trading partners — started looking slightly overvalued by the end of 1995. It ended up being about 9% overvalued by the time the crisis erupted, against its recent historical value, a divergence of about 6% per annum.

Most economies can live with such a small degree of divergence from historical value. On fundamentals, Thailand's currency did not necessarily need a drastic adjustment. But this should have alerted the authorities to the danger of linking the currency in a quasi-peg to the strong dollar. It would have been better to link it to a basket of currencies more correctly representing Thailand's trading partners, in particular the Japanese yen. On fundamentals, the baht could have remained at its inflated level for some more time, but it would have been such an expensive exercise that it would have hit a wall at one point in the not-too-distant future.

BOT had ample foreign currency reserves before the attack on the baht, in the vicinity of US$33 billion. Against about US$17 billion in M1 monetary mass, such reserves would, however, not have been sufficient to maintain a peg, let alone a currency board, but BOT had a sporting chance to repel mild attacks on the currency. Few international economists could actually perceive the rotten conditions undermining the baht, and this lack of perception was worth the equivalent of quite a substantial amount of foreign currency reserves. The problem stemmed from the fact that BOT did not know when to throw in the towel and so it embarked on wasting a gigantic proportion of its reserves in the defense of the baht. Even after it had become obvious to everyone else that the baht had to go, the BOT carried on defending it with unforgivable abandon. Central banks in Indonesia and the Philippines, and even to a degree in Malaysia, did not spend quite that much energy to delay the inevitable.

To make things worse, BOT is accused of having resorted to accounting tricks in order to conceal the extent of the damage from the public, external observers and, apparently, a large fraction of the Thai administration. They resorted to the old trick of entering into swap transactions where the spot component was revealed but the future component was, conveniently, not mentioned. It is an old trick long used by rogue currency traders to conceal losses, but the volume involved in this particular case is beyond imagination, as a total of close to US$30 billion was involved. Technically, that amount should have been deducted from official reserves which, after taking into account more visible spot transactions on the foreign exchange markets, had in reality fallen to about US$1.5 billion, close to technical insolvency (see also Chapter 10 on the arithmetic of foreign reserves). Note that, in truth, the net foreign reserves had not fallen by the full amount, since

Thailand at any time could theoretically attempt to seal reverse transactions and take the loss.[2] This would have restored some of the foreign reserves.

Apparently, BOT elected to publicize only the balance sheet entries, and not the off-balance sheet items. As per the balance sheet, the country's reserves remained high throughout the crisis, at US$32 billion in June 1997, just before the meltdown. But at the same time, the off-balance sheet entries secretly went from a relatively modest US$5 billion in December 1996 to a peak of about US$30 billion in May 1997. Normally, the two amounts should have been reconciled to indicate the net foreign exchange position. Since the off-balance sheet items were short in dollars and long in baht, meaning negative reserves, clearly the net reserves were close to nothing. As disclosing this disastrous situation would certainly have been detrimental to BOT's efforts to prop up the baht, one can understand the temptation to conceal the fact. On the other hand, there must have been a point when the net balance between the positive positions and the negative positions should have alerted the Thai government that it was time to give up the fight.

A lot of soul searching has taken place in Thailand, but it seems futile to put the blame on a scapegoat. Either the highest authorities in government knew, in which case they are to blame for letting it happen, or they did not know, which is hard to believe, and they are to blame for not knowing, comparable to Nixon and Watergate. Attempts have been made at accusing international speculators of having precipitated the crisis. About three-quarters of all swap transactions involve foreign private sector parties, as opposed to governments. It would be ridiculous to deny that speculators found in the Thai baht an easy target — yet some of them lost fortunes when the baht briefly strengthened — but one should be reasonable here. It takes two to tango, and the invitation to dance was clearly extended by BOT in its desperate search for immediately deliverable US dollars. After all, a US$/baht swap of the nature discussed here is nothing more than a baht holder begging a dollar holder to lend him his dollars against the use of baht for the duration of the contract. This is no different from other short-term borrowings of dollars collateralized with baht. In that sense, it is exactly as if BOT had obtained short-term IMF funds, to the tune of US$30 billion, for the purpose of defending its currency. Should a transaction of that magnitude be kept secret? Of course it should not.

The Thailand Meltdown

The proximate cause of Thailand's crisis, and probably the Asian crisis, was the sorry state of its finance companies. And yet, their total combined assets did not exceed the equivalent of US$40 billion. The outright failure of a single bank of that size, even in a relatively small economy like Thailand's, could not have precipitated the events that followed. All the more so in the case of the finance companies owing to the fact that their financial links with the rest of the financial institutions were fairly limited. For example, instead of relying on interbank funding, as the Malaysian non-banks did, they were issuing promissory notes directly to depositors. In addition, few of them belonged substantially to banks, although in many cases the bank shareholders were also the finance company shareholders. Table 4.4 illustrates the limited links between major banks and non-banks.

At a cost later estimated at about Baht 700 billion, the collapse and liquidation of a large number of finance companies in Thailand hurt the taxpayer rather than the banks. But it was very much offering a condensed version of what was to go wrong in most of Asia's financial systems.

Would it have been possible to avert the meltdown? No. The meltdown was inevitable, in the shape it took or in another shape, at some time in the very near

---

Foreign Exchange Swaps and Forward Transactions

Foreign exchange swap transactions are made up of a spot transaction and a reverse transaction in the forward markets for approximately the same amount. The spot transaction involves almost immediate delivery, in fact within 48 hours. The forward transaction calls for delivery at an agreed time, for example three or six months ahead. The forward rate is usually slightly different from the spot rate to compensate for the fact that one party will have the use of funds in a high interest rate currency (for example the baht) for six months, while the counterparty will play with funds in a low interest rate currency (for example the dollar) during that time. The owners of, say, US$1 million, part with their dollars immediately, in exchange for, say, Baht 25 million, with the understanding that, after six months, they will get their dollars back against the bahts, at a slightly higher rate.

This is a basic treasury transaction, and thousands of such transactions are made every day. Swaps can be created synthetically by the signing of separate deals with separate counterparties. Swaps can also be a part of more sophisticated transactions. The spot transaction (the first half of the swap deal) always enters the balance sheet itself because delivery of the currencies takes place almost immediately. Funds are actually paid or received in two currencies. The forward transaction (the second half of the swap deal) is only a promise to deliver and, therefore, it is entered as an off-balance sheet item. Funds will be exchanged later and, at that time only, will be entered in the balance sheet itself. Naturally, at the time the transaction is concluded, both sides of all swaps must appear somewhere in the accounts, one of them in the balance sheet and the other as an off-balance sheet item. Theoretically, they cannot be concealed. The net foreign exchange position, if any, is the algebraic sum of the positions recorded on and off the balance sheet.

TABLE 4.4 MAJOR FINANCE COMPANY AFFILIATES OR SUBSIDIARIES OF LARGE THAI BANKS (AMOUNTS AS OF DECEMBER 1996, IN BAHT BILLIONS)

	Finance company	Direct bank ownership (%)	Total assets	% of bank assets	Total loans	Total equity	Reported profits
Bank							
Bangkok Bank	Asia Credit	<10	61.9	5.40	50.7	7.6	0.9
	Union Asia	7	50.2	4.30	40.6	5.0	0.5
Thai Farmers	Phatra Thanakit	9	77.5	12.00	60.1	12.3	1.5
	CMIC	7	66.8	10.30	55.0	6.8	0.3
Siam Commercial	Dhana Siam	<10	67.5	12.50	51.3	11.6	1.1
	National	<10	70.8	13.10	54.5	10.3	1.2
Krung Thai	Krungthai Thanakit	82	54.5	7.60	45.0	6.3	0.9
Thai Military	Nava	20	58.4	17.60	47.7	8.4	0.9

Source: Thomson BankWatch Inc.

future. It is more relevant to examine whether it would have been possible to engineer a soft landing by reacting much earlier. For that to occur, it would have been necessary for the international community to realize much earlier that problems were looming. Their enthusiasm for Thai lending and investment would have been suitably damped and the crisis would have been much milder in nature. Furthermore, it would not have spread to the rest of the region as it did, with devastating effect.

A soft landing should have been engineered back in 1994, well before Thailand added the last 20% or 25% of growth to its economy. In late 1994, Mexico went through a short crisis, which prompted a question in the minds of investors in general: Mexico has done it again, what was the point in bailing it out the last time around? For a few weeks, emerging markets got really bad press and sentiment turned also against East Asia where several currencies came under attack. This took place in spite of the fact that very few similarities existed between the financial situation of Mexico and that of Asian countries. Partly through the coordination of the central banks of the region, and thanks to solid currency reserves, stability came back quickly to Asia's currencies.

Early in 1995, Thomson BankWatch analysts were poring, with terror, over some alarming statistics about the 15 Thai banks. They wondered whether the Thai banks would survive a serious crisis, of which a mild example had just been offered to us by the Mexico ripple effect in Asia. The statistics were describing the level of short-term US dollar borrowings the banks had in their books, and it was not a pretty sight.

There is theoretically nothing wrong for a bank in keeping some of its assets and liabilities in foreign currency as long as they are on the two sides of the balance sheet, and after adjustments for off-balance sheet items, roughly equal. The two sides should also preferably be matched in terms of maturity. The problem with Thai banks was that, at the end of 1994, they had short-term dollar liabilities that were not matched by short-term dollar assets, and they had too much of them.

Naturally, the banks swore that their dollar assets were short-term, on the grounds that their loan agreements with borrowers said so. In practice, this meant nothing since a substantial proportion of the money lent in US dollars found its way into highly non-liquid property investments and long-term projects. This would have been more or less tolerable had the banks maintained, for their own account, sufficient funds in quasi-liquid assets, for example government bonds, interbank deposits or marketable securities, to meet any unexpected call on their US dollar liabilities.

Unfortunately, few banks had more quasi-liquid assets than they did short-term dollar liabilities, and those that did only had a thin cushion against uncertainties.

The liquidity table was discussed (Table 4.5 and Figure 4.5) at various meetings and seminars that Thomson BankWatch was holding in 1995 and 1996. The rating agency warned its clients in no uncertain terms about the dire consequences for Thailand's banking system if either the baht was attacked, as happened briefly in the wake of the Mexican peso crisis, or the international financial community cut down their huge US dollar funding lines.

In the middle of 1997, both those situations developed. Perception of the Thai risk went negative, which put an end to the flow of short-term US dollars. This was the trigger that precipitated the Thai banks' fall into a non-liquid coma, inevitably followed for some of them by insolvency, and merger or liquidation.

TABLE 4.5   PERCENTAGE OF TOTAL ASSETS

	QLAR	Short-term foreign borrowing	+/−
Bangkok Bank	11.1	14.8	−3.7
Bangkok Bank of Commerce	7.4	7.4	0.0
Bangkok Metropolitan Bank	8.0	5.0	3.0
Bank of Asia	7.5	18.1	−10.6
Bank of Ayudhya	9.9	5.0	4.9
First Bangkok City	9.8	4.4	5.4
Krung Thai Bank	10.3	5.9	4.4
Laem Thong Bank	1.7	2.7	9.0
Nakornthon Bank	8.9	7.7	1.2
Siam City Bank	9.9	12.4	−2.5
Siam Commercial Bank	9.7	15.5	−5.8
Thai Danu Bank	9.7	8.5	1.2
Thai Farmers Bank	10.4	13.6	−3.2
Thai Military Bank	8.4	21.0	−12.6
Union Bank	7.7	5.8	1.9

QLAR = Quasi-liquid assets ratio
Source: Thomson BankWatch Inc.

FIGURE 4.5   Balance Sheet/Capital

1) Thai banks continue to maintain low levels of liquid assets.

2) Vulnerability of capital flight, high reliance on short-term foreign funding and minimal liquid assets provides a potentially lethal cocktail.

3) The next time a run on the baht, BOT may not (be able to) protect the currency.

4) If not, HOW WILL THAI BANKS FARE?

Source: Thomson BankWatch Inc.

BOT has long been seen as a benevolent regulator, always prompt and willing to give a helping hand to financial institutions in distress. Thailand's cultural traditions of smoothness and gentleness were to be found even in the way BOT would address important matters. In a famous example, BOT let culture interfere with efficiency in the case of Union Bank of Bangkok. For years, the two founding families had been fighting for control of the bank, with the result that no expansion could take place and no important decision could be made. At one point in the early 1990s, BOT came out to say publicly that, should the shareholders fail to find a compromise, BOT would step in and force a solution; however, to no avail. BOT's record as a mediator is rather poor, as was seen in other situations.

The case of Bangkok Bank of Commerce (BBC) was more serious, since it eventually resulted in considerable losses to the taxpayers. BBC was never a strong player and the fact was known both inside and outside Thailand. One would have expected the central bank to keep a close watch on developments, especially if depositors' money was at stake. In particular, a central bank should intervene whenever adjusted capital ratios fall to perhaps 2% or 3% of total assets, either by liquidating the bank, with the liquidators still finding enough to extract their pound of flesh, or by rehabilitating the bank under close surveillance. Nothing of that sort of action took place in the case of BBC. The fact that, at the end of the day, a loss of Baht 77 billion (then about US$3 billion) had to be recorded upon quasi-liquidation, against shareholders' funds of Baht 13 billion, certainly indicates that not even the minimum effort was made to ensure that BBC was properly monitored. Incidentally, the Thai government sought to disguise part of the BBC loss, which the taxpayers were made to swallow, through some creative accounting. Some BBC bad assets, beyond the first Baht 57 billion, were transferred to another entity, to die more discreetly.

As if this was not enough, in 1995, BOT had to face the embarrassment of seeing a Thai mid-size bank get caught red-handed by the US regulatory authorities for improper lending practices. Bangkok Metropolitan Bank (BMB) had, in its US branch's books, some questionable loans to individuals associated with the bank. BOT and BMB rushed to explain that this was an isolated case, that the amount involved, if lost, would not affect the bank's stability, and that everything was under control. Yet the episode generated the distinct impression that there were more serious management problems at BMB and that BOT was either not willing or not able to bring the bank back on the right track.

Episodically, in most countries, central banks are caught in difficult situations and it would be unfair to blame them for the misdeeds of their charges. In the particular case of Thailand, the political scene is very special in that business people and the military, in an unnatural alliance, run the country along lines that are difficult to grasp for an external observer. BOT is hostage to unseen and complicated arrangements making its task very difficult. But the BBC and the BMB episodes, coming more or less at the same time, started undermining BOT's strongest asset: its hitherto relatively good record. Thailand had always been forgiven for some weaknesses in the banking system, simply because BOT could be trusted to help out in cases of need. Not anymore. In particular, the all important matter of bank liquidity could no longer be overlooked. Thai banks have long exhibited poor, and weakening even more in recent times, quasi-liquid assets ratios (QLAR). Table 4.6 outlines the ratio for Thailand over several years.

In recent years, Thai banks have indeed been the least liquid of all Asian banks. Table 4.7 compares the QLAR of banks in some major Asian countries.

Clearly, Thailand was at the bottom of the class. The situation was barely tolerable with a good central bank staying in the wings, ready to help. With the loss of confidence in BOT, this was no longer possible. And this is why Thomson BankWatch started downgrading most banks in Thailand as early as 1995.

TABLE 4.6   QUASI-LIQUID ASSET RATIOS

	1988	1989	1990	1991	1992	1993	1994	1995	1996
Bangkok Bank	18.09	16.74	15.20	11.94	9.87	10.30	11.11	11.00	9.61
Bangkok Bank of Commerce	20.55	15.42	11.59	9.67	10.76	12.82	7.41	8.64	5.07
Bangkok Metropolitan Bank	18.26	16.37	17.94	12.30	10.76	10.53	6.98	7.70	5.98
Bank of Asia	15.42	14.36	16.56	0.45	10.89	11.40	7.48	6.99	6.58
Bank of Ayudhya	23.47	17.87	15.22	11.92	12.00	8.30	9.85	11.55	8.75
First Bangkok City Bank	23.05	23.37	14.54	10.74	11.64	12.27	9.77	9.28	6.10
Krung Thai Bank	17.24	15.66	14.65	13.91	8.26	10.20	10.32	7.23	6.67
Laem Thong Bank	19.54	18.35	15.01	15.76	16.90	15.38	11.67	12.37	8.17
Nakornthon Bank	20.32	23.42	14.16	11.64	8.43	9.40	8.85	9.93	7.60
Siam City Bank	19.57	16.01	16.23	14.17	10.14	11.01	9.22	8.13	8.26
Siam Commercial Bank	21.47	15.85	12.82	11.37	11.43	12.46	9.72	8.53	7.61
Thai Danu Bank	20.59	18.42	11.08	10.57	10.75	9.48	9.73	8.05	5.65
Thai Farmers Bank	17.90	17.24	11.89	14.73	12.40	13.39	10.35	8.53	7.82
Thai Military Bank	19.29	14.61	13.60	11.83	9.45	9.65	8.40	8.16	7.03
Union Bank of Bangkok	15.27	12.44	12.82	11.80	9.99	8.60	7.66	8.40	8.19
Total/Average	19.61	18.04	14.24	12.70	11.43	10.99	9.88	9.13	7.77

Source: Annual Reports

TABLE 4.7   QUASI-LIQUID ASSET RATIOS (%): AVERAGE OF DOMESTIC COMMERCIAL BANKS

	1994	1995	1996
HONG KONG (excl. HSBC)	45.78	43.51	41.96
SINGAPORE	41.10	38.33	36.69
SOUTH KOREA — Nationwide Banks	35.84	37.30	34.29
SOUTH KOREA — Provincial Banks	34.22	34.08	32.57
CHINA — Mainland	32.00	32.60	31.08
MALAYSIA	38.13	32.01	29.09
TAIWAN — Established Banks	24.75	23.42	23.95
PHILIPPINES	31.01	26.72	23.91
INDONESIA — State Banks	23.47	24.38	23.00
VIETNAM	22.69	21.39	22.44
INDONESIA — Private Banks	16.05	18.61	20.78
SOUTH KOREA — Specialized Banks	16.11	18.41	16.68
THAILAND	9.88	9.13	7.77

Source: Annual Reports

The Future

Although there is no specific deposit-insurance program in Thailand, the Financial Institutions Development Fund (FIDF) was created to provide stability to the banking system by supporting troubled financial institutions. This fund was first established in the mid-1980s under an amendment to the Bank of Thailand Act. Banks must contribute annually to the fund up to 0.5% of their year-end deposits. A committee chaired by the governor of the BOT manages the fund. The FIDF has traditionally been the vehicle of choice to invest in ailing financial institutions. In recent times, its many interventions have depleted its resources. The rescue of the sole Bangkok Bank of Commerce, which took place prior to the 1997 turmoil, cost the FIDF about Baht 57 billion. The magnitude of the losses faced by the finance companies, at Baht 700 billion, has definitely put an unbearable strain on the FIDF's capacity to rescue ailing banks. This means that the FIDF's formal guarantee in respect of other troubled institutions would have to rely on full government support.

For all their mismanagement of the early stages of the crisis, the Thais, at the time of writing, appeared as the most dedicated to fighting the crisis. The government seems willing to follow the IMF prescriptions. It looks increasing likely that Thailand will get out of the crisis much faster than the other distressed countries. One of the major obstacles to a resumption of growth is the unwillingness of several governments to clean up the mess. They should eradicate ailing companies and banks in order to restore an inviting climate for foreign investors. The resolution of the crisis as it affects the books of financial institutions is impossible until better bankruptcy laws are in force. This is one of the recommendations made by the IMF. In Thailand as elsewhere in Asia, the IMF has insisted on a prompt overhaul of bankruptcy laws. Thailand has lost no time addressing the problem.

Thailand is a good example of how Asia's economies were built without the support and the protection of modern legislation addressing such matters as contract law, trust law and bankruptcy law. Thailand has taken steps in the right direction. It is likely, however, that the full benefits of the new laws will not be felt immediately, and that the distressed corporate loans presently on the books of domestic and foreign banks will remain distressed for some more time.

This and other efforts will undeniably allow the country to measure the extent of the damage. To the extent that banking systems were at the source of the disaster, fixing them must be given the highest priority. At the time of writing, Thailand was well ahead of Korea and Indonesia. Several of its largest banks, including Bangkok Bank, Thai Farmers Bank and Bank of Ayudhya, have successfully gathered fresh capital funds, and most of the funds they found in Thailand. Other banks, mostly smaller institutions, invited equity participation from abroad.

Meanwhile the stock market index has plunged to the abyss, making it harder for anyone to insist on high valuations.

TABLE 4.8   STOCK EXCHANGE INDEX

	Dec. 93	Dec. 94	Dec. 95	Dec. 96	Dec. 97	15 Jun. 98
Index (THAIQIX)	1682.85	1360.09	1280.81	831.57	372.69	263.39
Base Dec. 1993 = 100	100	80.82	94.17	64.93	44.82	15.65

Source: Capital Information Services

Bankruptcy Laws in Thailand

Ever since they were approved under the Bankruptcy Act of 1940, bankruptcy laws in Thailand have made it extremely difficult for creditors to obtain redress against recalcitrant borrowers. After 12 years of painful preparation, amendments were passed in March 1998, making it possible for companies to reorganize, very much — but not entirely — like the reorganization allowed under Chapter 11 in the USA. At the same time, the rights of creditors are being better recognized, but substantial obstacles persist.

Under the old law, whose main principles are still in force, the only way creditors could obtain satisfaction was to apply to the courts. As secured creditors, they had to obtain the court's approval before starting proceedings for the recovery of debt through the realization of any collateral held by them.

The actual execution of any judgment obtained also needed further court approval. If unimpaired by procedural nuisances easily created by the debtor, the process would take a minimum of one year. In practice, it would easily take well over 5 years, by which time there was little hope of extracting anything approaching the original claim. Foreign secured creditors were in an even worse position, as they had to go through the motion of establishing that their country of domicile was granting Thai creditors similar rights — which were presumably better rights, as one can imagine!

Furthermore, if the claim was in foreign currency, the amount was frozen in its equivalent value in baht at the time the proceedings were initiated, meaning that any negative development in currency markets would eat away at the face value of the original claim. To make matters worse, any fresh money lent after the creditor knew the debtor to be insolvent would, in most cases, not be considered by the courts for repayment. Given the poor level of financial disclosure in Thailand, this knowledge was often a matter of opinion rather than a matter of fact, and reaching a conclusion before the courts in this respect was both time consuming and prohibitively expensive. It does not come as a surprise, therefore, that holding assets as collateral against loans was no real comfort to creditors. The best they could hope for was to be able to compromise with the borrower. Naturally, local banks are always in a better position than foreign banks in this respect, and this is true in any country. But stories circulate in Thailand about distressed borrowers paying out their last visible cent to local banks before declaring themselves unable to meet obligations towards foreign institutions.

After the 1998 amendment, at least an effort will be made to place all or most creditors in the same position. This includes new creditors, regardless of whether they knew that the debtor was insolvent when they lent, although they will enjoy no priority. But, in a way, this is going too far because, at the same time, the amendment is limiting the rights of secured creditors. Unlike in other countries where secured creditors are treated separately, in relation to the security they hold, the situation in Thailand is that secured creditors will have to establish before the courts either that the restructuring does not protect their rights, or that allowing them to execute their security does not impair the reorganization efforts. One can only guess at the courts' general attitude when such requests are made, but it is difficult to imagine that they will gladly agree to grant them.

The IMF has insisted on a prompt overhaul of bankruptcy laws in Thailand as well as in other Asian countries. It is likely, however, that the full benefits of the new Thai laws will not be felt immediately, and that the distressed corporate loans presently in the books of domestic and foreign banks will remain delinquent.

We are far from the stubbornness exhibited by the owners of finance companies in early 1997 when they insisted on outrageous prices for their shares. In addition, their accounts were hardly kept along internationally accepted accounting principles. But this remained a problem for some of the small banks. Foreign investors looked at their books and found loans whose documentation was missing. They found questionable appraisals of collateral values. Such missing information would usually prompt a downward negotiation of the price, so that the buyer is partly protected against the overvaluation of certain assets. But apparently, this did not work out too well and a number of banks for sale were left without a buyer. By early 1998, the Thai government took the extraordinary decision to force upon three banks a capital reduction. This is extraordinary as only Malaysia had used that weapon, and no East Asian country, not even Malaysia, had used it at any time between the mid-1980s crisis and the present one. The banks — First Bangkok City Bank, Siam City Bank and Bank Metropolitan Bank — saw their capital disappear and were invited to find fresh capital, without which they would be nationalized.

With some banks finding fresh equity in Thailand, others inviting foreign shareholders and most of the rest controlled directly or indirectly by the state, the Thai banking system seems ready to revive itself back to good health. Unfortunately, the non-banks remain a burden to the state, and this is likely to carry on diverting energies from more pressing matters. When the majority of the finance companies collapsed under the weight of non-performing loans, mostly real estate and consumer loans, the government stepped in to guarantee all the deposits, via the FIDF, to the tune of approximately Baht 1 trillion. It now appears that most of the assets funded by the deposits are impaired. The safest among the assets were transferred to a new bank called Radhanasin, while the government will probably write-off the balance, with the taxpayer paying for it all. Naturally, the temptation will always be there to conceal some of the bad news. One way to do so is to use the old trick of merging rotten finance companies into a relatively safe one, and to cook the books. There are sure signs that this is going to take place.

Thailand's woes are not over, but the country will emerge with its potential intact. The banking system needed a complete overhaul, which the crisis has precipitated. Five or six private sector banking groups will survive, and the rest will be lumped into a huge network of government-owned financial institutions whose capital ratios will remain negative for some time.

Endnotes

1. Those countries should realize that offshore centers must also be attractive from the point of view of international professionals. In addition to a solid legal framework and a soft tax regime, offshore centers must offer good communications, total intellectual freedom, an unrestricted flow of information and a high degree of cultural life. In Asia, only Hong Kong has ever achieved such objectives to a reasonable level.

2. If reserves in foreign currencies are exchanged for local currency, or committed to acquire local currency through a forward transaction, they disappear from official reserves but they do not necessarily represent a loss for the country. This is because the local currency so acquired can, at any time, be offered for sale against foreign currencies in transactions that would restore some or all of the reserves. There is obviously a limit to the amounts that can be transacted without upsetting some parameters like inflation, interest rates and, of course, exchange rates.

KOREA

Korea[1] became an early victim of the financial panic created by Thailand's woes. Its industrial and financial structures were begging for changes. Korea's banks were, on average, bankrupt well before the crisis unfolded. The financial panic simply precipitated a painful but welcome adjustment. The currency and the stock markets collapsed beyond reason, but this created a salutary change of attitude towards economic realities.

Korea is an extraordinary country in many respects. Recent observers would limit their views to the ills of an economic structure that needs considerable adjustment. To the seasoned analyst, though, South Korea's achievements in the last 35 years are absolutely stunning, with no parallel in any other country on the planet. Before turning to current problems, it is perhaps interesting to explore how the country negotiated, one after the other, the many hurdles on its way to become a major industrial power.

The Korean War during the early 1950s devastated a country that was already poor and without natural resources. For several years immediately after the war, Korea very much depended on grants and loans from foreign donors, particularly the United States. Savings rates were low, unemployment was high. Recovery from the war was the primary objective for Korea and little thought was given to strategic development beyond survival. Two positive points in particular could characterize Korea: a dedication to hard work and a high level of education. The Korean people share these attributes to some degree with other Asian countries, but, as it turned out, they put them to work with unrelenting passion.

The Korea Miracle

By 1962, foreign capital was financing an astonishing 82% of total investment, and the Koreans felt that such dependence, if allowed to crystallize, would impede their long-term development efforts. This is when a first five-year plan was elaborated, which favored the development of export-oriented industries, instead of the typical Third World import-substitution approach. Japan was of course on a similar track, and becoming increasingly successful. World trade was expanding rapidly and there were few trade barriers for Korean products. In the 35 years that followed the decision to focus on exports, real GNP grew on average by 8% every year, and the manufacturing sector's share of GNP grew from 14% to about 30%.

The 1970s were less promising than anticipated, as the world went through several shocks, including the quadrupling of oil prices in 1973. The decade saw a general tendency to more protectionism, and Korea reacted by reverting to its own cherished brand of isolationism, still the source of the many difficulties encountered by foreign firms, to penetrate Korean markets today. Import substitution became fashionable and, until the 1980s, a full one-third of all products needed an import license. The isolationism also promoted the uniquely Korean trait of concentrating all efforts on concerted actions to develop specific lines of products. In ten years, ship exports ended up representing 16% of all exports. Large construction companies signed huge contracts mostly in the Middle East. Korea was manufacturing heavy machinery, power generation equipment and other capital-intensive products. The light industry stopped getting the kind of attention and capital it had previously attracted, and agricultural development programs obtained mixed results.

Following a further increase in oil prices, and some political and social problems, Korea's economy actually contracted in 1980. The Koreans proved then, as they are about to prove now, that they can tighten their belts and carry on fighting. For example, it is remarkable that, in the early 1980s, central heating systems in Seoul, when they existed at all, were routinely suspended for 18 hours every day in the dead of freezing winters. Koreans can indeed cope with very tough times. In only a few years, the country was back on track, with low unemployment, low inflation and high growth. High savings were not enough to sustain the rate of investment and Korea started borrowing in earnest from the rest of the world. By the end of the decade, Korea was exporting textiles, electronic products, machinery and cars. By 1997, Korea was ready for OECD membership and its economy was the world's 11th largest.

Korea's Problems

Korea built its success on hard work. The economic model used called for a concentration of efforts in government-inspired specialization. And yet, Korea's economy is, strictly speaking, not in the hands of the state. Most of its success is due to family-owned conglomerates, or the Chaebols, that control most of the economy. The 30 largest Chaebols are said to control 85% of industrial Korea. They do not operate as holding companies, but rather like nebulous conglomerates, and their close links with politicians have brought them both economic success and the recipe for disaster.

There was a time in Korea's development when such concentration of power was useful, but the system has reached the end of its useful life. The conglomerates suffer from two main weaknesses: over-investment and cross-subsidy. It has been said that part of the problems encountered by the semi-conductor industry worldwide has come from over-capacity, in particular in Korea, which invested heavily in semi-conductor manufacturing. The same goes, for example, for the automotive industry. Korea is the only country of that size, fresh from developing-country status, with as many as four separate car manufacturers.

Cross-subsidies within conglomerates have turned out to be even more detrimental to the Korean economy. In most Western countries, if a subsidiary, division or sub-division is not viable, it may receive help for a limited time, but it is eventually liquidated if it cannot improve. Not so in Korea. Weaker members of the conglomerates will receive guarantees from other firms in the group so that they can carry on borrowing from outside. They can be close to death, but nobody will wish to notice. This is perverse as it can undermine the health of an entire group without advance warning: the group will patch over its problems and pent-up difficulties when they hit are all the more devastating. Incidentally, this is partly why Korean banks have been savaged over the years by credit losses that were, to a degree, unpredictable: a guarantee, usually pre-paid, that does not show to be worthless until actually called. As much as a bank can record the deterioration of a loan through incidents of late payment, there is little it can do in respect of tracking the strength of a guarantee.

The ability to properly monitor the creditworthiness of the guarantor has been a central issue. With a better credit culture, the easy acceptance of cross-guarantees could have been mitigated, if not completely eliminated.

The Chaebols have been instrumental in preventing the Korean government from opening up the economy. Much has been said about Japan's attitude in this respect, but the Korea market is almost as difficult as Japan's to crack from outside. The Chaebols have never been able to resist the temptation of expanding in a vast array of businesses across many industries. Overall, they were very successful and the problems affecting some of them only surfaced in recent years. But the families behind some of the Chaebols still believe that this crisis is no different from previous crises, only deeper, and that they can tough it out.

Another perverse effect of the concentration in so few hands is that it has become difficult for banks to diversify their risks. They are bound to find the same major names before them at every turn. This is all the more true because the Korean credit system has some similarities with that of Japan. In Tokyo, a group will have a main bank, concentrating on a few names for an unhealthy proportion of total borrowing. In Korea, the main bank is not necessarily the main creditor, but it is the designated supervisor company on behalf of all creditors. When Hanbo, one of the Chaebols, failed in early 1997, Korea First Bank, one of the five major commercial banks, was found to have an exposure on Hanbo equivalent to 60% of its own equity, which incidentally was inflated by creative accounting. Without such accounting tricks, Korea First Bank's true equity would have been much lower. Its true equity was in reality smaller than its exposure to Hanbo. The sad reality, not immediately apparent therefore, is that the Hanbo case would have been enough to bankrupt Korea First Bank, if other problems had not taken care of that. The same situation applies to some other names.

Such a wild expansion sometimes carries incidental problems, linked to human nature. Several corruption cases have erupted in Korea over the past three years, two of them involving prominent political figures. Corruption is widespread in Asia and often affects the highest levels of society. But how many countries would actually send two ex-Presidents to jail? Korea did, in a spectacular way. The cozy relationship between business and politics has largely been exposed.

As some academics suggest,[2] corruption at the top is perhaps a small price to pay for the unparalleled dynamism that countries can gather through the seemingly dangerous collusion between politicians, big business and banks. The benefits to the country in terms of growth largely outpace the social and economic costs of the inevitable corruption practices, and the inefficiencies they entail.

Trade unions are very powerful in Korea, or rather very vocal. They combine a militant spirit only found in socialist Europe with the kind of stubbornness that has seen Korea through its most difficult times. Labor laws make it extremely difficult for companies to lay off excess staff, but they were passed when Korea did not have industrial restructuring problems. New, more flexible laws were discreetly submitted by the government and passed in the early hours of a cold December day in 1996. When it came to enforce the new laws, riots erupted and the government had to relent. New sets of laws were subsequently examined and passed, but their enforcement has been explosive. Yet, they are Korea's only hope to attain the industrial flexibility needed to face some of its problems. They are particularly relevant in industries like banking, where considerable changes are called for in management methods and in the deployment of human resources. Only in 1998 did the banks get permission to actually shed staff.

The Korean won was savaged during the 1997 financial crisis, after years of stability. Table 5.1 shows the exchange rate at various dates.

TABLE 5.1   CURRENCY TABLE

	Dec. 93	Dec. 94	Dec. 95	Dec. 96	Dec. 97	15 Jun. 98
US$ per 1000 won	1.2374	1.2679	1.2908	1.1845	0.5896	0.6978
Base Dec. 1993 = 100	100	102.46	104.32	95.72	47.65	56.39
Won per US$	808.1	788.7	774.7	844.2	1695.8	1433.0
Base Dec. 1993 = 100	100	97.60	95.87	104.47	209.85	177.33

Source: Capital Information Services

Korea lacks capital funds. More accurately, it lacks funds invested as risk capital or long-term debt. The capital markets are so poorly developed that the huge growth witnessed over the past 30 years was not matched by and therefore could not rely on a parallel growth in equity funds. Total market capitalization in March 1998 amounted to about 10% of GDP, against about 130% in the US and 70% in Japan. Even before the collapse of the stock market, total market capitalization was much too low. The Chaebols have had to rely on huge borrowings. Their gearing ratios are among the highest in the world: many Chaebols, before the crisis erupted, had debt-to-equity ratios in the vicinity of 400% to 500%, and, for a few, the ratio jumped to 700% or 800% when their US$ borrowings expressed in won went through the roof. For comparison, the figure for gearing ratios in the US is about 70%.

There is spare money in Korean hands, like in all the distressed countries of Asia. Given the limitations put on the transfer of funds outside the country, most of that money is still in Korea and would be sufficient to recapitalize a number of companies. The funds remain concealed, however. There is a Belgian dentist[3] mentality, aided by steep taxes, leading to a substantial underground economy. The Koreans took the very pragmatic approach of permitting people not to use their real names in financial transactions. The fake-name approach was instrumental in recycling some underground money into the economy. The recent attempts at imposing the use of real names have simply sent some of that money back underground. If and when more pragmatism returns, substantial funds will again become available for visible investment.

The Korean Banking System

The Korean banking system is a disaster. It was, on average, already bankrupt at the end of 1996, ahead of the various big losses brought in by such names as Hanbo and Kia, and well ahead of the so-called Asian crisis. It is interesting perhaps to examine how it was at all possible for the situation to become so dramatic. It is important to understand that the accounts published by the Korean banks are not a faithful representation of their state of affairs. Everything looks too rosy. We shall explore some of the main factors affecting the truthfulness of account disclosure.

Most ratios make banks look better than they are. But before being so sadly negative, let us detour for a moment and examine the one ratio that the Korean banks, to the contrary, understate: the Net Interest Margin (NIM). A major reason why it is incorrectly stated is that Korean banks handle substantial deposits and loans under a different category called "trust accounts", a situation which leads to unusual entries in their financial accounts. The story of the trust accounts goes a long way to illustrate the strange mentality found in Korea, and incidentally in Japan as well, whereby a commitment is not a commitment, but rather a best-effort promise, or vice-versa. Parties to a contract do at times have to rely on the other party's sense of duty, or more appropriately their sense of shame.

TABLE 5.2   ECONOMIC INDICATORS

	1991	1992	1993	1994	1995	1996	1997	1998p
Currency								
WON/US$ (end period)	760.80	788.40	808.10	788.70	774.70	844.20	1,695.80	1,400.00
Real Exchange Rate, % change	−3.5	−2.6	−2.3	−8.7	−6.5	4.5	91.2	−10.7
Real Economy								
Real GDP, % change	9.1	5.1	5.8	8.4	9.0	7.1	5.5	−2.0
Fixed Investment as % of GDP	39.0	35.9	36.6	37.2	38.0	37.9	35.9	34.1
Official Unemployment Rate (%)	3.2	2.9	2.8	2.5	1.9	2.3	2.5	8.0
Money and Prices								
Retail Price Inflation (end period)	9.7	6.2	4.8	6.2	4.5	5.0	9.5	6.7
Lending Rate (%)	10.00	10.00	8.60	8.50	9.00	8.80	9.00	N/A
Reserves ($ billions)	13.70	17.12	20.23	25.64	32.68	33.02	27.70	31.50
Domestic Savings Rate (%)	36.2	34.7	35.2	35.6	35.0	33.1	33.0	34.9
Balance of Payments								
Exports (US$ billions)	69.58	75.17	80.95	93.68	123.20	129.80	138.70	150.00
Imports (US$ billions)	76.56	77.32	79.09	96.82	127.95	150.20	148.60	140.00
Trade Balance	($6.98)	($2.15)	$1.86	($3.14)	($4.75)	($20.40)	($9.90)	$10.00
Current Account Balance	($8.29)	($3.94)	($1.02)	($3.86)	($8.25)	($23.60)	($13.80)	$3.80
Current Account Balance, % GDP	−2.8	−1.3	−0.3	−1.0	−1.9	−4.8	−2.9	0.8
Foreign Debt (US$ billions)	39.73	44.16	47.20	60.00	82.10	112.10	137.40	154.00
as % of GDP	13.6	14.4	14.4	15.3	18.0	23.0	28.4	34.9
Debt Service Ratio (%)	7.1	7.6	9.2	6.8	7.9	9.3	11.4	12.2
Governmant Finance								
Gov. Surplus/Deficit as % of GDP	−1.6	−0.5	0.6	0.3	0.6	−0.3	−0.5	−2.0

Source: Thomson BankWatch Inc.

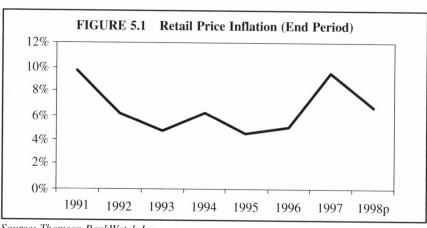

FIGURE 5.1   Retail Price Inflation (End Period)

Source: Thomson BankWatch Inc.

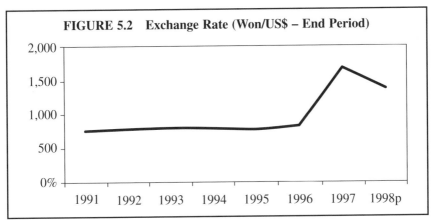

FIGURE 5.2   Exchange Rate (Won/US$ – End Period)

Source: Thomson BankWatch Inc.

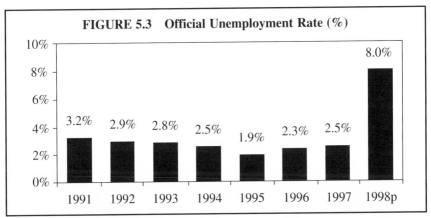

FIGURE 5.3   Official Unemployment Rate (%)

Source: Thomson BankWatch Inc.

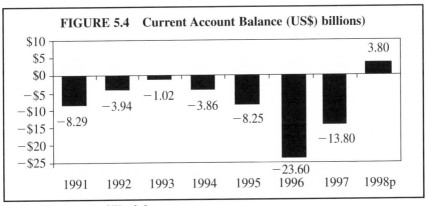

FIGURE 5.4   Current Account Balance (US$) billions)

Source: Thomson BankWatch Inc.

Korean Trust Accounts

In the classic definition of trust accounts, there is little risk associated with taking funds in trust and placing them on behalf of the depositor. The trustee receives a handsome commission. Any loss on the investment side translates into a shrinking of the liabilities to trust depositors. The bank's responsibility is limited to properly discharging its duties as a trustee. Assets and liabilities associated with trust operations appear as off-balance sheet items.

Trust accounts in Korea do not fall into that no-risk category for reasons that are both historical and cultural. Originally, the trust accounts were used as a way of circumventing the rigid government directives depriving banks of the right to set deposit interest rates and lending interest rates. Those restrictive rules did not apply to trust assets and liabilities. Theoretically, the banks were facing almost no risk in respect of those activities, which were originally rather small. Taking more deposits in trust, as opposed to taking them as bank deposits, was simply a way of obtaining more flexibility in pricing. The net interest margin of the trust accounts constituted a fee earned by the bank in its capacity as a trustee, and was entered in the main bank accounts as a component of non-interest income. This accounting treatment corrupts the consolidated figures and ratios in respect of both interest and non-interest income.

Culturally, however, it would seem that the bank's responsibility as a trustee was much wider in that depositors would not understand or tolerate a situation where the funds entrusted to the bank would be partially or totally lost. In other words, in case of trouble, trust depositors would claim their money back all the same. For quite a number of years, during the 1980s and early 1990s, the situation remained confused, with Korean banks themselves uncertain about the real risk to them of maintaining trust accounts in parallel to more traditional deposit products. Some banks would publish detailed trust accounts, some would not. As long as those trust accounts remained relatively modest, their impact on the overall risk profile of the bank would be limited and the external analyst would not give them too much importance. Korean banks tend to transfer funds from the bank account to cover casualties in the trust accounts that cannot be met by the trust income. Over the years, however, some banks became so dependent on trust account deposits that such accounts reached a size of approximately half of the bank accounts proper, making them much harder to dismiss as incidental. In the early 1990s, some banks started publishing consolidated accounts to include trust accounts. The main result of the switch was to reveal the weakness of many banks, as already low performance ratios were adjusted downwards: the numerator remained the same, but the sudden increase of the denominator depressed the ratios.

Some new accounting rules were expected in 1998 that would force banks to transfer the quasi-trust accounts to the banking account proper. Only the real trust transactions would remain under the trust accounts.

Naturally, the analyst is lost when exploring consolidated accounts since the entire income generated by the trust activities are accounted for in a single line of the main bank accounts. In the bank account, the result appears in non-interest income, while in reality they represent more than commissions and incidental costs generated by the trust activities. They largely represent the NIM, or the difference between interest received and interest paid in trust deposit taking and lending transactions. For that reason, the NIM exhibited by Korean banks is often understated and, as said before, this happens to be the only accounting ratio that looks too modest. After adjustment, the NIM of Korean banks is comparable to that seen in other countries, both industrial nations and Asian Tigers. After adjustment, the non-interest income is also within an acceptable range.

That was the good news. Now for the bad news. That the accounts do not correctly present the NIM and non-interest income is the least of the Korean banks' problems. It is the bottom line that shows Korea's predicament, since the banks' overall net income is savaged by the operating costs of one of the least efficient banking systems in Asia. Japan shares some of those characteristics with Korea, but if the comparison is made with the other three Asian Tigers, Korea is widely off the mark. Here is a table comparing efficiency ratios[4] in various Asian countries.

TABLE 5.3   EFFICIENCY RATIOS AMONG ASIAN BANKS: AVERAGE OF DOMESTIC COMMERCIAL BANKS (%)

	1994	**1995**	**1996**
Hong Kong	35.79	33.62	32.20
Singapore	41.97	40.40	40.66
Malaysia	43.95	44.13	42.58
Thailand	39.37	41.47	43.75
Indonesia	57.39	58.22	56.12
Philippines	60.39	58.99	56.28
Taiwan	58.07	57.84	56.49
China	68.63	67.01	69.47
South Korea	84.63	82.66	74.52

Note: A low efficiency ratio is a good one, according to this particular definition.
Source: Annual Reports

There are a number of factors influencing efficiency. Geography is important: it is more costly to maintain branches in small cities or on distant islands, and this is an important factor for the Philippines, China, India and Indonesia. More importantly, the average size of a transaction varies among countries: in relatively poorer countries, there are more transactions for each US$100 of assets than in richer countries, adding to the cost margin. Another factor is the asset structure: the cost of maintaining a single US$5 million interbank deposit is clearly lower than that of

Gross Profit Margin

The gross profit margin (GPM) is a ratio that looks at a bank's net profit, divided by average total assets, before provisions are put aside and before taxes are paid. Taxes are always best taken out of such comparisons, since there are vast differences across the region, while for comparison purposes, it is better to assume that virtually no bad loans are involved. The GPM measures a bank's capacity to generate wealth in safe and steady circumstances. Table 5.4 lists a few average ratios in several Asian countries.

TABLE 5.4   GROSS PROFIT MARGINS (%)

	1994	1995	1996
Philippines	2.68	2.71	2.89
Thailand	3.09	2.86	2.57
Hong Kong	2.13	2.30	2.46
Malaysia	2.14	2.14	2.39
Indonesia Private Banks	2.21	2.28	2.25
Indonesia State Banks	1.42	1.73	1.93
Singapore	1.68	1.67	1.66
Korea Old Merchant Banks	2.87	2.19	1.63
Taiwan New Banks	1.47	1.03	1.14
Taiwan Established Banks	1.05	1.01	0.98
Korea Nationwide Banks	1.09	0.57	0.48
Korea Specialized Banks	0.70	0.43	0.39

Source: Annual Reports

In emerging markets' commercial banking, it is not unreasonable to expect some assets to become non-performing. In the normal course of business, year in, year out, it is wise to assume that approximately 0.5% of total assets becomes delinquent, and an amount of that magnitude should be diverted every year to provisions. This should be deducted from the GPM, to give an idea of the net cash flow ratios before tax.

keeping 200 car loans of US$25,000 each in the books. More liquid banking systems are likely to be more cost-efficient and this should favor Hong Kong, Singapore, Korea, the Philippines and the sub-continent.

The cost margin[5] is defined as the cost, in terms of administrative and general expenses, of maintaining US$100 in assets. Such costs include salaries, rents, computers, telecommunications, transportation, insurance and other costs of a similar nature. Safe comparisons of cost margins are only valid between countries exhibiting relatively similar banking structures. Valid comparisons involving Korea can safely be made with banking systems in Hong Kong, Taiwan and Singapore. In the case of Hong Kong and Singapore, the cost margin analysis shows that, year after year, the commercial banks spend much less than their counterparts in Korea. The difference is an astonishing 1.6% of total assets. This means that Korean banks needlessly spend millions every year that would come in handy in strengthening their balance sheets.[6] In normal circumstances, an additional cushion of that magnitude would allow banks not only to face current loan defaults, but also to put aside comfortable provisions for a rainy day. That factor alone can explain why, over the years, Korean banks have become submerged under a deluge of non-performing assets that they could not attend to. Confronted with the same threat, Hong Kong or Singapore banks would have been able to build comfortable reserves against potential losses.

It can be clearly seen that Korean banks are inherently incapable of creating the cash flow that they need simply to survive, let alone the cash flow they need if they wish to grow. Looking at the 1995 figures — the last year when Korean banks were operating in almost normal circumstances — the GPM, at 0.57% of total assets for nationwide banks, is clearly much too low. After a precautionary provision of 0.50%, the nationwide banks would be left, before taxes, with a net profit ratio of 0.07% of assets. This translates roughly into a return on equity ratio of about 2%, appallingly low by any standards. What it means is that, even if there were no unusual needs for provisions — an overoptimistic view in the present circumstances — bank shareholders would be rewarded with very thin yields. Granted, a return on equity of 2% does not necessarily translate into a return on investment of 2%, since the share price will fluctuate around, and sometimes very far from the book value. But in Korea, a return on investment of about 2% or thereabout is definitely too low to attract any fresh equity funds.

The weak standing of Korean banks in terms of their capacity to generate cash flow is painfully dramatic when the analyst looks at the GPM as shown in Table 5.5.

Obviously, the Korean banks were doomed well ahead of the Asian crisis. Thomson BankWatch has been saying so for years. They cannot generate decent returns for their shareholders, let alone generate sufficient provisions for the mountain of non-performing assets built up over the years. The situation has been shaky for quite some time and it can be argued that, by the end of 1996, the banks were, on average, close to technical bankruptcy. This does not appear in the accounts, simply because the banks, with the blessing of the regulatory authorities, do not recognize all of their non-performing assets. It is difficult to quantify the amount of funds lacking in provisions against bad loans and bad investments. But it would not be wrong to say that, by the end of 1996, such provisions, if put aside along internationally accepted accounting rules, would have meant huge losses which would have wiped out the equity of most banks.

Asset quality has indeed never been very high among Korean banks,

TABLE 5.5   GROSS PROFIT MARGINS (%)

Nationwide Banks	1994	1995	1996
Shinhan Bank	1.52	0.87	0.74
Cho Hung Bank	1.62	0.86	0.67
Korea Exchange Bank	1.31	0.82	0.65
Korea First Bank	1.47	0.65	0.64
Hana Bank	0.88	0.48	0.60
Commercial Bank of Korea	1.07	0.84	0.59
KorAm Bank	1.06	0.55	0.52
Kookmin Bank	0.63	0.40	0.49
Daedong Bank	0.37	0.52	0.47
Hanil Bank	1.19	0.50	0.43
Peace Bank of Korea	0.40	−0.10	0.41
DongNam Bank	0.61	0.24	0.36
Donghwa Bank	0.74	0.09	0.34
Boram Bank	0.54	0.16	0.28
Seoul Bank	0.32	0.05	−0.41
Average — Nationwide Banks	1.09	0.57	0.48

Specialized Banks	1994	1995	1996
Export Import Bank of Korea	1.21	1.21	1.16
Korea Long Term Credit Bank	1.66	0.85	0.83
Housing and Commercial Bank	0.92	0.51	0.64
Korea Development Bank	0.85	0.63	0.51
Industrial Bank of Korea	0.36	0.30	0.19
National Livestock Coop. Fed.	0.75	0.15	0.10
National Agricultural Coop. Fed.	0.11	0.04	0.04
National Federation Of Fisheries Cooperatives	—	−0.36	0.04
Average — Specialized Banks	0.70	0.43	0.39

Provincial Banks	1994	1995	1996
Daegu Bank	1.35	0.81	0.85
Kyongnam Bank	0.69	0.81	0.79
Kyungki Bank	0.64	0.92	0.74
Chungbuk Bank	1.22	0.79	0.73
Jeonbuk Bank	1.03	1.13	0.70
Pusan Bank	0.68	0.82	0.67
Chung Chong Bank	1.00	0.95	0.60
Kwangju Bank	1.33	0.90	0.52
Kangwon Bank	1.06	0.53	0.43
Average — Provincial Banks	0.99	0.85	0.69

Old Merchant Banks	1994	1995	1996
Korean French Banking Corp.	3.47	2.42	2.04
Asian Banking Corp.	2.94	2.17	1.82
Korea International Merchant Bank	2.36	2.02	1.73
Saehan Merchant Bank	2.69	2.17	1.67
Hyundai International Merchant Bank	2.94	2.03	1.46
Korea Merchant Banking Corp.	2.93	2.33	1.11
Average — Old Merchant Banks	2.87	2.19	1.63

Source: Annual Reports

focused as they were on supporting the country's remarkable effort at industrialization. In recent years, but in particular in 1997, large amounts were lost to delinquent borrowers of large size, and this fact has been highly documented. In addition, small and medium-size companies have also been badly hit, as a result of an industrial structure largely inspired from the Japanese structure. In that system, large groups subcontract work to strings of smaller companies. This acts as a buffer when the economy slows down: the first victims are the small companies, while the big boys escape. Small companies are supposed to be more flexible than large ones, and able to readjust faster to adverse economic circumstances. In this system, large companies are spared and will ensure a degree of continuity that will benefit all economic agents. This theory works marvels in short cyclical downturns, but it cannot help small and medium-size companies in a long slowdown, which is exactly what has been affecting Korea over the past three years. As a result, beyond the Chaebols, Korean banks have been negatively affected by the poor performance of many small companies. Consumer lending, particularly in credit card loans, has grown considerably in recent times, a reflection of Korea's economic maturity. This activity has naturally also suffered from the downturn, adding to the banks' woes.

Reference has just been made to non-performing assets, rather than non-performing loans. Indeed, as if shaky loans were not enough, Korean banks have also piled up huge losses in equity investments. In some Asian countries — Taiwan is another case in point — it is possible for banks to become equity investors in other financial institutions and, more dramatically for Korea, in non-financial industries. In fact, this situation was even encouraged in Korea. It is not difficult to imagine that bank presidents[7] received calls from high-ranking officials begging them to lend a hand in efforts to prop up an ailing stock market. Many Asian governments have at times manipulated the stock markets. It is often difficult to do so openly, with state funds, but a banking system — or, worse, pension funds — can at times be coaxed into giving their support. This moral persuasion is very much in the Korean style. It found a fertile ground in banks that were desperate for additional sources of income, which the booming economy made very promising. Indeed, 1994 was extremely fruitful in that many Korean banks made exceptional profits on the stock market and used the funds to increase bad loan provisions. In 1995, however, the market started weakening considerably as can be seen in Table 5.6.

TABLE 5.6   STOCK EXCHANGE INDEX

	Dec. 92	Dec. 93	Dec. 94	Dec. 95	Dec. 96	Dec. 97	15 Jun. 98
Index (KOSPI)	678.40	866.20	1027.40	882.94	651.22	376.31	288.21
Base Dec. 92 = 100	100	127.68	151.44	130.15	95.99	55.47	42.48

Source: Capital Information Services

As a result of the market weakness, equity investments turned sour. The authorities permitted the banks to cover only 30% of the losses they would have faced had they marked to market their equity holdings. Very few banks were profitable enough to cover more than the minimum of 30%. Those who provided for losses beyond the minimum volunteered the information in their annual reports. The others remained carefully silent on the matter, misleading the reader about their real situation. This would be a minor consideration had the amounts involved not been so huge. But in 1995 alone, the major banks lost close to 20% of their own total shareholders funds to equity investments.

It should be kept in mind that those losses were affecting shareholders funds that were artificially maintained at inflated levels. It could be argued that, had those shareholders funds been properly adjusted for bad loan provisioning, the major Korean banks would have been rendered bankrupt in 1995 by their equity investments alone. To make things worse, the stock market kept falling in 1996 and 1997. What equity investments did to weaken Korean banks in 1995 was repeated and amplified in subsequent years. Predictably, fearful of the effect on capital ratios, the authorities carried on permitting banks to hide a substantial part of their equity losses. Banks were required to cover only 30% of their equity losses in 1995 and 1996, and 50% in 1997.

In the middle and at the end of 1996, the six major commercial banks had stock losses as detailed in Tables 5.7 and 5.8.

TABLE 5.7   INVESTMENT LOSSES — JUNE 30, 1996: AVERAGE OF DOMESTIC COMMERCIAL BANKS

Major banks	Unrealized losses (Won billion)	In proportion of equity (%)
Cho Hung Bank	333	24
Commercial Bank of Korea	276	23
Hanil Bank	393	28
Korea Exchange Bank	233	25
Korea First Bank	361	30
Seoul Bank	296	26

TABLE 5.8   INVESTMENT LOSSES — DEC. 30, 1996: AVERAGE OF DOMESTIC COMMERCIAL BANKS

Major banks	Unrealized losses (Won billion)	Provisions put aside (%)
Cho Hung Bank	614	30
CBK	486	40
Korea First Bank	573	31
Hanil Bank	602	37
Seoul Bank	505	30
Korea Exchange Bank	408	30

Source: Thomson BankWatch Inc.

Hell Breaking Loose

As a result of this sorry state of affairs, the Korean banking system entered 1997 with shaky accounts. Officially, the average BIS ratio of the 25 commercial banks was down to 9.14% in 1996, a level still respectable by international standards. In reality, the estimated amount of non-performing assets in the major banks was, at the end of 1996, larger than their combined capital funds. Averages always conceal substantial differences between strong names and weak names. Shinhan Bank, KorAm Bank, Kookmin Bank, Hana Bank, some merchant banks and, by a smaller margin, some other institutions, were ahead of the pack and definitely far from bankrupt. But one should accept that when a string of large failures started affecting Korea in early 1997, most of the banks were already on their knees.

The Hanbo Steel (January 1997), Sammi Steel (January 1997), Jinro distillery (April 1997) and Kia group (July 1997) cases hit an already moribund banking system. It did so in a devastating way for some banks because they had a large concentration of loans on the failed groups. A table showing the exposure of each of the major banks to the large corporate problems of 1997 would illustrate a sorry fact: that the concentration of exposure to single names would have been enough to send some of the banks to intensive care. This would have been the case had they started 1997 in a healthy state, something we all agree would be an overstatement.

External observers, exclusively armed with official statistics and the annual reports published by the banks, would certainly derive the impression that Korean banks, while not claiming to be among the strongest in the world, would pass any basic creditworthiness test. Korea has become a major industrial country, admitted to the circle of OECD countries, and it would be unbecoming for its banks to be seen as suffering from any weakness. Therefore, capital ratios must be seen as conservative. The usual way governments achieve this mystification is by playing with provisioning rules. The non-performing assets (NPA) classifications can be stretched to accommodate the most appalling situations. As discussed above, this was the case for equity investments.

The NPL classification rules in Korea have long been extremely loose. By official definition, NPLs would only comprise loans that have been non-performing for over six months. Even assets classified as normal would include those on which no interest was paid for three months. Using these narrow definitions, the official NPLs were only 4.5% of total credit — including consolidated loans, guarantees, L/C bills bought, import usance bills, credit cards accounts, etc. — at the top eight commercial banks at the end of 1996. Estimates by Thomson BankWatch put the real ratios at that time at over 12.5% of total credit. The official NPL ratio was about 6% at the end of 1997. A more accurate calculation for the year 1997 would see the NPLs at about 15% and one could fear that up to 30% of total lending would be impaired by the end of 1998.

Merchant banks are an interesting case of uncontrollable madness, although it is important to realize that there are two main categories of merchant banks: those created in the early 1980s with foreign financial institutions, and those created in the 1990s. Of the six old merchant banks, at least three are still quite safe. The 24 new merchant banks are much weaker, and a number of them had to be closed by the authorities. Most of them belong to large groups and they entered the market at a time when the Korean banking system was already facing difficulties. There were few safe prospects for them in the market and they ended up concentrating their lending in the most dangerous assets available: the bottom end of South East Asian corporate borrowers seeking short-term dollars, the capital markets of Eastern Europe and South America, and the weaker Chaebols at home. When KIA collapsed in 1997, three merchant banks were found to have lent over 120% of their own capital to the group. This is an extreme case, but many of the new merchant banks had unconscionable exposure to a string of bad names. When the crisis hit, what had been a shaky situation turned into a disaster.

The one positive factor in favor of Korean banks, in the midst of the Asian crisis is that they are relatively less exposed to real estate than their counterparts elsewhere. Traditionally, they have limited their direct exposure to real estate to about 12% of total lending, which is about half of what it is in Indonesia and Thailand, and a quarter of what it is in Hong Kong. Unfortunately, all over Asia, including Korea, property is used as collateral. When things go sour, this factor becomes very relevant and there is the fear that Korean banks will soon be found having more property exposure than they bargained for. Prices have not gone as high as elsewhere in Asia, but they are under pressure from the glut of land awaiting sale by troubled companies. Many distressed companies are tempted to unload some real estate in order to meet their obligations, and they are all trying to do so at the same time. The market may soften considerably as a result. In fact, in the early months of 1998, property prices were falling at an average rate of about 2% to 3% per month. So, even though there was no excessive behavior by lenders and developers in respect of real estate, this factor might very well become as relevant to Korean banks as it is to banks in other parts of Asia. Banks themselves are already booking losses as a result of the disposal of foreclosed property.

Korea is the only one of the five distressed countries that has compounded its problems at home with a large dose of problems imported from other countries. As discussed earlier, Korean banks could not find good returns at home. They turned to international lending and investment with an enthusiasm that was not matched by a relevant level of skills and credit control. Over the past few years, Korean banks have amassed large amounts of debt issued by corporate and sovereign borrowers in Eastern Europe and in the CIS countries. Not all such investments are necessarily risky, but some of them may end up adding to Korean banks' woes. Worse are loans and investments in the likes of Thailand and Indonesia, where Korean banks found the large interest margins that they thought would improve their profits. Needless to say, many corporate borrowers in South East Asia will default on their obligations, chiefly among them those borrowers

The Korea Asset Management Corporation

Among the possible solutions to the bad loan problem always lies the "good bank-bad bank" concept whereby a special vehicle is created to park shaky loans transferred from the books of weak financial institutions. The banks are given a chance to start afresh with a clean portfolio. This approach was selected in a number of countries and under a number of guises. In Korea, this took the shape of the Korea Asset Management Corporation (KAMC), which is supposed to purchase from banks, without recourse, those bad assets that are collaterized, and to act as a broker for the recovery of some of their collaterized impaired assets. Unfortunately, the KAMC in its first version lacked teeth. The funds available to it were pitifully limited: Won 10 trillion at the end of 1997, equivalent to about US$6 or 7 billion, funded by bonds, by loans from the government and by loans from local banks and financial institutions. This was nothing in comparison to the magnitude of problem loans. In addition, KAMC's mission was limited to supporting the banks where they least needed it. Bad loans that are collaterized are the least painful for the banks to keep in their books: if they are properly collaterized, it is only a matter of time before they can be liquidated with limited losses. Furthermore, collaterized NPLs are only a small fraction of a mountain of bad debts in the banks' books. KAMC's original target of buying out about Won 20 trillion of such debt was too modest.

There is a fear that the KAMC approach is, once again, a way of diluting the problem, of sweeping it under the carpet. The actual discount at which the assets are sold is putting a supposedly exact figure on the value of the transferred assets. This is not the case, as the sale price will be adjusted once KAMC actually liquidates the underlying collateral. In the meantime the bank records a limited loss, as the discount on assets transferred to the KAMC in 1997 was on average 35%. But the asset burning the pockets of a bank suddenly disappears. The asset is now burning the pockets of the KAMC, where it can sit for years before becoming an issue. The KAMC will of course, like the CCPC in Japan, not recognize bad assets for what they are until a political decision to do so is taken. The one positive effect of the KAMC sales is on the banks' capital ratios, since those sales will eliminate large chunks of assets from the books of the banks. They are replaced with bonds guaranteed by the government, so they carry a reduced risk weightage, and they also earn around 12% for the banks. Yet at the same time, losses previously concealed in the books will suddenly have to be recognized through the discount in the transfer price to KAMC, eliminating an opportunity to cover up potential non-performing assets.

> On May 20, 1998, the Ministry of Finance and Economy (MoFE) announced a financial reform package that included the issue of government-guaranteed bonds by the KAMC, to the tune of Won 25 trillion (80% of it in 1998, 20% in 1999). The funds would be used by KAMC to buy about Won 50 trillion of NPL from banks at a discount of approximately 50%. This is closer to what is needed, but it is still too little.

who were happily paying large margins, up to 500 basis points, or 5% above interbank interest rates. Korean lenders eagerly sought business from such borrowers, and the full impact of their inability to repay their loans has yet to reach the books of Korean banks.

Korea and the IMF

When a crisis of confidence hit Asia after the debacle in Thailand, the solvency problem of Korean financial institutions became compounded by a liquidity problem in foreign currency. Unlike Thai banks, the Korean banks were sufficiently liquid in that they were maintaining enough quasi-liquid assets in their books, mostly in local currency, to meet, within reason, any unexpected call on their liabilities. Their inability to repay foreign currency loans had more to do with the lack of dollars available in Korea than they had with the availability of liquid funds in won. When it became difficult to renew short-term obligations in US dollars, too many dollars were sought by banks to meet those obligations than were available in the market. In the end, Korea needed both an extension of some dollar-denominated obligations and a won exchange rate that would reflect the surge in demand for US dollars.

Considering Korea's figures on the debt front, in particular the huge amounts borrowed in the short-term, it would have been impossible to convert enough short-term debt to longer-term obligations, in order to match the immediate need for US$ with the immediate availability of US$. There was no option available other than to beg funds from the IMF and from major countries. The crisis was hitting Korea at the wrong time, as presidential elections were to take place in December 1997, with the winner taking his job in February 1998. The IMF asked from all three presidential candidates a commitment to adhere to its conditions for the loans, and fortunately none of the candidates refused to agree, for what this was worth. This is no small feat in a country that was still in a state of denial about the whole affair.

The IMF conditions for the loans were very strict, more so than in Thailand or Indonesia, for the reason that no mistake could be made with Korea. Its economy is as big as those of Indonesia, Thailand and Malaysia combined, and a failure to stabilize it would lead to further trouble in the rest of the region, including Japan, perhaps leading to global destabilization. Also Korea should not fall into the trap of amortizing its problems over the next several years. The example of Japan was in everyone's minds, where the financial crisis had already endured for eight years, with no real solution in sight. Japan could afford the delay, Korea could not. Korea's industrial capacity remained unimpaired and it would have, above any other Asian country in distress, a credible claim to the world's tolerance for a slow recovery. But this would encourage a status quo that, in the end, would undermine Korea's chances to recover fully.

The IMF economic reforms addressed quite a large spectrum of the problems explained in earlier paragraphs and could be divided into the following:

- Low growth, high interest rates, current account surplus, flexible exchange rate policy
- Foreign reserves to grow to US$30 billion by mid-1998
- Small fiscal surplus, cuts in expenditure, assistance to small and medium-sized companies
- Rehabilitation of the merchant bank sector
- Recapitalization of Korea First Bank and Seoul Bank
- Bank restructuring
- Establishment of proper controls of the banking system
- Opening of the financial and equity markets to foreign investors
- More transparency in financial statements
- New bankruptcy laws
- New labor laws

This was a tall order, and there were doubts as to whether all objectives could be achieved within a reasonable timeframe. The Chaebols, meanwhile, collectively announced that they would launch an ambitious export drive aimed at creating a current account surplus of US$50 billion in both 1998 and 1999. They said that the 500 largest companies in Korea should be able to shave US$30 billion per year off their imports and increase their exports by US$20 billion. In exchange for their determination, they apparently started pressuring the government to increase export financing, which had suffered as banks were seeking to reduce overall lending, to install the holding company system and to go ahead with the labor laws which would make it easier for Chaebols to lay off staff.

In response, the government indicated that it did not wish to see a further concentration of power, materialized by the holding company system. It was also concerned that reducing imports would be too much of a belt tightening exercise, leading to incidental problems. It also confirmed that the Chaebols would be required to shrink their debt-to-equity ratio to a maximum of 200% before the end of 1999, although no suggestion was made as to how to achieve that result.

What the government and the Chaebols were to negotiate upon would have to rely on the assistance of the people of Korea. The success of the economy in the past 35 years was largely due to the courage and determination of an entire generation of workers. Many were close to the end of their professional life, and were now seeing the fruits of their hard labor disappear before their eyes, while the new generation had, like in Japan, only known the better times. The cradle to grave mentality has slowly permeated the Korean mentality. Few understand why Korea should suffer. Many accuse the IMF of imposing unreasonable reforms. The "IMF=I'm Fired" slogan is not dissimilar to the "No to Maastricht" slogan seen in some European countries. There the reforms imposed by the Maastricht Treaty organizing the finances of the European Union are seen as responsible for the impoverishment of a nation. More educated rioters would realize that the reforms would be necessary regardless of the European construction. The same goes in Korea with regards to the IMF reforms. Naturally, it is at times convenient for politicians to deflect problems and to direct the rioters to other targets. There are no "Maastricht lay-offs" in Europe, but in Korea many companies organize "IMF sales" attributing their woes to some external diktat.

Among the liberalization measures suggested by the IMF, while dictated by Korea's desire to take its place among the rich nations, is the need to open up full control of local companies to foreign investors. The negative list of firms remaining out-of-bounds to foreigners has shrunk considerably following the 1997 crisis. Yet, for cultural reasons, it is difficult to imagine foreign companies buying heavily into Korean companies. Even assuming, which is definitely a stretch, that accounts are presented in conformity with generally accepted accounting principles, and that important matters like the protection of minority shareholders and the bankruptcy laws are properly addressed, one would have to cope with an immense cultural divide. Korea shares with Japan the belief that working for foreign companies is not done. In a cradle to grave system, one does not change companies. Taking a job with foreigners, even those eating Kimchi,[8] would make it difficult to reintegrate into the cocoon of a Korean company afterwards. Korean workers have long demanded a premium to work for foreigners, and a couple of international banks a few years ago suffered so tremendously in labor disputes that they simply closed shop. There will no doubt be a number of spectacular takeovers by foreigners, but it looks highly unlikely that the cultural divide will disappear. Foreign investors will remain shy until they feel more tolerated.

The Future

Bleak is the word that comes to mind. Thomson BankWatch had estimated the NPL at well over Won 40 trillion, probably close to Won 60 trillion. In a surprising show of transparency, the Ministry of Finance announced, on May 20, 1998, that non-performing loans would reach Won 100 trillion. This figure does not include precautionary loans, which are often dismissed as current loans that see occasional delays in repayment. Including them would propel the figure to Won 112 trillion. It is fair to say that actual bad loans may very well never reach that figure. Yet the amount is staggering and adjustments for the fact that authorities are usually hiding something would propel it to horrendous levels. The Korean government says that the Won 100 trillion in NPLs will likely translate into Won 50 trillion in losses for the banks. This represents more than twice the aggregate amount of capital funds available to them. Incidentally, this is the first time that an Asian government has openly stated that its banking system is bankrupt.

The MoFE released details on May 20, 1998 of what it hopes will mark the end of the first stage in the Korean authorities' efforts to clean up the sick local financial sector and create a solid base for rehabilitation and revitalization of the country's depressed economic state. For several months before that, Korean bankers and their regulators remained in what can only be described as a state of denial; there was a crisis in the country and elsewhere in the region, but the financial system was, they believed, sufficiently resilient to tide them over. New efforts at transparency are welcome. Whether it is realistic to expect a full recovery on the strength of the May 1998 measures is another matter altogether. At the end of 1996, the 40 largest banks and merchant banks had an aggregate Won 30 trillion in shareholders funds. The MoFE places the total amount needed to recapitalize the Korean financial industry at Won 50 trillion (equal to the total possible losses on the proposed NPL disposal program assuming that the current market value of total estimated NPLs is 50%), plus a further Won 4 trillion which is required for banks to meet the minimum 8% BIS capital adequacy ratio now in force in line with IMF guidelines, irrespective of the bad debt disposal program. In other words, the government is telling us that its banking system had, in early 1998, after adjustment for bad loans, aggregate shareholders funds of about minus Won 20 trillion. This translates into a BIS-style capital adequacy ratio of minus 5%, for the banking system on average.

Against this, loan loss reserves totaling Won 9 trillion already existed in early 1998. The government will commit Won 16 trillion for recapitalization, through the Deposit Insurance Company. This leaves Won 25 trillion which banks will need to source themselves to cover their losses. Given their appalling record at generating cash flow, and the cloudy horizon overshadowing the economy, their only option is straight recapitalization. Few investors — domestic or foreigners — however, will be tempted to buy, given the present sorry state of their accounts. The issue of subordinated debt is a possibility. Nationalization increasingly looks like the only real solution, perhaps after an attempt at prolonging the agony through mergers.

We live in interesting times. Hectic certainly in Korea.

Endnotes

1. For the sake of simplicity, we shall refer to South Korea as "Korea", as many commentators do. The South Koreans themselves call their country "Republic of Korea" without clarifying that this only refers to the south of the Korean peninsula.

2. Wade and Radelet in particular.

3. Until better controls put an end to the practice, Belgian dentists were the world's most skilled income tax evaders and they found in Luxembourg and Switzerland easy havens to squirrel away their excess cash receipts.

4. The analyst's lot is not a happy one. Here is a ratio, used mostly in North America, that tells him the reverse of what he would expect: the lower the efficiency ratio, the higher the efficiency.

5. The reader will find average cost margins among the region's banks in Table 8.3.

6. Banks operate on very thin profit margins. As a rule of thumb, a commercial bank is comfortable when it generates, after provisions and taxes, a profit roughly equal to 1% of total assets. Wasting 1.6% on inefficiency can make the difference between fat profits and slow decay.

7. Until 1995, the government was selecting the top two executives of all the major banks, even in the private sector, rotating them among the banks. At present, the major private sector banks still need government approval for the selection of their top managers. One can imagine that the government's influence has barely diminished.

8. Kimchi is a Korean dish made of cabbage and prepared in a variety of ways. The favorite garlic-flavored version is responsible for the dominant smell that permeates the Seoul subway system in the morning. No foreigner can penetrate the Korean mind without first learning how to appreciate Kimchi.

INDONESIA

The Asian panic hit Indonesia more than any other country. Its currency was savaged. The banking system ground to a halt and most banks passed under government tutelage. Among the countries in distress, Indonesia is the worst case. More than anywhere else, it is possible to put a finger on what is wrong with its financial system. Yet little can be achieved until a more fundamental question is addressed, that of the political and social system. The very people who were instrumental in writing Indonesia's success story are also at the source of its present predicament. The Indonesian people deserve a quick and peaceful resolution of the present crisis. Any delay in finding a way out is inflicting further suffering and making a positive outcome more elusive. General Suharto's relatively quiet departure from the scene in May 1998 is likely to precipitate events.

The Banking System

From independence in 1946 to the banking reform of October 1988, the banking scene in Indonesia was dominated by a string of state-owned banks, originating from a structure in place when the country was a colonial outpost. Each of the banks had, theoretically, a specific mission of promoting certain sectors of the economy. They were reporting to Bank Indonesia (BI) and therefore indirectly to the Ministry of Finance which would dictate everything from interest rates to the list of the beneficiaries of bank loans. Indonesia was staunchly anticommunist but, ironically, the structure of its financial system was not very different from that of communist China. The five state-owned banks (Bank Dagang Negara, Bank Bumi Daya, Bank Negara Indonesia 1946, Bank Rakyat Indonesia and Bank Exim) still exist. They have been badly mauled by the crisis. But the sad truth is that, before the crisis hit, all of them were either close to bankruptcy or already beyond repair.

Over the years, a few private sector banks were established. By 1988, they were together handling about 15% of all banking services in an environment where a number of directives and restrictions were imposed on them. Foreign banks were tolerated, but generally restricted to the Jakarta district, and many would simply direct to their branches in Singapore or elsewhere whatever corporate loans their Jakarta representative would bring to the table.

Some Indonesian tycoons would also invest outside of Indonesia, and they became important clients for foreign banks. Corruption was rampant. Foreign bankers were invited on luxury cruises and escapes to idyllic retreats. Many a foreign bank ended up paying dearly for its naïveté, but this was part of the price to pay for partaking in Asia's development. The mid-1980s crisis affected mostly Malaysia and Indonesia and it brought substantial losses to foreign banks.

In 1988, Indonesia decided to liberalize its banking sector in a way that no other Asian country had ever seen, or was to duplicate after that. Basically, the Indonesian authorities told all and sundry that anyone with some spare cash could come forward and apply for a banking license. It would be naïve to think that there were no other criteria applied,[1] but it meant that, for about seven or eight years, banks sprang up like mushrooms. On their very frequent visits to Jakarta, the BankWatch analysts would compete for the highest number of new bank names spotted on the way from the airport to the city. The joke went that any group of four old ladies playing bridge on a Monday afternoon could suddenly decide to pool their stakes and get a bank license by the end of the week. By the next Monday, the bank would be operating. Everybody and her cousin had a bank license. Over the years, a number of small banks ended up in the hands of larger competitors. No doubt this was the only option if the owners wanted to avoid the embarrassment of a failure. In fact, some of the largest private sector banks grew as much by acquisitions as they did organically.

It is often said there are too many banks in Indonesia. But, with a total of about 221 commercial banks at the end of 1997, the number remained modest for a country of close to 200 million people. Comparisons are difficult across countries due to the fact that there are multiple definitions of banking activities, and one should include all minor versions of money lending. It can be argued that there were not too many banks in Indonesia, only too many banks that could grow uncontrollably and, worse, reach a level where they could start playing with dangerous toys.

The temptation for would-be bankers was to rapidly reach a size sufficient to gain a much coveted private foreign exchange license, which would open the door to the lucrative world of import and export trade finance, foreign exchange transactions and, later, foreign exchange derivatives. Until 1995 when the authorities started feeling embarrassed by the number of applications, there were no specific rules on how to obtain that license, except perhaps asset size, but being well connected certainly helped. Originally, a large proportion of the small list of private sector banks held private foreign exchange licenses, but, as the pool of commercial banks grew, only about 20% of them enjoyed the privilege.

With the private foreign exchange license came more profits, and with them the opportunity for banks to go public at inflated premiums. Most of the banks had been founded by individuals or by families. With a bit of luck, going public at the right moment with only 15% of the shares was likely to pay the family back their entire stake in the bank, and they would enjoy, free of charge, the remaining 85% forever after. For that to happen, they needed a shallow stock market, trumped-up financials and gullible investors, all ingredients readily available in the early 1990s in Indonesia. Those observers who today lament the spectacular collapse of the Jakarta Stock Exchange should realize that, for many a small punter, bank shares had already fallen considerably from their heights well before the 1997 crisis.

Gaining a larger market share by gathering deposits was the name of the game and the country witnessed an extraordinary war between the banks, especially acute in the early years of the decade. The legendary toaster, which would have been a luxury for some small Indonesian depositors, was replaced with lavish gifts and lotteries, distributing four-wheel drives and Mercedes-Benzes with little restraint. The growth of the most aggressive private sector banks was extraordinary, perhaps only matched — on paper — by banks in countries experiencing hyperinflation. Increasing deposits at a yearly pace of 50%, 60% or more was all too common. There were two reasons for that growth. Firstly, the authorities intentionally left the best part of the growth to the private sector, as a way to deflate the role of state sector financial institutions. Secondly, the country was growing rapidly, with a real GDP growth in the vicinity of 8%, and money supply, as measured by M2, expanding by more than 20% every year. Indonesia had long been "underbanked" and was making up for it largely through the growth of private sector money lending. Some of the growth at major banks came from the acquisition of small financial institutions, sometimes from the rescue of troubled institutions. In fact, very few banks actually failed during the growth period, but many small players were forced into mergers.

Banks needed capital to sustain growth, hence the importance of having access to the stock market. Without the huge share premiums paid by 11th hour investors, such capital would not have been found. It would be wrong to assume that Indonesian banks were not profitable, or at least, potentially profitable. As in many emerging markets, banking services are extremely expensive and translate into the transfer of small money from the masses to big money for a privileged class. Indonesian banks have, in the past 10 years, enjoyed the benefit of very large net interest margins (NIM) (Table 6.1) and interest spreads, a measure of the difference between the average interest paid on deposits and the average interest received on loans.[2]

The NIM, being the bread-and-butter of Asian banking, should normally dictate the level of net profit, but the relationship is affected by two other factors: non-interest income and administrative expenses. There is nothing unusual about the level of non-interest income in Indonesia,[3] but administrative expenses are among the highest in Asia. There are a number of reasons for these to be high, among them the huge geographical spread of the country where communications and transportation costs are substantial and it is difficult to run viable commercial banking operations in a small distant community. The average size of a typical

TABLE 6.1 NET INTEREST MARGIN (%)

	1994	1995	1996
Philippines	4.92	4.79	4.89
Korea — Old Merchants Banks	6.39	4.83	3.79
Indonesia — Private Banks	4.11	3.82	3.66
Thailand	3.98	3.74	3.61
Malaysia	3.03	3.19	3.47
Hong Kong	2.64	2.84	2.99
Korea — Provincial Banks	2.08	2.99	2.98
Indonesia — State Banks	3.03	2.98	2.61
Korea — Specialized Banks	2.51	2.29	2.23
Singapore	2.06	2.03	2.03
Korea — Nationwide Banks	1.68	1.64	1.67
Taiwan	1.06	1.68	1.53

Source: Annual Reports

TABLE 6.2 INDONESIA'S FUNDAMENTALS

	1991	1992	1993	1994	1995	1996	1997	1998p
Currency								
Rupiah/US$ (End period)	1,992	2,062	2,110	2,200	2,308	2,348	5,400	7,500
Real Exchange Rate (% change)	−4.6	−4.0	−7.4	−4.9	−3.7	−4.9	118.4	−8.1
Real Economy								
Real GDP (% Change)	7.0	6.5	6.5	7.3	8.1	7.8	4.7	−5.0
Fixed Investment as % of GDP	35.0	34.6	36.1	33.0	29.0	31.0	31.0	28.9
Official Unemployment Rate (%)	2.7	2.6	2.5	2.5	2.3	2.2	3.0	n/a
Money and Prices								
Retail Price Inflation (End period) (%)	9.4	7.5	9.7	9.2	8.6	6.6	11.6	47.0
Lending Rate (%)	N/A	24.03	20.59	17.76	18.85	19.22	21.82	34.00
Reserves (US$ billions)	9.26	10.45	11.26	12.13	13.71	17.90	19.30	20.80
Domestic Savings Rate (%)	32.6	35.7	35.2	36.1	35.8	36.0	27.1	31.9
Balance of Payments ($ billions)								
Exports (US$ billions)	29.14	33.97	36.82	40.05	45.42	51.00	53.38	60.40
Imports (US$ billions)	25.87	27.28	28.33	31.99	40.92	48.00	41.54	40.00
Trade Balance (US$ billions)	3.27	6.69	8.49	8.06	4.50	3.00	11.84	20.40
Current Account Balance (US$ billions)	(4.26)	(2.78)	(2.12)	(2.79)	(7.02)	(7.80)	(9.56)	9.00
Current Account Balance (% GDP)	−3.6	−2.2	−1.3	−1.6	−3.9	−4.0	−3.9	3.0
Foreign Debt (US$ billions)	79.78	88.30	89.48	96.50	109.20	115.00	129.00	140.00
as % of GDP	65.1	66.4	58.9	57.4	55.8	51.8	60.9	71.0
Debt Service Ratio (%)	34.0	31.6	33.8	30.5	31.4	31.7	29.9	28.0
Governmant Finance								
Gov. Surplus/Deficit as % of GDP	−0.4	0.2	−0.2	−0.5	0.8	0.5	−1.0	−3.2

Source: Thomson BankWatch Inc.

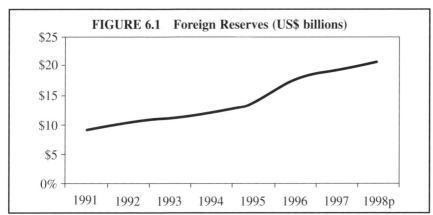

FIGURE 6.1 Foreign Reserves (US$ billions)

Source: Thomson BankWatch Inc.

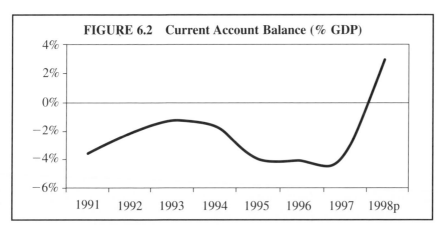

FIGURE 6.2 Current Account Balance (% GDP)

Source: Thomson BankWatch Inc.

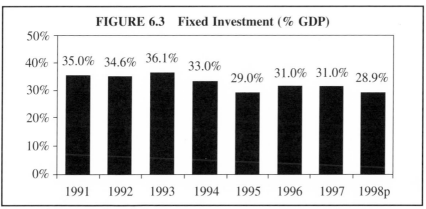

FIGURE 6.3 Fixed Investment (% GDP)

Source: Thomson BankWatch Inc.

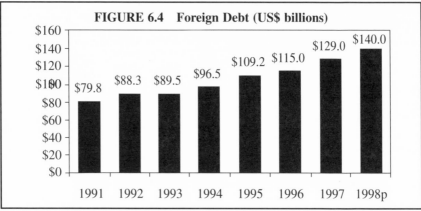

FIGURE 6.4   Foreign Debt (US$ billions)

Source: Thomson BankWatch Inc.

transaction in Indonesia is also lower than in Hong Kong or Taiwan. Bank managers have also been profligate when it comes to their own comforts, and bank owners, for obvious tax reasons, among others, have tended to live off the beast as much as they can. As things stand, Indonesian banks are — or at least were, before the crisis — profitable, and would have been extremely profitable if run under more rigid principles as far as expenses were concerned. Tables 6.3 and 6.4 shoe recent profitability ratios.

TABLE 6.3   PROFITABILITY: AVERAGE — PRIVATE BANKS

	1993 (%)	1994 (%)	1995 (%)	1996 (%)
ROAA	0.96	1.18	1.19	1.18
ROE	12.77	14.74	15.18	15.88
NIM	3.89	4.11	3.82	3.62

Source: Annual Reports

TABLE 6.4   PROFITABILITY: AVERAGE — STATE BANKS

	1993 (%)	1994 (%)	1995 (%)	1996 (%)
ROAA	0.48	0.43	0.60	0.72
ROE	10.93	8.40	10.50	11.85
NIM	2.67	3.11	3.23	2.91

Source: Annual Reports

The Wild East

If there were a prize for the most creative bankers in the wildest banking environment in the world, certainly the Indonesian banking system would be a clear winner. Although banks in Japan, Korea, Thailand and some other Asian countries have long entertained the financial world with extraordinary tales, they are nothing compared to the Indonesian banks.

One of the country's largest private sector banks, Bank Pacific, was among the first banks to establish its head office in a brand new building in the south of Jakarta. That took place in the early 1980s and the building was comparatively attractive. This prompted the following report by the representative of a foreign bank visiting Bank Pacific to discuss interbank facilities: "Figures not available. But lunch was good, management nice, new headquarters beautiful. Let us give them US$10 million."

Where else in the world would you find a bank, under the control of the central bank after an earlier quasi-failure, go bust because the owner's daughter went wrong in a pet project? The same Bank Pacific, majority-owned by a Suharto brother-in-arms, went under in 1996 when its guarantee was called on a failed resort development project. The otherwise charming daughter of the owner (and, until a restructuring in 1995, Managing Director of the bank) was promoting the project through an associated finance company. Indonesia's very own central bank had long been a substantial minority shareholder of Bank Pacific and had representatives on the Board of Directors. See nothing, hear nothing, say nothing — this is Indonesia.

The Bank Duta story is a good illustration of a certain style prevailing in Indonesia's capital markets. Until it went public in 1990, Bank Duta was in the hands of three charity foundations headed by General Suharto. Bank Duta went public with 25% of its shares, leaving the balance in the hands of the foundations. There is nothing unusual with this arrangement. However, only a few weeks after going public, the bank announced huge foreign exchange losses that would wipe out the entire proceeds of the recent flotation. The losses were so huge as to be incompatible with normal banking transactions. They were also too big to have been piled up in only a few weeks, and it would have been impossible for the previous owners, contrary to what they rushed to claim, to be unaware of them before the share issue. The backlash from the markets was, for once, so strong and unexpected that the previous owners had to backpedal and make good the losses, although it is not clear where the money came from. The manager in charge of treasury at Bank Duta, who claimed to be innocent of the crime, was duly arrested and kindly requested to spend some time in jail for the crime.

There is one aspect that distinguishes the Indonesian banks from most of the rest of Asia, and it has to do with related party lending. This notion pertains to the granting of credit facilities to persons or companies associated with the owners of the bank. It is not difficult to imagine that such lending activities do not usually comply with normal notions of prudent credit control. In addition, it makes the idea of minimum capital ratios totally obsolete, since the owners in fact owe the bank money beyond their capital investment. This is discussed in Chapter 3.

Indonesian bankers are Asia's most skilled related party lenders. It is a national pastime, which is not surprising when most banks belong to families or to industrial or commercial groups. The temptation is there, and there is little that can be done by regulators. They know what is going on — everybody in Indonesia does — but they are totally helpless. Either they cannot prove their case, or the cheaters are beyond reach, thanks to their connections. The rules call for a limit on related party lending of no more than 10% of the bank's equity — down from 25% a few years ago. However, five years ago when Bank Summa failed, it was rumored that the bank was found to have 55% of total loans[4] to related parties.

Efficiency is extremely low at Indonesian banks. In their defense, it is difficult to remain efficient in a country covering 5,000 km, with thousands of islands and a poor population. Yet, stories abound of competitive bids in distant cities where private banks would install a new branch and steal away, at a cost, the only bank staff available from the couple of banks already fighting over limited business opportunities.

Liquidity has long been a problem in private sector banks (see recent ratios in Tables 6.5 and 6.6). Opportunities to lend seem to have always exceeded the deposits available. This has often made Indonesian private sector banks prone to liquidity crises. In the early 1990s, runs hit several banks, including a major name. The Minister of Finance had to appear on television to ask depositors to show some restraint.

TABLE 6.5   CAPITAL/LIQUIDITY AND FUNDING: PRIVATE BANKS

	1993 (%)	1994 (%)	1995 (%)	1996 (%)
Equity/Assets	7.74	8.16	7.58	7.27
Equity/Loans	11.50	11.24	10.63	10.34
Loans/Deps.	80.65	86.24	84.57	81.79
QLAR	20.71	16.05	18.18	20.16

Source: Annual Reports

TABLE 6.6   CAPITAL/LIQUIDITY AND FUNDING: STATE BANKS

	1993 (%)	1994 (%)	1995 (%)	1996 (%)
Equity/Assets	4.51	5.76	5.71	6.35
Equity/Loans	6.60	8.32	8.31	9.04
Loans/Deps.	105.18	94.86	96.04	94.59
QLAR	24.08	24.92	23.98	22.43

Source: Annual Reports

By 1995, asset quality had improved in Indonesia from the abysmal level seen in the early 1990s, but clear signs of deterioration were visible prior to the crisis. The limited credit culture of Indonesian banks has always been a problem. What made Indonesian banking an accident waiting to happen was the unbridled credit growth that followed the 1988 deregulation. Early in the decade, growth was particularly wild. Some banks would grow by over 50% or 60% a year. Naturally, one would not expect the credit culture and the credit skills to grow in harmony. Having said that, it is undeniable that, as devastated as the banking sector might be today, it would have been in even worse shape if state-owned banks had carried on running the show. Political patronage is the single most important explanation for the fact that state-owned banks were carrying, before the crisis, two-thirds of all delinquent loans in the country.

Property lending has recently been a substantial driver of total loan growth, since that sector alone grew by 35% every year in the past three years. Officially, property lending accounted for around 20% of total lending before the crisis — unofficially closer to 30%. It had long been relatively safe in that most of the lending was directed at landed property. In recent years, however, some developers multiplied their investments in commercial, office and condominium real estate, to the point where many loans have become shaky. Another phenomenon is the "village", a city out of the city, built entirely by developers where nasty surprises are in the making after some banks had offered sweet deals to buyers in order for friendly developers to unload some of their inventory. Concerns about property-related exposures have led the central bank to put a selective freeze on fresh lending.

NPLs have soared in Indonesia following the crisis, and no accurate figure is available. Even before the crisis, the real level of NPLs was understated, as banks were routinely restructuring most delinquent loans. A delinquent loan would remain classified as performing until up to three months after the bank saw the last payment. Just for the pleasure, let us confirm here that by the end of September 1997 — that is well into the crisis — one of the largest private sector bank was claiming to have no more than 1.9% in NPLs. It is probably useless to add that banks are not any more professional when it comes to the adequacy of their bad loan provisions.

The Crisis

There have been wild fluctuations in the currency markets of the five distressed countries since July 1997, but none of them saw as much of that action as Indonesia. Mainly in the second half of 1997, the rupiah went up and down like a yo-yo, with intra-day amplitudes in excess of 10%, the result of economic and political uncertainties as much as the relative lack of liquidity. Substantial amounts must have been made or lost in the first few months of the crisis. The stock market also saw ample fluctuations (Table 6.7). Recent high figures do not sustain the

The Indonesian State-owned Banks

Indonesia is the only one of the five distressed countries where a very substantial proportion of total commercial banking assets is in the hands of state-owned banks. To summarize how they fare, it is best to listen to the following piece of wisdom, well established in the circles of cognoscenti in Jakarta: those borrowers who intend to pay the money back borrow from private sector banks, while those borrowers who do not intend to pay the money back should address their requests to the state-owned banks. It is as simple as that. Proper credit culture is abysmally lacking in Indonesia, but much more so in government banks where, typically, one could be blamed for not being politically correct. If it appeared that a borrower should, on purely commercial and objective grounds, not be given the funds applied for, the instinct of conservatism would dictate a cautious attitude. However, before he was rejected, it would be wiser to first check whether or not the borrower was well connected. A good job in the quasi-civil service is worth a little caution now and then.

The state-owned bank situation became so embarrassing that, in 1995, a mysterious list of recalcitrant borrowers was leaked to the press and the government announced that those borrowers who were able, but not willing, to pay back their loans to state-owned banks would be pursued. And, for good measure, they would be prevented from leaving the country until the matter was cleared. Miraculously, the NPLs on the books of state-owned banks, ranging from 12% to 30% of total lending, started shrinking significantly. The one government-owned unit that remained beyond repair was Bapindo, a development bank said to have long had the highest concentration of dud loans south-east of Rangoon. One such loan exposure for an amount of US$650 million was to Eddie Tansil, the brother of Rahardja, of the Harapan group, himself famous for his ventures into real estate in Singapore in the early 1980s, and fondly remembered by some European banks. Tansil was arrested, found guilty of misappropriation of the funds and jailed for years. For reasons that have yet to be explained, he escaped from prison soon after and was never seen again.

In Indonesia, as in other Asian countries where state-owned banks control a sizable proportion of the market, the authorities try and make sure that such banks keep posting acceptable figures so as not to attract negative comments from external observers. A good many analysts, hailing from countries where accounts are a more faithful representation of a bank's state of affairs, still rely too blindly on figures and ratios. One should not blame the Indonesian government for misleading those simple minds.

Are performance ratios relevant to state-owned banks? Liquidity is never a problem, since the Ministry of Finance or the Central Bank can always extend additional funds. State-owned banks are often used as a source of financing for the government: it is seen as a relatively efficient way of mobilizing savings that government capital market issues might not reach. In countries where state banks are dominant, it is an easy tool to control credit growth. The various rules governing bank liquidity as a cushion against fluctuations in cash flows are superseded by government objectives for its budget. More often than not, liquidity ratios of state-owned banks have no meaning whatsoever.

Capital ratios are no problem either. To the extent that they provide a protective cushion for creditors and depositors against a failure by the bank owners to swallow operating losses, clearly the high creditworthiness of a government bank owner should be sufficient. Capital ratios lose any significance. Furthermore, since a major factor affecting true capital ratios is asset quality, it is easy to imagine that governments give themselves a degree of flexibility in assessing the true quality of loans in the books of state-owned banks. The authorities can decide which loans are going to be considered non-performing and, if the situation gets unbearable — meaning the capital ratios would be too negatively affected — they can issue government bonds in lieu of cash for the replenishment of shareholders funds.[5]

Profitability figures are trickier to play with, if only because untrained observers tend to focus on them. Nonetheless, it has been a tradition that governments would play with profit figures of state-owned banks to get them to fit into a respectable pattern. The rule of thumb is that, between 0.20% and 0.30%, the ROAA of such an institution is pretty acceptable. Nothing fancy, nothing dangerous, a good showing when, after all, a state-owned bank has social responsibilities and its primary objective is not to be profitable. It is much more difficult to play with profitability ratios than with other ratios as profits can actually be counted. Yet state-owned banks have always seemed to hit the proper range of profitability ratios. If the year was good, the banks were told to deflate profits by increasing their bad loan provisions, which they were always cruelly short of. If profits were below the expected range, some arrangements had to be made. For example, in the mid-1980s when the rupiah met with several sudden devaluations, the central bank would call state-owned banks in need of profits with advance warning of the devaluation, so that they could take large long dollar positions. Other more subtle tricks were used like soft loans at concession rates or the payment of fees for certain services.

The Indonesian government has become so good at coaching its banks into the right profitability range, that it even succeeded in engineering a gradual improvement in their return on assets ratio (ROA) to about 0.60% in 1995 and 1996. Why would it do so, when banks were badly in need of bad loan provisions? Simply because two or three of the state-owned banks were slated for privatization. Who would buy into a bank that posted low profit ratios? In Indonesia, an ROA of 0.20% translates into a return on average equity ratio (ROE) of roughly 4.5%. With a ROA of 0.50%, the ROE can reach 12% and be more palatable. This trick allowed the government to unload Bank Negara Indonesia 1946 (BNI) on unsuspecting investors.[6] But, to be fair, BNI was in much better shape than the other state-owned banks and buyers were interested in a future stream of dividends, while government support still offered strong protection.

TABLE 6.7   STOCK EXCHANGE INDEX

	Dec. 93	Dec. 94	Dec. 95	Dec. 96	Dec. 97	15 Jun. 98
Index (JKISP)	588.760	469.640	513.847	637.432	401.712	406.5
Base Dec. 1993 = 100	100	79.87	87.28	108.27	68.23	69.04

Source: Capital Information Services

comment made by a foreign securities house that only 20 listed companies could face their obligations.

A major reason why the currency fell as much as it did was the appetite for dollars of the Indonesian speculator himself. When the rupiah started weakening, people in Jakarta reacted like they did in Bangkok. Those who had a negative open position in dollars — they borrowed dollars and converted into rupiah — rushed to the exit, trying to secure dollars before the rupiah fell too much. They were joined by thousands of local speculators who did not have any position either way, but who wanted to seek refuge in a safe currency while it was still cheap to acquire. They were invited to partake in a beautiful one-way bet and they built up huge long dollar positions. Everybody rushed at it, even for modest amounts. So much so that quite substantial amounts were disbursed in US dollar notes, not the typical way a large corporation would want to keep its dollars until the time came to reimburse its loans. Clearly, some of the demand was coming from individuals. At one point, several banks were permitted by the authorities to close some branches, not because they had run out of rupiah, but because they had run out of US dollar notes. Everyone wanted to hold dollars. The highly visible and brilliantly staged selling of wads of US dollar notes by persons close to the regime, ostensibly to support the value of the rupiah, was just the unwinding of a tiny chunk of those highly rewarding positions.

The rupiah had fluctuated from Rps 2,300 for one US dollar in early 1997, to over Rps 15,000 at the height of the crisis. At one point, it stabilized at about Rps 9,000 for one US dollar and some commentators, including one famous Asian politician,[7] lost their basic arithmetic bearings when they started saying that the rupiah had lost 400% of its value. No asset of that kind can lose 400% of its value, for if that were the case, it would have a negative value and you would have to pay someone to buy the rupiah from you. It would have been more correct to talk about a 75% devaluation, since it would take only about 25 cents at that level to buy the same Rps 2,300 that a dollar was buying before the crisis. Almost all currencies are quoted on a "per unit of dollar" basis, but in fact their value should be calculated, as they are in the futures markets, using the reciprocal, that is on a "per unit of currency" basis. It remains correct to say that dollar-priced products have increased by about 400% in rupiah terms, but this is another story. Using the reciprocal, one can compare the real situation as shown in Table 6.8.

TABLE 6.8 CURRENCY TABLE

	Dec. 93	Dec. 94	Dec. 95	Dec. 96	Dec. 97	15 Jun. 98
US$ per 1000 rupiah	0.4739	0.4545	0.4332	0.4258	0.1851	0.0681
Base Dec. 1993 = 100	100	95.91	91.41	89.85	39.06	14.37
Rupiah per US$	2110	2200	2308	2348	5400	14675
Base Dec. 1993 = 100	100	104.27	109.38	111.28	255.92	695.50

Source: Capital Information Services

Indonesia has seen its currency devalue much more than that of other countries during the crisis and yet, it would seem that the country had been better than its rivals in managing its currency over the past few years. The rupiah was devalued several times in big steps during the mid-1980s crisis, and the Indonesian authorities learned something about currency management. In a clever move, they let the rupiah slide down every year after that in a managed way so as to absorb some of the overvaluation that would otherwise have been built up in the currency. This was a much wiser move than seen in Korea and Thailand, where leaders stuck to a more rigid link to the dollar. This brought an invaluable benefit to Indonesia when the crisis erupted: very little was wasted in what would have been a futile attempt to prop up the currency. To be honest, this view should perhaps be reviewed now that it has been revealed that Bank Exim, a government-owned bank, took a substantial position in support of the rupiah just before the currency collapsed. How many more positions of the same nature were taken by other state-controlled institutions, financial or non-financial, is something that the usual lack of disclosure in Indonesia will not allow external analysts to figure out.

The rupiah clearly overshot any reasonable readjustment target, but an additional problem made any stabilization difficult. By coincidence, Indonesia was also facing a political crisis. General Suharto was seen by many as needing some rest, after 32 years in power. Riots and quasi-unanimous dissent eased him out. Habibie stepped in, possibly short term. The only problem was that the succession had not been well prepared. Suharto is a very intelligent man and an extremely clever politician. A lot more than you think was hidden behind his smiling face. He was the one who steered his country out of poverty in one generation, by setting targets and adroitly using whatever tools he could. Human rights activists and do-gooders found flaws in his deeds, with a degree of justification, but they probably realized that running a country of that size and complexity on the ruins of colonialism, war and communist insurgency is not a simple task. Suharto had the intelligence to understand that, without the financial support and business acumen of the small Chinese-Indonesian community, development would have been much slower. His only problem was perhaps, in the last few years of his reign, that he had ears for his family only, whose abnegation and devotion to public service is not established, to put it mildly. Cronyism is embedded in the Asian culture, and nepotism often follows. Yet Suharto was no Marcos, as far as can be seen for the moment. But there is mounting popular pressure in Indonesia for a full investigation into the family's financial dealings, and some monopolistic deals with the Suharto family have already been cancelled.

The Greeks, who invented democracy, also knew that it is wiser to let dissenting voices express themselves, to meet their arguments, and to let the people decide who has to have the upper hand. Pure democracy probably was not what Asia needed in its high growth era. Rice and directives were more relevant and they produced miracles. Maturity and wealth eventually brought the need for more accountability from the leaders, and for a degree of democracy. Suharto did not allow any meaningful opposition to grow, and he made the mistake of not nurturing a credible successor for himself. At one point not long ago, the situation was still manageable in that few people were openly insisting on a change of regime and therefore a smooth changeover would have been possible. However, faced with these uncertainties, many wealthy Indonesians voted with their feet and went to the banks to buy substantial quantities of dollars. Considerable amounts have left the country for safer havens.

The Future

Indonesia played cat and mouse with the IMF for some time, eventually signing an agreement that Suharto had no intention to abide by. The government announced a surrealistic budget.[8] In a theatrical gesture, 16 banks were forcibly closed, including three banks belonging to the first family. One of them, Bank Andromeda, immediately found a way out: the family bought a tiny bank called Bank Alfa and transferred all assets and liabilities of Bank Andromeda to the new bank. Signage and stationery were changed overnight, and that was the end of the matter.

More seriously, can the rupiah be stabilized? As said earlier, the Indonesians had their share of problems with the currency in the mid-1980s and the managed, gradual devaluation of the rupiah in the 1990s kept them aware at all times of the possibility that fresh problems could affect them again. This did not prevent the private sector from borrowing huge amounts in US dollars (at last count, the amount was US$80 billion). Any company that borrows in such a way is aware of the danger and takes a calculated bet that the rupiah will not fall more than the interest differential between dollar and rupiah. If it does, the company can still take a loss and survive, provided that the fall is reasonably small. Unfortunately, however it is calculated, the rupiah's fall went well beyond the capacity of most companies to swallow the loss. Even at Rps 5,500 for one US dollar (hinted at one point as a managed stabilization rate), the fall was unbearable, and the currency will never again see a level as high as Rps 5,500.

If the currency falls by a substantial but tolerable margin, most companies can still be nurtured back to health. Even if the currency temporarily falls too far, companies with staying power can survive; they recognize their currency losses in their accounts, but are not forced to crystallize the losses at depressed levels. Companies without staying power in the shape of unimpaired assets are forced to buy back their dollars at too high a level. If the currency falls dramatically and remains at low levels, the situation becomes unmanageable. Inflation starts creeping up, bad loans increase, liquidity disappears and wealth is destroyed. This is why Indonesia was desperately and vainly trying to stabilize its currency in the first months of 1998, against the background of political uncertainty. A distinguished American university Professor, Dr Hanke, made a convincing appeal to Suharto to consider the establishment of a currency board. This could not succeed. It was debatable whether Indonesia could, in the future, exhibit the financial discipline necessary to the maintenance of a currency board.

More importantly, the level suggested for the conversion was a rich Rps 5,500 to the dollar. This was overoptimistic considering the speed at which inflation was hitting Indonesia, and getting worse by the day. Also Indonesia did not have the kind of reserves needed for a currency board at that level, or, for that matter, at any level below 11,000. But the main reason why such a proposal could not be tolerated by Indonesia's lenders is that it would have given a free ride to a selected few. Most Indonesian speculators would realize that getting out of the rupiah at 5,500 to the US dollar was the last chance to do so at such a good level. After that, the reasoning would go, an even more calamitous meltdown would engulf the economy and propel the dollar to dizzying heights against the rupiah. Needless to say, in a country where there is no level playing field between the well connected and the merely well-to-do, let alone the poorer people, only a privileged few would have had access to the last dollars available from the central bank under the quasi-currency board. This would have meant distributing to a few people the last crumbs of wealth left in the country.

Slightly more acceptable is the proposal to institute a system, applied with success in the Mexican crisis, whereby the central bank converts the foreign currency debt of domestic companies into rupiah debt at a fixed rate, and swallows any fluctuation in the currency. At least this allows borrowers to count their losses, to face them if possible, and to plan for the future, while avoiding cross-default situations. Here again, there would probably be a transfer of wealth from the taxpayer to a few beneficiaries, but a judicious selection of the conversion rate would make it less painful. That conversion rate, or for that matter whatever rate would be selected for a currency board or a peg, is a very important factor. Too high, it chokes the economy. Too low, it allows more of that unhealthy transfer of wealth. Many Indonesian borrowers who claimed they could not pay their US dollar debts had in fact ample means to do so, but had little to lose by stalling. It was indeed unlikely that the rate of conversion selected for a peg or for a Mexican-style deal would be worse than the market rate. This in fact largely explained the movements in the value of the rupiah, in sympathy with supposedly secret negotiations. Inevitably, whatever arrangement was eventually to be selected, it would be unfair. But would the rescue of the economy not be worth it? The present arrangement[9] entitles participants to buy US dollar at the best 20-day average market exchange rate occurring from the date the program becomes operational until June 1999.

It would be wrong to say that the Indonesian authorities had not reacted to what they could perceive as a potential banking crisis. In 1996 and early 1997, a number of measures were taken to coordinate a soft landing for the banking system. It turned out to be too little too late, but at least it shows that Indonesia was less in a state of denial about its problems than Korea and Thailand. In 1996, the government imposed individual lending growth limits on the banks. Many banks exceeded the limits — this is Indonesia, after all — and the sector grew 24% against a target of only 17%, but it showed some restraint after the wild growth of the early 1990s. In 1997, the target was fixed at 18%. There will, of course, be a contraction of the rupiah part of a bank's loan portfolio, owing to the situation, but the dollar part of the books has exploded when expressed in devalued rupiah. It was not uncommon for a bank to have 40% of its activities in dollars prior to the crisis. With the rupiah falling from about 2,300 to the US dollar to about 14,000 to the US dollar, the 40/60 distribution of assets along currency lines has changed into a 240/60 distribution. This is likely to make irrelevant any measure of portfolio growth. Incidentally, it is also sending the typical BIS ratio from 10% to a paltry 3%, and this ratio has yet to see the impact of adjustments on account of loan losses.

Just for the record, as such measures have lost much of their meaning in the present crisis, the authorities have imposed minimum capital ratio requirements to be attained in stages up to September 2001. In 1996, the government also sought to limit the number of banks firstly by imposing capital and capital ratios threshold for the granting of a foreign exchange license and, subsequently, by putting an indefinite moratorium on all new banking and finance company licenses. The central bank started encouraging mergers. This book contains a number of negative comments about the merger mania in Asia. The Indonesia situation is the most relevant to those comments as not a single one of the rescue mergers contemplated in 1997 and early 1998 would fall into the only safe category, whereby a good large bank swallows a weak small bank. We only saw wild suggestions to merge together equally weak names.

Assuming the rupiah can be stabilized and the political crisis solved, Indonesia will wake up with a huge hangover. Rebuilding a financial structure will be long and painful. A growing number of Indonesian banks are overwhelmed by substantial credit losses, while many of them are facing liquidity problems. The Indonesian government is pumping liquidity into the ailing banks. Right after Suharto's resignation, Bank Central Asia suffered a deadly run in its deposits. It was the largest private sector bank, long considered as safe as a state-owned bank, as it was owned by friends and family of the former President.

Indonesia has put together a special vehicle called Indonesian Bank Restructuring Agency (IBRA) whose ambition is to rehabilitate ailing banks. Some of the sector's major names, including Bank Danamon, BDNI and BCA have already come under IBRA management. At the time of writing, the trigger for IBRA to take over a weak bank was for it to exhibit an excessive need for liquidity or to have exhausted its capital funds beyond a certain threshold.

Indeed, liquidation is inevitable for most names. Whether this takes the shape of mergers or dismemberment, or straight liquidation, it makes no difference. At the end of the day, the government will get less for whatever assets it can put its hands on than it will pay out to depositors. One difference, though, lies in how much the shareholders will lose. It would be socially and legally unacceptable if the shareholders of failed banks could escape losing their entire equity in the banks. If at all possible, they should also be made to pay back the loans they have granted themselves. Nothing short of an immediate nationalization of the failed banks will achieve this result.

Former Finance Minister Mar'ie Muhammad shares this view. But in June 1998, the economic daily *Bisnis Indonesia* quoted Sjahril Sabirin, the central bank Governor, as saying that there was no plan to liquidate or freeze the operations of the banks presently under IBRA. This is sending the wrong signal. It may put an end to the average person's withdrawal of all deposits from such banks, but it will make the overall cost of liquidation much higher for the Indonesian taxpayer.

The Indonesian government's effort at stabilizing the banking system through IBRA was a good idea, but it is creating a number of secondary effects which would all disappear if IBRA was empowered to impose immediate nationalization of failed banks. It should not be difficult for the government to issue adequate decrees to that effect, and it is unlikely that the dispossessed owners of the failed banks could successfully challenge the decision before the courts. If Indonesia is serious about putting an end to crony capitalism, this would be a good — and urgent — first step.

Most financial institutions are way beyond rehabilitation. The only other solution, besides nationalization, is for them to seek foreign capital. But foreign capital will only be forthcoming if assets offered for sale carry a price tag

Indonesia Bank Restructuring Agency

The creation of the Indonesian Bank Restructuring Agency (IBRA) was a welcome move. However, the way it has operated so far falls short of meeting the targets such an institution should have achieved. Furthermore, one could certainly fear that IBRA may have created the conditions for the owners of failed banks to get away unscathed. Although the original intention was for IBRA to take over the troubled assets and write down shareholders' investments against the losses, to date it has not invested in banks or taken over their assets. All it has done is substitute management of the ailing institutions with managers from state-owned banks.

Press reports in early June 1998 indicated that an audit of a number of the banks under IBRA control revealed substantial gaps between reported and actual asset and liability figures. No matter how these differences came about, and the reports indicated diplomatically that it may have been "differing accounting treatments", the result was that the ultimate cost of rescuing the banks will be far higher than originally estimated.

A bank can be insolvent or illiquid to a point where a careful rehabilitation is still possible. This usually involves close scrutiny by the authorities while the bank uses its unimpaired cash flow generation capacity to restore its capital through retained earnings. Most of the ailing banks of Indonesia have gone beyond that point and they are simply beyond repair. No amount of rehabilitation will save them, unless capital is restored with an injection of fresh funds.

Indonesia has opted not to liquidate such banks, for fear of creating social and economic chaos, even though the government has promised to reimburse depositors in full. Instead, those failed banks are simply being administered by IBRA, which is a serious mistake.

IBRA is manned by managers or retirees seconded from state-owned banks. They are certainly very capable, but they are not likely to have learned many of the tricks needed to run private sector banks in turmoil, let alone private sector banks that are bankrupt or have run out of liquidity. IBRA was supposed to remove the previous management from the banks. Unconfirmed rumors indicate that IBRA has in fact found it expedient to ask the owners of the failed banks to help them with management decisions, and this has created a new moral problem. Even from outside the banks, previous owners can influence decisions. Although it would be unjust to accuse all such owners of taking advantage of IBRA, some are said to have made use of the situation to pump more funds out of the banks for themselves and their allies. Related party lending is so widespread that some bank owners owe more to their banks than the capital they would lose if the bank was to go bankrupt and be liquidated. By extending the period during which such unhealthy arrangements can thrive, IBRA is making the matter of inevitable liquidation immensely more difficult.

accurately reflecting the underlying value of assets. In most cases, this is close to impossible. We may very well see a blanket nationalization of most banks, followed by several years of rehabilitation. The government may also select some healthy assets from several failed banks and sell them as a package to a foreign investor, together with a retail banking network.

Private sector foreign debt has become unbearable on account of the rupiah's collapse. In early June 1998, international creditors agreed to freeze the principal of the corporate debt for three years, a gesture that was forced upon them by the realization that there was no alternative. It is debatable whether many companies will ever be able to generate the cash flow they need as the foreign exchange losses might represent dozens of years of profits. The deal has at least achieved two objectives: there will be less immediate pressure on the exchange rate, since fewer dollars will be bought in the near future, and international lenders will be able to defer embarrassing decisions on bad loan provisions.

The Chinese Indonesian control a vast proportion of the country's commercial and industrial structure. Thousands of them lost their lives in the revolution that brought Suharto to power in the 1960s, as they were targeted as scapegoats for Indonesia's ills. But the community stayed on and prospered. If they go this time, the whole system will collapse. But can they go? It has been argued that, regardless of the political developments, the Chinese-Indonesian community would not be in a position to abandon ship. If they were to flee the country, they would have to leave behind their considerable fixed assets, in the shape of factories, office buildings and land. But this is only partially correct. The Chinese-Indonesian families also control most of the private sector banks, and related party lending is rampant. It would not be particularly difficult for any of them to borrow from the banking system in amounts approaching the assets that they would have to leave behind. Such funds could easily be transferred to Singapore or Hong Kong. A revolution could seize their local assets, but it would have to foreclose on their liabilities. The local banks would fail, leaving the taxpayer to cover the losses. The present legal infrastructure of Indonesia would make it very difficult for the country to recover loans extended to bank owners. There is no evidence that any of this has taken place, but it is not difficult to realize that any political idea of seizing Chinese-Indonesian assets would be both a political error and a sad miscalculation. Former President Suharto knew this. Are his successors going to be as enlightened?

Indonesia is in the midst of a serious social and political crisis that makes attending to the economic crisis a daunting task. Yet there are a number of positive points that will support Indonesia in its recovery. A sizable proportion of the US dollars borrowed by Indonesians were sunk into meaningful investments, as opposed to what happened in Thailand, Korea and Malaysia, where a high degree of malinvestment took place. Indonesia has natural resources, a young population, a large market and a cheap and relatively reliable work force. There is no reason to think that the dynamics that sustained the country's development in the past two to three decades have been permanently destroyed.

Endnotes

1. Banking skills, however, were apparently not required.
2. The Net Interest Margin is not equal to an average interest spread, since the total liabilities that carry funding costs and the total assets that produce interest are not necessarily equivalent. For example, capital funds on the liability side and fixed assets on the asset side do not generate interest entries. Like many ratios, the Net Interest Margin is imperfect, but it allows sensible comparisons.
3. In Indonesian commercial banks, non-interest income is usually consistent with their commercial banking activities.
4. One should realize that 55% of total loans, for a typical Indonesian bank, is roughly equivalent to 500% of total equity, a level clearly beyond the limit.
5. The bonds-for-loans trick has long been a method favored by governments on the sub-continent.
6. As I mentioned at the time BNI went public, I would have gladly become a shareholder had the Indonesian government paid me to take the BNI shares, on account of the negative net asset value. That the share price almost doubled shortly after flotation is a sure sign either that Indonesian punters are immature or that misinformation still works quite well.
7. Malaysian Prime Minister Mohathir Mohamad in March 1998 at the Dubai International Emirates Forum.
8. In early 1998, the Indonesian budget was based, among other unrealistic factors, on a high level of Rps 5,500 per dollar, widely "out-of-the money".
9. Inevitably, the arrangement will be modified as better solutions are found.

MALAYSIA 7

At the time of writing, Malaysia had been spared the worst of the crisis and is still hoping to avoid begging help from the IMF. It seems, unfortunately, that the country will be seriously hit by the second wave of the crisis. Financial panic reached Malaysia in 1997, with a battered currency and a weak stock market. This panic has acted as a revelator for the many shortcomings of Malaysia's financial system which, let us be reasonable, would have hit the country in any event at some point in the near future. If this is a crisis of growth, then Malaysia is a target of choice, as the expansion of its economy over the few years before the crisis was getting out of hand. Unbridled growth was leading to unsustainable imbalances.

Multicultural Complexity

Blessed with natural resources, a good geographical location and a population of manageable size, Malaysia is a country that could have done rather well, if not for some idiosyncrasies that are difficult for foreign observers to grasp.

Malaysia is an interesting melting pot of races and cultures. The original Malay people — the bumiputra, literally "sons of the land" have had, over the centuries, to endure the influence of a great number of invaders, not all of them friendly. The region of Malacca saw Portuguese and Dutch colonists being replaced with Arab traders, Indian settlers and Chinese laborers. More recently, the English occupation did little to develop a national identity. Independence in the 1960s created dramatic situations, including uneasy relations with Singapore and Indonesia, while communist insurgency, born with World War II, remained a serious challenge to stability. The search for racial harmony led to an unwritten rule, as is often the case in Asia. History books report that early Chinese settlers in the 19th century would, out of necessity, search for new economic activities. They would explore the country's rivers upstream and sail down the rivers with raw material and other products. The Malay population would remain on the plains and simply establish checkpoints along the rivers to redistribute the wealth through various taxes. The Chinese, who are good at business, would give up administration and politics to the Malays, while perhaps the Indians, who are good dialecticians, would have a go at Law. The three main groups would flourish in parallel and everybody would be happy ever after.

By 1970, it became clear that this division of labor was creating an underclass of bumiputras, who were left behind in the race for development. Enter the New Economic Policy (NEP), whereby the state would tinker with market forces and organize a transfer of wealth from the well-to-do to those in need. There is nothing extraordinary in that policy, as it is the mainstay of many a nation's distribution of wealth, but in Malaysia the division was along racial lines. Bumiputras, who represented half of the population of Malaysia in 1970, only had 4% of its capital wealth. The intention was to have them reach a target of 30% of that wealth. One of the main tools for this redistribution was to periodically impose a transfer of up to 30% ownership in Chinese-controlled businesses to Malay investors at preferential prices. For the Chinese, this was the price to pay: accept this unusual form of taxation and subsidy, and enjoy the freedom of creating more wealth for yourselves — and incidentally for your Malay compatriots, while someone else will look after the country's administration. This worked out relatively well, except for the fact that special arrangements were found by some to circumvent the rules, with the result that some of the wealth ostensibly transferred to the Malay community found its way back to Chinese hands. By 1997, it is estimated that the bumiputras were controlling only about 20% of the capital wealth of the country.

The backlash against Chinese-Indonesians during the early 1998 riots in Indonesia has given rise to interesting comments on Malaysia's NEP. As unnatural and economically inefficient as the NEP may be — according to each person's opinion — it protects the Malaysian Chinese from social tensions. The NEP has undeniably helped redistribute wealth among Malaysians of all races, with the result that Malaysia does not exhibit the enormous wealth disparity that divides Indonesia along racial lines. There are definitely modest and outright poor Chinese people in Indonesia, but one would find many more such people in Malaysia, where people therefore have less of a tendency to associate wealth with racial origin. This situation may very well spare Malaysia some of the racial tensions seen in Indonesia.

Malaysia is not the largest Muslim country in the region. Indonesia for example, with its 180 million people, is much larger. So is Bangladesh. But Malaysia is the most radical of them all, as if it had been possible to reinforce the bumiputra identity through the unifying religious principles of Islam. There are a number of non-Malay who are Muslims, and a number of bumiputras who are not Muslims. Also, there is no restriction on other religions, but, by and large, Malaysia identifies itself with a certain kind of religious state which permeates the lives of all in the country. There are prayer rooms in banks and official buildings. (Incidentally, there are chapels in some bank buildings in the Philippines.) In some

Malaysian states, Islamic principles are translated into laws that apply, directly or indirectly, to all.

The political scene is relatively stable, at least compared with the revolving door politics seen in other Asian countries. Prime Minister Mahathir Mohamed is a good politician and an educated man. He is a medical doctor. In the 1970s, he wrote a book, soon banned in Malaysia, titled *The Malay Dilemma*. It was a courageous, honest and surprising description of his country, giving some interesting views on the relative weaknesses of the Malay people when compared to other ethnic groups in Asia. Naturally, the comparisons were made essentially against the Malaysian Chinese, who comprise only about a third of Malaysia's population, and who are generally seen as having achieved a higher level of economic advancement than their Malay compatriots.

Malaysia is full of contradictions. Curiously enough, it seems that Malaysia was the only country in the region that sided, discreetly, with Saddam Hussain during the Gulf War in the early 1990s. This surprising political decision was not official, but anybody exposed to government-inspired comments during the Gulf War would have forged that impression. Years after Egypt has made peace with Israel, Malaysia still forbids Israeli citizens from entering the country. There has been an on-and-off relationship with Singapore and with Indonesia. The love-hate relationship with the colonial power at one point resulted in a "buy British last" campaign. Japan, the invader of yesteryear was welcomed as an investor and, at times, a model. Matsushita is now behind 6% of Malaysia's GDP. The country has managed its internal contradictions with remarkable success so far.

The Banking System

The market was long dominated by Bank Bumiputra, a state-owned institution. Although it has a wide range of activities, and generally acts as a commercial bank along the same lines as its competitors, it was created with the ambition of fostering the development of the bumiputras, or local Malays. It therefore came as a surprise to the financial community when Bank Bumiputra lost its entire equity in a single sour loan to a flamboyant ethnic Chinese gambling on Hong Kong real estate.[1] The bank lost a similar amount on distressed local loans. It will probably go down in history as the only bank in South East Asia to have lost, in one year, more than the profits posted by all the country's other domestic banks, playing havoc with all peer comparisons for quite a while.

The Malaysian financial system is characterized by the fact that non-banks play an important role. There are merchant banks, finance companies and securities houses complementing a string of 21 domestic and 16 locally incorporated foreign banks. This is quite substantial for a relatively small country.

As is often the case when trouble is brewing, deposits move from local banks to foreign banks. This phenomenon is particularly sensitive in Malaysia where foreign banks carry the burden of history. When Malaysia gained independence, foreign banks, especially HongKongBank, Citibank and what is now Standard Chartered Bank, were controlling a large share of deposits and loan volume. This situation was unique in Asia, as no other nation freshly liberated from colonial oppression had to tolerate the presence of such a large proportion of foreign financial institutions. Local banks started growing faster than foreign banks soon after independence, but to this day, foreign banks still control 21% of all deposits and 23% of all lending in commercial banking. It was only in September 1994 that Malaysia took the dramatic decision to eliminate the foreign banks, simply by forcing them to incorporate locally. Furthermore, for those that insisted on maintaining ownership at the 100% level, there were limitations on their possible expansion. A few foreign banks declined and promptly sold their Malaysian operations to local entities. Those who stayed on opted for full ownership, in spite of the restrictions attached to their choice.

Malaysian banks suffered tremendously during the mid-1980s crisis, to the point where the official figure for NPLs in the domestic banking system was a huge 34%. This ratio was volunteered by Bank Negara Malaysia, the central bank, in a rare display of openness, totally unprecedented in Asia at the time. Bank Negara Malaysia has its critics. The most vocal accused the institution of having gambled away billions of dollars in foreign exchange transaction in the 1980s. Indeed, Bank Negara Malaysia was moving markets at the time. Unsettling was a more appropriate word for their activities, and legend has it that some central banks around the world warned them in vain that it was a dangerous game to play. Granted, Bank Negara Malaysia was not an astute foreign exchange player, but the mid-1980s crisis brought two lessons that made it one of the best bank regulators in Asia: you must apply the rules strictly and you must be transparent. Rules in Malaysia may not be good enough yet, but banks are strongly invited to follow them; the annual report published by Bank Negara Malaysia has long been the best in the region. Every year, it has published the level of NPLs in the industry, coming down from the dizzying heights of 1986 to more manageable levels in recent years. Yet, of course, one should still question the validity of such statistics in that some of the improvement was the mechanical effect of an expansion of lending, where the NPLs of the past are diluted by fresh, and hopefully better quality, loans.

As usual, the bank analysts tried to reconcile the statistics of the central bank with the figures revealed individually by all the banks. This is one of those wonderful cases where the sum of the parts is not equal to the total.[2] According to each of the banks, the problems referred to by the central bank were always pertaining to the bank next door.

In the 1980s, banks were routinely counting as income the interest capitalized but never actually received from delinquent borrowers. At present, Malaysia has some of the region's best rules for provisioning and for the recognition of bad or NPLs.

Another remarkable feat seen in Malaysia and nowhere else in Asia until 1998 is the determination of the regulators to force bank shareholders, when appropriate, to take their losses. In the mid-1980s, three Malaysian banks were deemed too weak for rehabilitation or rescue by merger, and the government decided that it would force shareholders to reduce capital and find fresh investors. Only Malaysia's most vicious detractors would point out that some of those banks had substantial foreign shareholders,[3] while other weak banks were nurtured back to health. Or so was the ambition, or perhaps the gamble: indeed, without the remarkable development of the region's economies since the mid-1980s, it would have been difficult for those weak names, burdened with dud loans, to survive.

The gamble paid off, but it can be argued that some of the weak banks would have gone under had the present Asian crisis hit them two or three years earlier. As things stand, some banks are still licking their old wounds and they did not enter the crisis in the best of shape. It is to be feared that some of them will suffer a severe relapse in the coming months. Credit growth for the whole of 1997 (but note that in Malaysia many banks do not publish accounts at the end of the calendar year) was still 27%. This was not very different from the 30% average growth recorded over the previous three years. This is all the more worrying because, as a percentage of GDP, lending is about 170%, one of the highest intermediation levels in the world. In fact, Malaysia shares with Thailand and Korea the highest credit-to-GDP ratios, all three in a range going from 130% to 170%. Early in 1998, the authorities set themselves a more modest growth target for lending at 15% by the end of the year. The weakness of the economy will ensure that figure is not exceeded.

As will be explained later in this chapter, the financial system has lent with abandon against shares, much more so than in any other country in the region. Securities houses and merchant banks are the usual victims when share gambling turns wrong, and their mistakes would normally not have any influence on the health of the commercial banks, which should operate on a different level. In Thailand, for example, the disastrous developments that affected the viability of finance companies also touched the banks, but the finance companies were not borrowing much from banks, and the banks had relatively modest stakes in them. The two systems were almost watertight. Not so in Malaysia. Banks do own finance companies and merchant banks and they do lend them money. Sime Bank offers a ready example. Sime Darby, a respectable Malaysian conglomerate, bought UMBC, a bank on the way to rehabilitation, and put its name on it just two years before the crisis. Sime Bank met its fate when the group's securities house, technically a subsidiary of the bank, ran into trouble. The bank itself was not the strongest in the country, but could have survived on its own. There had been hopes that Sime Darby would be able to turn it around. The link with its non-bank affiliates made it impossible.

Nevertheless, there are good bankers in Malaysia, and good banks, like MayBank, Public Bank and some other names. At the other end of the size spectrum, some very small banks are relatively safe in that they have always thrived as modest money-lending boutiques, taking only short-term self-liquidating risks, mostly in trade related transactions. Major problems are likely to hit mostly middle-size banks, especially those run by new owners whose experience as commercial bankers is limited.

The Crisis

The Asian panic reached Malaysia by contagion from its neighbors. Malaysia was hit without real justification in 1997, but it should be accepted that the country would have met its fate some time in 1999 or 2000, owing to a number of negative factors inexorably piling up.

First among them is the property market. It is very fragile. Office and retail sub-sectors are forecast to face a serious oversupply problem post-1997. To the credit of Malaysia's regulators, when problems started hitting the country's neighbors, in April 1997, Malaysia took a number of measures to cool down the banking system. In particular, those measures aimed to limit lending secured by shares and facilities to the property sector. This last guideline was considerably diluted when vested interests started suggesting it would kill the property market and create more problems than it was solving. As a result, exemptions were allowed. They are so wide that the measures only have a limited effect. In any event, this is shutting the door after the horse has bolted, as the property market is already seriously in trouble. Strategic decisions in such matters take years to affect supply. The considerable oversupply of office, retail and residential space over the 1999-2000 horizon would have created problems even without the regional crisis. Table 7.1 outlines the most recent estimates for the supply in the property sector.

TABLE 7.1   PROPERTY SECTOR

	Dec. 1996 (million sqm)	Dec. 1997 (million sqm)	Dec. 1998 (million sqm)
Office space	3.4	4.0	5.4
Condominiums	5.6	6.5	8.3
Retail	1.4	1.7	3.1*

*Includes 851,000 sqm under construction in 1998
Source: Thomson BankWatch Inc.

In retrospect, the changes affecting the banks' asset mix and asset growth in the past few years are frightening. Loan growth, from over 30% in 1995, stabilized at a still high 27% in 1996 and 26% in 1997, with most of the growth directed at property and business services. By the end of 1997, over 28% of total lending was directed at real estate, not an excessive ratio. But individual figures for some of the smaller banks are in a range of 32% to 46%. Moreover, it is the growth of the exposure that is frightening: in 1996 alone, lending for the construction of commercial complexes and office buildings grew by 51%. There was less worry on residential properties, as strong demand still existed before the crisis at the lower end of the price spectrum. However, condominium units are already suffering and it is obvious that the regional crisis and the economy's slowdown will dampen demand over the whole range of the residential market. In terms of supply, much more worrying is the office sector. At last count, total office space was expected to increase by around 55% and retail space by around 60% by the end 1998, a leap difficult to digest even in the best of circumstances. As stated earlier, direct exposure by the banks is not exceptionally high, but another problem is going to hit them. Most collateral value held by the banks in the form of property has not been "marked-to-market", in the present case revalued downward. When this takes place, loan loss provisions will have to rise drastically, and loan loss coverage is bound to decline.

A second potential disaster is the recent weakness of the local stock market (Tables 7.2 and 7.3). Malaysia is very focused on stock market activities. In fact the stock market is a giant casino, making up for very restrictive laws on gambling. Before the crisis, its market capitalization, at a huge level of 300% of GDP, was much higher than that of major OECD countries.

TABLE 7.2   STOCK MARKET MELTDOWN

Price indices	Dec. 1996	Dec. 1997
Composite index (points)	1,238	594
Market capitalization/GDP (%)	323	136
Market capitalization (RM billion)	807	376
Total companies listed	621	708

Source: Capital Information Services

Even recently, after the collapse of the region's stock markets, Malaysia's ratio of market capitalization to GDP was seven times that of Korea and 20 times that of Indonesia. As much as Asia's financial troubles found their source in the weaknesses of its banks, Malaysia is adding another dimension to the picture. The central bank report indeed indicated that, at the end of 1997, a full 9.3% of the banking system's lending in Malaysia was directly or indirectly exposed to the vagaries of the weak stock market.[4] Naturally, the real figure is likely to be much higher since the official classification often misses the final destination of funds. This proportion is vastly superior to anything seen in the rest of the region and will cost some Malaysian financial institutions dearly.

Weak stock market conditions do not hurt Malaysian banks' shareholders funds directly as they do in Japan, since Malaysian banks normally do not hold equity investments outside of their own financial subsidiaries. But the weak market creates problems for banks in two important ways. The market's weakness effectively dries up an important source of financing for many companies, causing them to turn to banks for interim financing, which is getting more risky for the banks and more expensive as interest rates increase. It also diminishes the collateral value held by banks against several types of loans, most importantly margin-trading loans. By nature, securities houses carry the highest proportion of share financing loans, but several banks are involved in such activities beyond reason. Table 7.3 lists of some of them.

TABLE 7.3   BANK EXPOSURE TO SHARE FINANCING

Bank	Percentage share financing exposure*
Arab Malaysian Bank	13
Arab Malaysian Merchant Bank	20
Bank Bumiputra	11
PhileoAllied Bank	10
RHB Bank	12
Maybank	16
Bank of Commerce	10
Multi-Purpose Bank	10

*Could be understated
Source: Thomson BankWatch Inc.

Banks have remained extremely secretive about their strategy in the face of a collapsing market. It is not clear whether they would exercise their rights under the "forced -sell" rules when share prices fall below the maintenance margin (usually fixed at an average 60% of the outstanding loan), for fear of making the situation even more delicate.

TABLE 7.4   STOCK EXCHANGE INDEX

	Dec. 93	Dec. 94	Dec. 95	Dec. 96	Dec. 97	15 Jun. 98
Index (KLCX)	1275.32	971.21	995.17	1237.96	594.44	452.24
Base Dec. 1993 = 100	100	76.15	78.03	97.07	46.61	35.46

Source: Capital Information Services

One should remember that the Thailand crisis was triggered by defaults in finance companies. But in Thailand, the non-banks were operating pretty much independently from the banks. In most cases, the relationship was limited to banks holding a minority stake in one or more non-banks. Even where the investment was more substantial, banks were not lending to their subsidiaries. By contrast, in Malaysia, the relationship between banks and the various finance companies, securities houses and merchant banks is more intimate. Table 7.5 shows the relationship between banks and security houses.

TABLE 7.5   SECURITY FIRM RELATIONSHIP

Bank	Direct securities subsidiary (%)	Indirect subsidiary via group/investment holding companies (%)
Public Bank	70	—
MayBank	100	—
Bank Bumiputra	100	—
Sime Bank	100	—
Perwira Affin Bank	—	50
RHB Bank	—	100
PhileoAllied Bank	—	100
Arab Malaysian Merchant Bank	—	100
Bank Utama	—	100
Hong Leong Bank	—	100
Southern Bank	—	70
Bank of Commerce	—	100

Source: Thomson BankWatch Inc.

The share of total loans to manufacturing firms fell from 19% in 1995 to 9% in 1996. By the end of 1997, loans to the finance and business services sectors were a high 35% of total lending. Business services include non-banks, securities houses and holding companies whose exposure to property and stock is usually high. It is not difficult to see how dangerous the situation had become and how the crisis in Thailand acted as a late — much too late — wake-up call for Malaysia.

A detailed analysis of bank asset quality brings in some good news and some bad news. On the positive side, capital ratios along BIS guidelines were high at 12.4% in 1995, 12% in 1996 and 11% in 1997. Also there appears to be a high coverage of official NPLs, at 101% in 1996 and still a strong 91% in September 1997, against only 48% in the trough of 1987. This seems to provide some comfort to the banking system.

It should be remembered however that, under the new guidelines forcing the recognition of loan delinquency after three months instead of six months, NPLs would mechanically jump by over two percentage points, reaching about 5.3% at the end of 1997, according to official statistics. One should adjust for the fact that restructured loans disappear from statistics and that other arrangements make it possible to minimize official NPLs. As such, a better estimate of what lies ahead in terms of NPLs would be approximately 15% in mid-1998 and probably much more by the end of the year — the official figure was just shy of 10% at the end of March 1998. A positive point, however, is that Malaysia has relatively stringent rules on the actual recognition of non-performing assets. Also on the positive side is the fact that local banks have lent relatively little in foreign currency, compared to Thai banks. But some Malaysian companies have borrowed in US$ and the decline of the ringgit has hit them as surely as the decline of the baht has ravaged the Thai domestic borrowers. This is bound to affect their ability to service their debts in all currencies, including the ringgit. Table 7.6 shows the collapse of the local currency.

TABLE 7.6   CURRENCY TABLE

	Dec. 93	Dec. 94	Dec. 95	Dec. 96	Dec. 97	15 Jun. 98
US$ to ringgit	0.3704	0.3906	0.3937	0.3968	0.2577	0.2442
Base Dec. 1993 = 100	100	105.45	106.29	107.13	69.57	65.93
Ringgit per US$	2.700	2.560	2.540	2.520	3.880	4.095
Base Dec. 1993 = 100	100	94.81	94.07	93.33	143.70	151.67

Source: Capital Information Services

When the crisis erupted in mid-1997, about 48% of Malaysia's total foreign debt was accounted for by the private sector, with about 75% of the total expressed in US$. The public sector debt is, according to the government, mostly long term in nature, making it less of a burden in terms of immediate liquidity. Infrastructure projects carried out by certain bank clients, both from the public and the private sector, are heavily exposed to currency fluctuations due to a high import content, for example power plants, mass rapid transport system, ports and commercial buildings. By the end of December 1997, Malaysia had only about US$21 billion in foreign reserves.

By early 1998, it was recognized that many non-bank financial institutions were in serious trouble and the government engineered a rescue operation through mergers. It forced the smallest and the weakest non-banks to seek partners. The ambition was to regroup non-banks into eight units. It is perhaps appropriate at this stage to reiterate the view that mergers are not necessarily the best solution when a vast proportion of the institutions are in trouble. Mergers will only result in the creation of larger but still weak entities. By the end of March 1998, the 39 finance companies were either integrated in their parent bank, merged with a bank or consolidated into six larger finance companies. Market sentiment is jittery especially in respect of finance companies and local banks despite repeated assurances by the government. Heavy withdrawals of deposits from local banks led to transfers to foreign banks. But recently such transfers have somewhat stabilized after Bank Negara's assurance.

TABLE 7.7   ECONOMIC INDICATORS

	1991	1992	1993	1994	1995	1996	1997	1998p
Currency								
Ringgit/US$	2.72	2.61	2.70	2.56	2.54	2.52	3.88	3.70
Real Exchange Rate, % change	−3.66	−8.74	−3.37	−8.89	−4.18	−4.58	51.20	−11.64
Real Economy								
Real GDP, % Change	8.7	8.5	8.3	9.2	9.6	8.2	7.0	2.0
Fixed Investment as % of GDP	36.3	36.9	37.0	41.5	43.0	44.8	45.0	42.1
Money and Prices								
Consumer Price Inflation (%)	4.4	4.7	3.6	3.7	3.4	3.8	2.8	7.0
Real Lending Rate (%)	8.13	9.31	9.05	7.62	7.60	9.20	8.40	11.05
Reserves (US$ billions)	10.89	17.23	27.25	25.42	23.77	25.00	21.70	22.00
Domestic Savings Rate (%)	28.9	28.4	29.5	29.8	35.2	38.4	40.0	40.2
Balance of Payments								
Exports (US$ billions)	33.71	39.83	46.22	56.91	68.51	75.00	78.10	81.00
Imports (US$ billions)	33.32	36.68	43.21	55.33	72.18	75.50	73.50	77.50
Trade Balance (US$ billions)	0.39	3.15	3.01	1.58	(3.67)	(0.50)	4.60	3.50
Current Account Balance (US$ billions)	(4.18)	(2.17)	(2.81)	(4.15)	(7.30)	(6.20)	(5.00)	(1.50)
Current Account Balance, % GDP	−8.9	−3.7	−4.4	−5.9	−7.8	−6.4	−5.0	−1.9
Total Foreign Debt	17.81	19.96	23.30	24.77	30.60	33.90	31.00	33.20
as % of GDP	39.9	36.4	38.7	36.9	38.5	40.1	31.2	33.0
Debt Servicing Ratio (%)	7.7	6.6	7.8	7.7	7.6	7.3	6.1	6.1
Governmant Finance								
Gov. Surplus/Deficit as % of GDP	−4.4	−4.2	0.2	2.4	0.5	1.0	1.3	2.5

Source: Thomson BankWatch Inc.

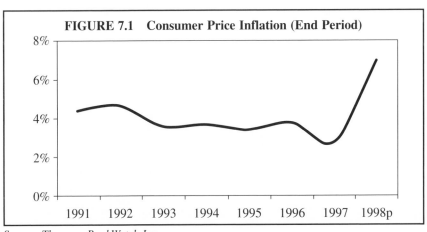

FIGURE 7.1   Consumer Price Inflation (End Period)

Source: Thomson BankWatch Inc.

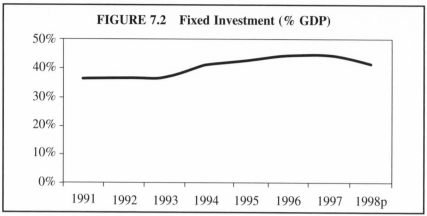

FIGURE 7.2   Fixed Investment (% GDP)

Source: Thomson BankWatch Inc.

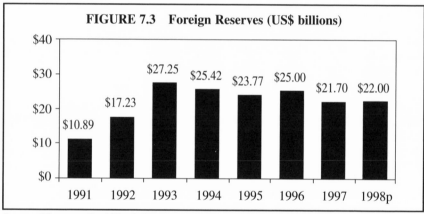

FIGURE 7.3   Foreign Reserves (US$ billions)

Source: Thomson BankWatch Inc.

FIGURE 7.4   Foreign Debt (US$ billions)

Source: Thomson BankWatch Inc.

The Future

At the time of writing, Malaysia is the only one of the five distressed countries that had not yet seen a change of the top team. The same people in charge during the build-up period leading to the crisis are still there today. Changes in Korea and the Philippines came naturally as senior posts were up for election. The Thais and the Indonesians have squarely put the blame on the teams in place before the crisis erupted. In Malaysia, the politicians are very shrewd, and they have had remarkable success in deflecting any domestic criticism to concentrate the wrath on foreigners. In a simplistic way that seems to appeal to the Malaysians, the West is accused of conspiring to put an end to Asia's, and particularly to Malaysia's, development. If the situation were not so tragic to many, the battle of words at the top would give it a touch of comedy.

Is Malaysia another Thailand in the making? Probably. Is the Asian crisis going to hit Malaysia as devastatingly as it did Thailand? Probably not. There are a number of similarities, the most striking being that the currencies and the stock markets have declined sharply. There are differences as well. At various stages of development, there is an oversupply of property in both countries, but the lower end of the property market in Malaysia was healthy before the crisis erupted, while even that sector in Thailand was overpriced and is now in shambles. Asset inflation was much more pronounced in Thailand. Malaysia was much less reliant than Thailand on foreign currency short-term borrowings. Transparency and the regulatory environment are better in Malaysia. Yet Malaysia is much weaker than Thailand in respect of the relationship between the various segments of the financial system, and in respect of the exposure of financial institutions to the ailing stock market. It would be impossible to determine which of those positive or negative factors will be of the highest relevance to the evolution of the crisis, but it looks difficult to remain optimistic for Malaysia.

On the positive side, Malaysia can claim to have a relatively strong central bank, capable of implementing tough regulations. The country has been, so far, politically stable. Malaysia can learn from the way Thailand, Korea and Indonesia have handled the crisis.

Malaysia is determined not to seek help from the IMF, which is comforting in a way. Some commentators have suggested that the conditions the IMF would undoubtedly attach to its support package would create serious social and political problems. Among the IMF conditions always stands a clear recommendation that all market imperfections be ironed out. This would imply for Malaysia a traumatic revision of the rules redistributing wealth, education support and other government-sponsored support schemes along racial lines. Riots with racial overtones have taken place over the years in Malaysia as well as in Indonesia. The Indonesian riots of early 1998, with their broadside attacks on Chinese businesses, are a reminder that some tinkering with equity is sometimes useful. The Chinese

Indonesian have accumulated wealth in a proportion vastly superior to that seen in Malaysia, where the seemingly unnatural redistribution of wealth to bumiputras may have taken some steam out of potential racial disturbances. Alas, one should not count too happily on that: human greed makes people quickly get used to wealth and we always build our expectations from ever-higher bases.

George Soros Against Dr M

These would be good characters for a James Bond film. More seriously, this is a story that has kept many amused and some frightened. There is nothing better than a war of words to illustrate the deep feelings of East and West. The currency crisis started on July 2, 1997 with the flotation of the baht. By the end of July 1997, Malaysia's ringgit had suffered but was still relatively strong. Prime Minister Dr Mahathir Mohamad named George Soros as the man behind the attack on the currency. At the end of August 1997, during Malaysia's independence celebrations, he added… "If we do not strive to protect our independence, directly or indirectly, colonialists will return to colonize us." Dr M, as the Prime Minister is often called, lashed out at currency traders during the IMF meeting in Hong Kong in September 1997. In a keynote address, he said: "…currency trading is unnecessary, unproductive and immoral. It should be stopped. It should be made illegal." After a reference to the Mexican crisis, he said: "Now we know better. We know that economies of developing countries can be suddenly manipulated and forced to bow to the great fund managers who decide who should prosper and who should not." He described the "guiding principle of a group of ultra-rich people…For them, wealth must come from the impoverishing of others. Their weapon is their wealth."

He said, in reference to liberalization: "All along, we tried to comply with the wishes of the rich and mighty. We opened up our markets… But that was not enough: we were told to slow our growth, that it was bad for us, that we would overheat." Dr M said, in various speeches, that currency traders were "ferocious animals", that currency trading was "secretive and shady" and that the current events were "a move by Western industrialized nations to keep Asia poor."

In the heat of verbal exchanges, prior and subsequent to the IMF meeting, Dr M is said to have used the words "moron" and "Jewish plot" to describe his adversaries. George Soros retorted that Mahathir was a "menace to his own country" and that his suggestion to ban currency trading was "so inappropriate that it does not deserve serious consideration." Soros went on to explain some basic principles sustaining the international financial system.

Soros is intelligent. His arguments are technically perfect. He is a master of his trade. That he usually benefits from his strategic decisions is undeniable. That his trading decisions impoverished Asian nations is not established. That his attitude is part of a conspiracy to destroy Asia is preposterous. Months after the crisis erupted, at the request of Malaysia, neutral observers examined the role of hedge funds — Soros' usual trading vehicle — and established that they played a very minor part in the currency turmoil. Soros declared that, with the exception of a paltry US$10 million position, he took no position against Asian currencies after the crisis erupted.

Mahathir is intelligent. He is a politician. He often speaks to a captive domestic audience. He is charismatic and emotional. His country did suffer from colonial oppression. Mahathir's arguments are technically flawed, but he speaks for many Asians whose grasp of the intricacies of international finance is limited. Unfortunately, Dr M's interventions invariably hurt his home currency. Watching his moods has become as important to foreign exchange dealers as watching economic fundamentals, very much like, in the old times, astute dealers were watching the human behavior of European leaders in order to guess whether they would adjust their national currencies.

At a conference in Tokyo on June 4, 1998, Mahathir said that a new breed of foreign capitalists was threatening the region, and Asia could not stop them without the West's help. He warned of a violent backlash, involving a "guerilla war". "The people will show their resentment against those outsiders who will lord over them once again" he said, adding that, "Sooner rather than later, they will think of regaining control over their economies. They will regard this as a new war of liberation."

There is no point in blaming Dr M for what he said, except to the extent that he has now created a lingering feeling in international circles that perhaps Malaysia will not be the right place to invest, when Asia rebounds. Now that the dust has settled on the first part of the Asian crisis — mostly the currency adjustments — it is abundantly clear that there was no plot by the West to weaken Asia. Most of the currency trading has involved Asian players. Soros is no more responsible than anyone else is for what happened. Dr M was barking up the wrong tree.

Yet Mahathir has a point. There is a serious danger of a return to a certain brand of colonialism, especially if banking systems fall into the hands of foreign financial institutions. But is a wholesale takeover of Asia by the West realistic? Japan, to whom Asia is a natural hinterland, has over the years commercially "invaded" the region with more success than anyone could ever dream of. While this dominance is obvious in the automotive industry and for a number of electric and electronic consumer items, Japan is far from a quasi-colonial domination over the rest of Asia.

The IMF would also insist on more transparency and better protection of minority shareholders. A few unsettling episodes have taken place where the authorities permitted or fostered the unhealthy restructuring of ailing companies. Some of them are said to be linked to politicians or to political parties. In short, while nobody should level the same accusations at Malaysia that were leveled at the Philippines in the 1970s and Indonesia in the 1990s, it looks increasingly difficult to rank Malaysia among the cleanest countries of Asia.

Malaysia was heading towards a crisis in any event. The economy was clearly overheating. Investments in prestigious but unwise projects were bringing serious imbalances in the economy. The Petronas twin towers, briefly the tallest in the world,[5] are adding too much office space to the capital city. The new Kuala Lumpur International Airport (KLIA) is too big and too far away, while the old Subang airport was still serviceable. The railway linking KLIA to the city may not be completed for years. Malaysia's own Silicon Valley-style corridor will likely remain a dream for some time. Then there is the Bakun Dam, a huge hydro-electric project, and much more.

While the private sector was largely responsible for the malinvestment that felled the Thai banking system, it is the public sector that carries that opprobrium in Malaysia. Yet, banks can run up delinquent loans on their own in the private sector: they do not need any prompting from the government to do so. The situation has become much more serious than the authorities would have admitted earlier on. Malaysia correctly states that its dependence on foreign currency borrowing was fairly limited, sparing the banking system currency-led problems. This reinforces the view that the present difficulties would have hit the country independently from the currency crisis, which has acted only as a catalyst.

Hong Kong has always attracted the darker side of Malaysia's wild capitalism. The Carrian case[6] will remain a sad memory for all involved. More recently, rumor has it that some well-connected Malaysian firms have borrowed funds from the Hong Kong subsidiaries of Malaysian financial institutions in order to finance dubious investments in other countries. Such firms do not have to go that far to find offshore funds. Malaysia has establish in Labuan (East Malaysia) a self-contained offshore center. It is far from reaching the excesses of Thailand's BIBF, but more than 50 banks operate from there, including Malaysian banks. Together the banks had extended over US$17 billion in US dollar offshore loans in 1997, of which US$11 billion went to Malaysian companies. Some of the funds borrowed by the companies were invested abroad, mitigating the foreign exchange risk, but most of the funds ended up in countries whose currencies went down during the financial panic. The amounts involved are more modest than those which destroyed Thailand's banking system, but they are still very substantial and they will likely create serious headaches for Kuala Lumpur.

In early June 1998, details came out on Malaysia's Asset Management Corporation (AMC), a government-funded vehicle that will acquire dud loans from banks. NPLs in the banking system are rising rapidly. The official figures, subject to the usual adjustments, at the end of March 1998 pointed at a ratio of NPLs to total lending of 9.3%.[7] The AMC will be funded by government-backed bonds to the tune of Ringgit 25 billion (approximately US$6 billion). The AMC will select distressed assets and buy them from banks at a discount, so that the banks will be able to start lending afresh. Although the announcement repeatedly stressed that AMC will act in full transparency, some observers have wondered whether it would be at all possible to avoid favoring some distressed banks over others. The very fact that the asset sale will be made at a discount and without recourse brings about the question of whether the assets can be marked-to-market on a really transparent basis. Proper pricing is a difficult task in the best of circumstances, but Malaysia is in a serious crisis.

With some substantial variations, the AMC runs into the same conceptual problem as Japan's CCPC, Korea's KAMC and Indonesia's IBRA: it goes only half way down the road to nationalization, while it opens itself to accusations of selective favoritism. The government says that AMC will buy dud loans from banks at market-driven value. This achieves nothing in terms of solvency. The banks are better placed than anyone to collect their own delinquent loans. It is very doubtful that the banks, should they keep the loans in their books, would eventually collect less than the transfer price: if that was the case, then the transfer price would obviously be too high, negating the claim to neutral transparency. The AMC approach does achieve something in terms of liquidity though, since the banks will receive cash for their loans and will be able to lend again, as the plan goes. But if creating that liquidity was the aim, then the central bank could achieve it through other means, much more straightforward than the convoluted AMC arrangement.

Meanwhile, a de-facto nationalization has taken place owing to the fact that the central bank has guaranteed all deposits of banks, merchant banks and finance companies. In such a situation, the banks' assets are virtually at the disposal of the authorities. Should the crisis deepen, it is probably the only way out. A full-scale nationalization of all weak financial institutions would have the added benefit of preventing the international financial community from putting its hands on Malaysian banks, if this is politically important.

Endnotes

1. This is the very famous Carrian case. In the hands of George Tan, an ethnic Chinese, Carrian gambled in huge real estate transactions in Hong Kong with funds whose origin was never clearly established.
2. No amount of figure crunching by analysts could ever get the figures to match.
3. Perwira Habib Bank had Habib Bank of Pakistan as a shareholder, while Banque Nationale de Paris was behind Oriental Bank.
4. The proportion was likely to be over 20% for non-banks and, among banks, the average was concealing large variations.

5. Until a tower in Shanghai took over the title. The Petronas Towers are a highly visible symbol of the overinvestment in office space, but it is far from being the only one.

6. See note 1 above. The Carrian case was extremely embarrassing in the context of Malaysia's attempts at social engineering along racial lines.

7. It would not be surprising to see the real level of NPLs reach 30% by the end of 1998.

THE PHILIPPINES 8

The Philippines central bank — Bangko Sentral ng Pilipinas or BSP — has reacted swiftly to the crisis affecting East Asia and, more importantly perhaps, it has acted in one voice and has made its position well known both domestically and abroad. With US$12 billion in reserves in March 1997, against US$45 billion in debt, the central bank took the wise decision not to fight market trends. A few days after the Thais gave up on the baht (on July 2, 1997), the Philippines let the peso float (on July 11, 1997). There was no point in defending the currency, although some funds were spent to manage the depreciation. From its high levels in the early 1990s, the inflation rate had gone down substantially in the mid-1990s, but it was still too high and the overvalued peso was undermining the country's competitiveness. A currency adjustment looked increasingly desirable.

The banking system in the Philippines was not as vulnerable as in some neighboring countries. No stranger to financial calamities, the Philippine government had already done much to put the industry's house in order prior to the crisis. Although IMF tutelage and the Ramos era economic reforms had done much to revamp the banking system, in early 1997, the central bank wisely began introducing a number of prudential measures designed to protect the banking system. The measures included a 20% cap on loans to the real estate sector (30% if cheap housing loans were included), a real estate loan-to-value ceiling of 60%, and more stringent rules on NPL recognition and provisioning. The government also imposed a 30% liquidity cover on the foreign exchange liabilities of the banks' foreign currency deposit units, and in the wake of the devaluation, restricted the banks' freedom in keeping open positions and tightened the regulations governing the computation of the positions. In addition, it imposed prior approval for the sale of non-deliverable forward exchange positions[1] to non-residents, a move to protect the peso from Dr Mahathir's — imaginary or real — enemies.

Because its banking system went into battle in relatively good shape, the Philippines is arguably in the best position of the five countries hit by the currency and asset crisis in 1997 to swallow its problems. Fifteen years ago, however, the sobriquet so often applied to the Philippines - "the sick man of Asia" — was essentially correct. At a time when almost all East-Asian countries outside of Indochina were developing at breakneck speed, the dictator Ferdinand Marcos, his friends and his family were happily plundering the country. Worst of all, they were plundering the seed rather than the crop, and the hundreds of millions siphoned away translated into billions in lost opportunities.

The Philippines is not particularly well endowed by nature. Limited mineral wealth, almost no local energy (the country imports 95% of its energy needs) and frequent devastation brought by the summer monsoon have long taught Filipinos that their development could only be built on people. Education — and particularly the education of women, often neglected in other parts of Asia — has, over the years, reached Western-style levels. But the sad state of the country's economy resulted, during the 1980s and 1990s, in the migration of tens of thousands of workers, mostly to wealthier Asian countries and to the Middle East. Among them were highly educated bank staff who, like Pakistanis in the Middle East, could be found as expatriates in the more affluent countries in the region, such as Indonesia or Hong Kong. Large numbers of Filipino sailors are on the payroll of international shipping lines, and there are nurses from the Philippines in many countries. Yet the largest contingent of overseas workers are probably the maids or "domestic helpers" employed in Hong Kong and in Singapore. Financial circumstances have sometimes created extraordinary situations where the maid from the Philippines has a university degree, while the lady of the house has little or no education.

The Philippines has squandered years of hard work and development and it is no exaggeration to say that the country fell, in one generation only, from one of the best performing nascent economies of Asia to one of the poorest. Yet through the ordeal, the country's banks, having been overhauled following the Marcos years, have chugged along and remain in surprisingly good shape.[2] In the last three or four years prior to the 1997 crisis, the Philippines banks, on average, were the most profitable banks in Asia. They were also the most highly capitalized banks (Table 8.1), and ranked reasonably well in the liquidity league.

TABLE 8.1   LEVERAGE (TIMES): AVERAGE OF DOMESTIC COMMERCIAL BANKS

1990	1991	1992	1993	1994	1995	1996
9.58	8.86	7.85	7.46	6.87	6.88	6.90

Note: Any leverage ratio below 12 times is strong.
Source: Annual Reports

Philippine banks could boast of some of the best bank managers in Asia. Modeled on American standards, their accounting norms were above those of most Asian countries. The body of the car might have been damaged but the power train was still able to put rubber to the road.

The country's authorities have reacted swiftly to show that there should be no chain reaction collision among Asian economies and that the troubles in Thailand, Indonesia and Korea need not cause a similar demise in the Philippines. Government officials roamed the world with a relatively good story: that the Philippines is in much better shape than the IMF Three. They have a point as, whatever the main and incidental causes of the crisis, the Philippines would enjoy the benefit of the doubt if tested against many of them. Just to take an example, the Philippines did not grow as fast as its neighbors in the three years preceding the crisis (GDP growth is the last three years was only 5% to 6%, against 7% to 9% in Thailand, 8% to 10% in Malaysia and 7% to 8% in Indonesia), while its banking system is in much better shape. Consequently, even though it missed the benefits of explosive growth, it also avoided the excesses.

Not all is perfect; far from it. The Philippines has long been rated below investment grade and is likely to remain there for some time. But there are some indications that the Asian Crisis is not going to devastate the country as it has done or will do to most of its neighbors: GDP growth fell to 5.1% in 1997, against minus 0.4% in Thailand, 7% in Malaysia and 4.7% in Indonesia.[3]

The Banking System

One striking feature of the commercial banking system in the Philippines is that it is very small, and certainly so in relation to the size of the country and its population. By the end of 1996, total assets of commercial banks were the equivalent of about US$70 billion, less than the assets of a great many single banks in Asia. The largest bank in the country did not even reach the modest size of US$10 billion. The 1997 figures show a decline resulting from the lower value of the local currency.

A strong point of the banking system is its relative transparency, based on accounting systems closer to Western standards than those of many other East Asian nations. This is in part a legacy of the American colonial era and the close ties maintained between the USA and the Philippines in the ensuing decades. The central bank (BSP) has taken a proactive stance towards bank supervision and, as bank regulators go in Asia, it is among the best. The legal system is fairly developed, if cumbersome and insolvency and foreclosure laws are regarded as fairly effective, especially when compared with neighboring jurisdictions.

Another less obvious characteristic of Philippine banks is that families or groups of families own banks and major shareholders often play a role in day-to-day management. This in other countries would be a negative point, but the Philippines is an obvious exception. Leading banks have high caliber management, many with international experience and education from the elite business schools in the USA. The larger banks are technologically more advanced than many other Asian banks. Staff training is emphasized, not surprisingly in a country that gives much importance to education in general.

TABLE 8.2   ECONOMIC INDICATORS

	1991	1992	1993	1994	1995	1996	1997	1998p
Currency								
Peso/US$ (end period)	26.65	25.10	27.70	24.42	26.21	26.29	39.50	41.00
Real Exchange Rate (% change)	−23.5	−14.7	2.8	−20.9	−3.6	−4.8	45.1	−5.3
Real Economy								
Real GDP (% change)	−0.6	0.3	2.1	5.3	5.7	5.7	5.1	2.4
Fixed Investment as % of GDP	20.3	22.2	24.3	25.5	22.3	23.0	25.8	24.3
Money and Prices								
Consumer Price Inflation	18.7	8.9	7.6	9.1	10.9	8.4	5.1	9.1
(End period)								
Lending Rate (%)	23.07	19.48	14.68	15.06	14.68	14.84	16.26	15.25
Reserves (US$ billions)	3.25	4.40	4.68	6.02	6.37	10.03	9.50	8.80
Domestic Savings Rate (%)	17.6	16.6	17.1	16.2	14.7	18.0	19.4	18.0
Balance of Payments								
Exports (US$ billions)	8.84	9.82	11.38	13.48	17.45	20.54	25.23	31.80
Imports (US$ billions)	12.05	14.52	17.60	21.33	26.39	32.30	35.94	39.80
Trade Balance (US$ billions)	(3.21)	(4.70)	(6.22)	(7.85)	(8.94)	(11.76)	(10.71)	(8.00)
Current Account Balance	(1.03)	(1.00)	(3.02)	(2.95)	(1.98)	(3.56)	(4.00)	(2.70)
(US$ billions)								
Current Account Balance	−2.3	−1.9	−6.0	−4.6	−2.6	−5.0	−6.8	−4.7
(% GDP)								
Foreign Debt (US$ billions)	32.45	33.00	35.93	40.00	39.45	43.00	45.00	47.00
as % of GDP	70.4	60.8	64.9	60.8	51.5	54.6	76.8	81.3
Debt Servicing Ratio (%)	23.0	24.4	25.5	18.9	16.4	14.8	13.3	11.0
Governmant Finance								
Gov. Surplus/Deficit as	−2.1	−1.2	−1.5	1.1	0.5	0.3	0.0	−0.2
% of GDP								

Source: Thomson BankWatch Inc.

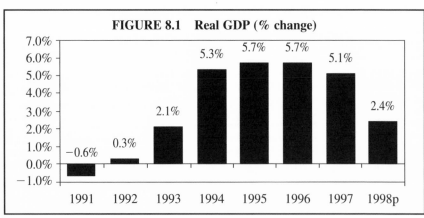

FIGURE 8.1   Real GDP (% change)

Source: Thomson BankWatch Inc.

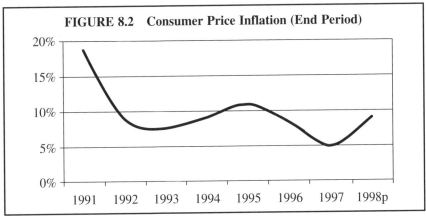

FIGURE 8.2   Consumer Price Inflation (End Period)

Source: Thomson BankWatch Inc.

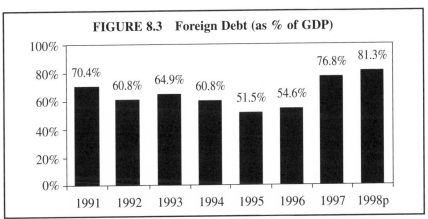

FIGURE 8.3   Foreign Debt (as % of GDP)

Source: Thomson BankWatch Inc.

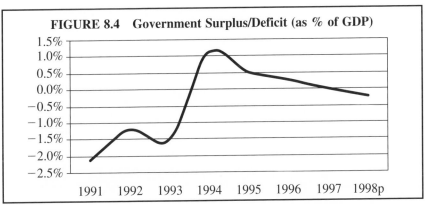

FIGURE 8.4   Government Surplus/Deficit (as % of GDP)

Source: Thomson BankWatch Inc.

The Philippines banks are rich — well, except PNB perhaps — and profitable. So what is wrong, if anything, with them? What is wrong is that this prosperity is artificial. It rests on a cartel-like structure which maintains high interest margins. This is not to say that the cartel is in immediate danger of disappearance, but one day the government may wake up to the reality that it eats away at the competitiveness of many companies. The cartel creates a permanent and unhealthy transfer of wealth between depositors and borrowers on the one hand, and commercial banks on the other hand. There is little competition among banks and they have long been able to rely on massive net interest income. This situation has led, over the years, to a great complacency in respect of expenses: since income is so ample, there is little incentive to control expenses. This has placed the Philippines at the bottom of the list in Asia when it comes to efficiency. A typical bank in Manila spends more than three times what a typical commercial bank would spend in Hong Kong or Singapore, on rents, salaries, cars, computers and power lunches. If the average Taiwanese bank were as wildly profligate as the average Philippines bank, it would go bankrupt in about five years, with its capital wasted on expenditure alone.

This profligacy is unbelievable, considering the modest salaries, by international standards, paid to bank staff. Naturally, the geography of the Philippines, with hundreds of small islands and distant cities impose, like in Indonesia, a number of constraints making it difficult to run banks with the same efficiency as in Hong Kong or Singapore. Furthermore, cost margin calculations relate costs to total assets. The average transaction in the Philippines probably pertains to an amount that is about one-tenth of the average amount transacted in Hong Kong, on the basis that the GDP per capita is about one-tenth of that in Hong Kong. Processing a single transaction largely takes the same administrative input everywhere. Since many banks belong to families and are run by them, perhaps the managers find it tax efficient to reward themselves with comparatively high salaries. It is hard to put a finger on those factors. It remains that banks in the Philippines are, by many measures, extraordinarily inefficient, as can be seen in Table 8.3 comparing cost margins across Asia.

Watching the present trend in net interest income, it is certainly possible that the fat margins may very well collapse before the banks can reasonably address the expenditure problem. This event, which might very well occur in 1999 or 2000, could result in a cataclysmic alteration in the status of Philippine banks. It is conceivable that such a calamity could be avoided. As noted, Philippine banks' high costs can be attributed to some extent to geographical problems and, to a lesser extent, to a somewhat slow pace of technological development. The banks will be able to achieve faster cost reductions by intensifying their technological investments. Similarly, mergers and acquisitions would create economies of scale. One should remember the Lilliputian size of some of the country's financial institutions. If technological progress and consolidation occur rapidly enough, Philippine banks may escape the problems posed by a collapse of margins. But this outcome is by no means assured. As Table 8.4 shows, margins remained high in 1996 but profitability ratios will deteriorate in 1998 and 1999.

The Case of the Missing Billions

Just in case the reader might feel inclined to consider the Philippines as a paradigm of accountancy virtue, here is the strange story of the missing billions of Philippines National Bank (PNB). The largest bank in the country and once fully owned by the state, PNB has long been seen as a kitty bank by successive governments for the promotion of noble social ideas. In the Marcos era, the noble social ideas involved transfers of funds to a selected few, not necessarily in need. This created huge holes in PNB's accounts, which the government agreed to fill in 1987, to the tune of P71 billion (in the vicinity of US$3.5 billion at the then prevailing exchange rate). The amount was gigantic, considering that the country's GDP was only P683 billion at the time.

A few years later, when the bank was fully rehabilitated, the government sold off 43% of PNB to the public. But, unbeknownst to the happy new shareholders, the Treasury was sitting on a claim of Pesos 26.32 billion against PNB against a set of bad loans transferred to the government. The 1994 annual report of PNB did mention something about accounts previously transferred to the National Government in 1986, with a subsequent rebooking by the bank in 1993, but it was difficult to infer from the accounts that P26.32 billion were still due by the bank. Surely, the amount was large enough to attract and deserve attention: P26.32 billion represented then about US$1 billion, no small sum for PNB, or anyone for that matter.[4] In fact, it represented 18% of PNB's total assets, 132% of its equity and 13 times its 1994 profits. But little was done to highlight the existence of the claim. Not only would ordinary investors have had a tough time discerning its existence and magnitude, but it was almost impossible for Thomson BankWatch analysts to figure out how the bank had managed to enter those strange transactions in its books. Dozens of calls, visits and faxes failed to shed light on the matter. It was as if no one at PNB had ever heard about the missing billions. Eventually, the analysts discovered the amounts well hidden under some customer deposits.

After partially privatizing the bank, the government decided to act on its claim. Not surprisingly, the shareholders screamed. Ultimately, the government decided to give up some of its claim on the grounds that PNB — still a government-controlled bank — had suddenly[5] been able to find some documentary evidence that contradicted it. Unfortunately, no such documents were found in respect of the last Pesos 4.7 billion. This amount the bank had to swallow over seven years against recurrent profits.

TABLE 8.3   COST MARGINS

	1996
Philippines	3.73
South Korea — Specialized Banks	3.50
South Korea — Provincial Banks	3.37
South Korea — Old Merchants Banks	2.95
Indonesia — Private Banks	2.75
Indonesia — States Banks	2.49
South Korea — Nationwide Banks	2.26
Thailand	2.00
Malaysia	1.66
Taiwan	1.35
Hong Kong	1.17
Singapore	1.14

Source: Annual Reports

TABLE 8.4   PROFITABILITY: AVERAGE OF DOMESTIC COMMERCIAL BANKS

	1993 (%)	1994 (%)	1995 (%)	1996 (%)
ROAA	2.84	2.6	2.06	2.12
ROE	18.34	16.28	16.25	17.14
NIM	4.81	4.89	4.79	4.92

Source: Annual Reports

The Asian crisis may aggravate the problem by encouraging the influx of foreign competition. Indeed, after the July 1997 devaluation, interest rates jumped and liquidity melted down, ultimately constricting interest income to a trickle. The Philippines was the first Asian country to really open its doors to foreign banks, after years of isolation. Initially, some selected banks were permitted to open 100% foreign owned branches, although networks were limited in size. Subsequently, President Ramos came out with the surprising offer for foreign investors to acquire up to 60% of local banks, with almost no restriction. Foreign banks had just begun to take advantage of the new liberalization when the crisis erupted. Their presence is bound to have a further negative impact on bank margins.

The currency crisis and the general slowdown of the economy are affecting banks in the Philippines in a much smaller way than they are affecting the banking systems in other countries of the region. The cash flow generated over the years has allowed the banks to achieve several objectives. Firstly, any need for loan loss provision has been met immediately out of recurrent profits. This has permitted the banks to enter the crisis almost with a clean slate. Secondly, the banks have been able to improve their capital adequacy ratios well above international guidelines, to the point that many of them are capitalized at more than twice the norm. Thirdly, the belated growth in lending, witnessed over the last few years only, was supported with adequate adjustments to equity funds, something the average bank in the rest of South East Asia has not been able to achieve.

The banking system is indeed very well capitalized. On average, its equity-to-risk assets ratio was 17% at the onset of the crisis. The ratio has been gently sliding down over the past few years, but it remains at the top of the class. A cruder calculation exists, based on leverage, which compares total liabilities to equity. The leverage ratio is useful because banks in many countries do not disclose enough information for an accurate estimate of the more refined equity-to-risk assets ratio. On that basis, as Table 8.5 shows, the Philippines banks are at the top of the class in Asia.

TABLE 8.5 LEVERAGE (TIMES)

	1994	1995	1996
Philippines	6.87	6.88	6.90
Singapore	7.74	7.37	7.55
Hong Kong (excl. HSBC)	8.71	8.19	8.18
Thailand	11.69	11.38	10.91
Indonesia — Private Banks	11.26	12.19	12.73
Malaysia	15.08	14.25	14.23
Taiwan — Established Banks	18.93	18.15	15.58
South Korea — Nationwide Banks	22.24	24.83	25.99

Source: Annual Reports

The Philippines banks have been in that position for years. Furthermore, as is the case in Hong Kong and Singapore, banks have long been sufficiently profitable to be able to take good care of non-performing or bad loans as they came along. The rules for early recognition of problem loans also happen to be better than in many other countries. As a result, not only are the capital ratios comfortable, but also they are largely based on correct figures, which is more than can be said for most of the region.

Asset quality which had been steadily improving reached its best level just prior to the crisis. NPL to total loans for the upper tier Philippine banks were in the vicinity of 3%.[6] It would be naïve, however, to assume that banks in the Philippines have nothing to hide in respect of weak loans. Smaller banks outside the universe of institutions covered by Thomson BankWatch generally displayed poorer asset quality, while the industry as a whole saw NPLs double in 1997. They may very well double again in 1998. How bad the situation might be is anyone's guess. Thomson BankWatch has most recently estimated that the top 25 banks will see NPL levels increase to as much as 10–12%. More weakly capitalized and less well managed institutions are likely to see levels worse than that, spurring consolidation in the sector. The regional crisis will act as a ruthless revelator. Several warning signals have emerged in 1997 and 1998, including the failure of two small banks (Monte de Piedad and Orient Bank) and some major corporate insolvencies. But, even assuming that many more loans will turn sour, the local banks in general can swallow more bad news than their counterparts in other major East Asian countries.

The Crisis

When the Asian crisis contagion spread, both the peso and the stock market took a hit, and the Philippines started suffering simply for being part of the group of East Asian countries about which the world had sudden doubts. Tables 8.6 and 8.7 show the extent of the damage.

TABLE 8.6 CURRENCY TABLE

	Dec. 93	Dec. 94	Dec. 95	Dec. 96	Dec. 97	15 Jun. 98
US$ per perso	0.03610	0.04098	0.03815	0.03800	0.02510	0.02359
Base Dec. 1993 = 100	100	113.52	105.68	105.26	69.53	65.35
Peso per US$	27.70	24.42	26.21	26.29	39.50	42.39
Base Dec. 1993 = 100	100	88.16	94.62	94.91	142.60	153.03

Source: Capital Information Services

TABLE 8.7 STOCK EXCHANGE INDEX

	1993	1994	1995	1996	1997	15 Jun. 98
Index (PHISIX)	3241.86	2785.81	2594.18	3170.56	1869.23	1746.86
Base Dec. 1993 = 100	100	85.93	93.12	122.22	58.96	53.88

Source: Capital Information Services

On the surface, if the trigger of the crisis was the realization that Asian countries were borrowing too much in foreign currency, then the Philippines should have been largely spared. In September 1997, its total foreign currency debt was only US$46 billion, equivalent to 56% of GDP. According to the central bank, 81.5% of the debt was long-term. More importantly, it appears that almost half of all the liabilities of its commercial banks in US$ (45% exactly) were to Philippines nationals, considerably better than Thailand with 1%. The Philippines figure jumps to 72% when only deposits — as opposed to borrowings by the banks — are considered: overseas workers repatriate close to US$6 billion in savings every year and many of them keep their savings in US$ in local banks, something relatively unknown in neighboring countries. There is no such situation in any of the other distressed countries.

When it comes to a liquidity crunch where foreign lenders insist on repayment of the short-term debt, a banking system that holds half of its liabilities onshore is in a very strong position. Small local depositors are not likely to insist on immediate repayment. In case of panic, the government can freeze such deposits, as Pakistan did in June 1998 in the wake of sanctions imposed on it after its nuclear tests. In contrast to the Philippines, Thailand was in a much weaker position: the foreign currency liabilities of Thai commercial banks were almost entirely to foreign lenders. It should be kept in mind, though, that bank debts are only a portion of total external debt.

Less relevant, but still deserving attention, is the fact that many domestic borrowers in US$ in the Philippines claim to have a natural hedge against their exposure in the form of US$ earnings. Some people optimistically suggested a proportion of 80% of all such borrowers have a natural hedge. Utilities have long-term US$ debt but claim to be able to price their products accordingly — meaning that the price in local currency goes up dramatically — while many companies with US$ liabilities are export-orientated and will carry on generating US$ cash flow. While this situation is true in higher proportion in the Philippines than in Thailand, Korea or Indonesia, it remains that such reasoning is not entirely correct. In practice, demand for utilities is not totally inelastic and the pricing in local currency will have to be adjusted downward. The same goes for exports, especially when the local content is low. Certainly, exporters will generate US$ receipts, but it is very likely that the devaluation of the various regional currencies will greatly alter the sales volumes and the terms of trade, and consequently a smaller amount of US$ proceeds will be generated. Also, some inputs are priced in US$ and, as in other countries, will impair the ability of local companies to benefit fully from the devaluation.

The Future

The Philippines is, of all the countries in distress in East Asia, the country that is most likely to suffer from a mechanical adjustment to domestic prices on account of the devaluation of the peso. Indonesia has met with considerable inflationary pressures, but for different reasons. The Philippines imports 95% of its petroleum products and its geography results in a high dependence of many prices on energy and distribution costs. The government controls domestic energy costs, but there is a limit to its ability to subsidize them. Fortunately, the recent lowering of oil prices has had a mitigating effect.

The country maintains one of the lowest domestic savings rate (18%) in East Asia. In a context of high growth, this potentially translates into current account deficits, to make up for the funds missing in support of investment. It also has a negative impact on the interest rate structure. Both factors constrain development. Foreign direct investment would be welcome in the Philippines, but a recent incident may very well dampen the enthusiasm of all but the boldest investors. The venerable Manila Hotel, headquarters of General MacArthur during World War II, was up for sale. A group of investors from South East Asia submitted the winning bid, and the transaction was concluded. A local investor who lost out in the bidding applied to the Courts to have the deal cancelled on the grounds that the Manila Hotel was a national heritage, and should not be sold to foreigners. The local investor won the case. This is a reminder that a contract is not always a contract, even in the Philippines.

On a positive note, the structure of the country's economy does not show the kind of imbalances found in Korea, where, for example, the largest companies control an enormously high proportion of the economy. The Philippines economy is not concentrated in quite so few hands, and the large companies have relatively healthy balance sheets. The same cannot be said for many smaller size commercial, construction and services companies whose appetite for financing propelled gearing ratios, in recent years, to dangerous territory.

After years of moderation, loan growth and deposit growth started climbing steeply. From a recent low of about 10% in early 1992, banking sector lending has since been growing much faster. Lending grew by about 40% in both 1995 and 1996, and growth remained high until the middle of 1997. As perilous as this explosion could be for asset quality, it was simply an adjustment by the Philippines banking system after years of relative stagnation. Domestic credit as a percentage of GDP was extremely low during the ten years or so of isolation following the 1983 debt moratorium. In 1993, the ratio started climbing, but by 1997 when it reached about 70%, it was still relatively modest by international standards and, more relevantly, by East Asian standards (Table 8.8).

Growth per se is not necessarily a weak point. What the statistics do not show, however, is that the growth registered among Philippines banks in very recent times conceals large disparities in the types of loans affected by the growth.

TABLE 8.8   ESTIMATED LEVELS OF INTERMEDIATION

	Loans/GDP (est. 1997)
Japan	200–220
Korea	160–170
Malaysia	140–160
Thailand	130–150
Taiwan	120–130
USA	55–60
Philippines	60–70*
Indonesia	50–60

*This range in the Philippines is more than double what it was in 1991.
Source: Thomson BankWatch Inc.

The growth rate of foreign currency loans was much larger than that of local currency loans, a dangerous trend if the crisis had not put an end to the practice. Human nature never changes. The temptation to borrow and lend in US$ has been difficult to resist. Seeing that many banks in neighboring countries were playing the game, and that foreign lenders were prepared, after years of caution, to lend more to Philippines banks, one can hardly put all the blame on local institutions. Wherever blame lay, the result was that total lending in foreign currency grew by 58% in 1995 alone, and by another staggering 98% in 1996. Admittedly, this was from a low basis, but it was nonetheless insane. If not for the huge capital ratios posted by the Philippines banks, this would have sent a very negative signal to external observers. Table 8.9 gives some details about the likely deterioration of asset quality.

TABLE 8.9   ASSET QUALITY INDICATORS

	1994 (%)	1995 (%)	1996 (%)
Asset growth	24	33	25
Loan growth	31	45	35
Foreign currency loan growth	N/A	58	98
Provisions/loans	2.2	1.7	1.5
NPLs/loans	2.3	2.0	2.1

Source: Annual Reports

In 1997, the central bank imposed a punitive 30% liquidity reserve on foreign currency borrowing, but it was too late to stem the flow. As previously mentioned, a variety of other preventive measures were taken in 1997 with the view of preventing a meltdown. Among them were stronger provisioning requirements, which were probably of little relevance since the banks already have fat capital ratios. Perhaps more coercion in the matter of running expenses would have been more salutary.

In the Philippines, as in most other countries, banks are not permitted to take significant foreign exchange positions. They are supposed to match their assets and liabilities in all currencies separately, with any difference covered by off-balance sheet items if need be. In theory then they should never suffer from a violent devaluation of the local currency. Unfortunately, there are two reasons why the theory could potentially fail to apply to Philippines banks. The first one they share with other banking systems: a client who has borrowed in foreign currency has in fact often created for himself a foreign exchange position. He may fail to find enough dollars or pesos to meet his obligations, now that the dollar is more expensive to acquire.[7]

The second reason is that, owing to the structure of their balance sheet, banks in the Philippines always carry a huge net negative US$ position (the amount, according to central bank statistics, exceeded US$19 billion in October 1997). Naturally, they balance the negative position with a positive position in US$ forwards, which appear in off-balance sheet accounts. But the peso has collapsed and all the banks' counterparties in US$ forwards are on the losing side of the transactions. Most of them will not renege on the deals, especially if the losing position is balanced against a winning one in their books.[8] But some of the counterparties may very well not have a counterbalancing position and, faced with a huge loss, would not be able to deliver. Their failure would transfer the currency loss to the banks, with disastrous results. If such problems exist, they will affect the banks in their 1998 accounts.

Certainly property lending is as prominent in the books of Philippines banks as in Thailand, Malaysia and Indonesia, but there is no real estate glut, while asset inflation has not affected the market beyond luxury condominiums. It is fascinating to observe that luxury apartments were being built in large quantities, and put up for sale at approximately US$800,000. Out of a population whose per capita income is US$1,200 — this is the country's figure at the end of 1996 — how many households can afford to acquire such luxury accommodation? Yet hundreds of them have been built. But overall the banking system has not overindulged in lending to mad developers like in Thailand, Malaysia and even Indonesia. NPLs, officially in a low range of 2% to 3% since 1994, as noted are bound to jump to as much as 10% or more in 1998, but, if this prevision holds true, even with the usual adjustments, the situation will still be manageable.

Since the authorities have taken no substantial measures to curb general expenditures in Philippines banks, it is highly possible that the looming problem of efficiency will turn into a disaster ahead of the timeframe suggested by Thomson BankWatch. The devaluation of the peso and the general slowdown of the region's economies are likely to affect the banks' asset quality, thereby reducing their ability to meet gigantic running expenses as they have in the past. As discussed, the disaster is avoidable if proper measures are taken to reduce expenses and increase efficiency. Laws designed to protect workers and an administration committed to greater economic democracy (albeit in the context of maintaining economic and financial reforms) do not necessarily bode well in this endeavor.

The Asian crisis has hit the Philippines by contagion, more than for any other reason. At best, the crisis is likely to force a number of mergers on the banking community, which will enable the remaining players to achieve requisite efficiency levels. The critical question remains: will efficiency improvements occur before the banking system suffers a major breakdown brought on by excessive cost structures held up by artificially high margins kept in place by a cartel?

Endnotes

1. Non-deliverable forward transactions are those where, at maturity, the position is reversed in the spot market. Theoretically, only the net loss is transferred from the loser to the winner, although the two transactions are often entered separately in the books. Deliverable forward transactions usually complement genuine trade or investment positions and the funds are actually delivered at maturity. But the vast majority of forward transactions are non-deliverable. By restricting their volume, a government can hope to reduce the strength of an attack on the currency.

2. This is of course a statement about their relative strength in comparison to the distressed banks of the rest of the region. There is little doubt, however, that even the Philippines banks face substantial difficulties.

3. The Philippines had less to lose than its fast-growing neighbors in 1997 and the comparison will be more relevant in 1998.

4. One should also question the ethical position of a government that sells a bank to private investors without telling them about a liability the state owners created themselves and over which they had full control.

5. The process that led to the "discovery" of the documents remains a mystery.

6. In recent years, only banks in Hong Kong and Singapore have generally been better than those in the Philippines in respect of the true level of their non-performing loans.

7. This has in fact been the single most important factor that has affected the viability of otherwise safe Indonesian banks.

8. The immediate counterparty in a transaction may very well have no foreign exchange position at all, as is expected from banks, but someone, somewhere down the line, must have a foreign exchange position.

OTHER EAST ASIAN COUNTRIES

O ther countries in Asia have exhibited weaknesses that are very similar to those which have brought the five distressed countries to the crisis. It would be interesting to detour and explore some of these countries, trying to understand what makes them different, if anything, why they escaped and whether a similar crisis could hit them in the near future. China and Japan would certainly deserve a separate study but they make only a modest appearance in this book.

China

The Chinese banking system is in shambles. It was originally meant to operate as an extension of the ministry of finance of a communist country. Outside of their role as giro centers,[1] banks were to gather deposits in order to finance the government budget. On the asset side, they were to direct loaned funds — or rather disguised subsidies — to state-owned corporations in need. With no regard for the economic justification of state-owned enterprises (SOEs), the communist state was the ultimate treasurer of political and social decisions. SOEs with spare cash at the end of a period would deposit the funds with banks. Should their own funds be short, the SOEs would borrow from banks. In addition, a gigantic IOU system was developed, also called "triangular debt", whereby it became more expedient for companies to delay payments rather than seek relief from the banking system. Regularly the triangular debts would be cleared or netted among SOEs, with a resulting positive or negative net entry in their bank accounts.

Even though their contribution to the country's total net wealth creation is modest, it is estimated that about 85% of the working capital of China's SOEs are financed by the banking system, a ratio that even the overextended Korean Chaebols could not match until recently. Depending on what conceptual approach is selected to measure the SOEs chances of survival, anything between 25% and 45% of them will never be able to reimburse their loans. A simple mathematical operation would show that potential loan losses are larger than the aggregate equity of all commercial banks in China. The system is virtually bankrupt. As mentioned in Chapter 11, there is nothing wrong with a bankrupt banking system, as long as liquidity is maintained. In China, a bad loan is not a bad loan until the government says it is. With creative accounting, it is possible to keep the system alive for quite some time. There are encouraging signs, most notably in the northern part of the country, that China will stop throwing good money after bad to loss-making SOEs, but this is likely to carry a huge social cost.

There should be a limit to the free ride enjoyed by the government. Bank deposits in China represent a fiscal deficit[2] that cannot grow forever. At one point it must be addressed. Fortunately, China does not have a wide fiscal deficit and can certainly stretch it. The government announced in early 1998 that it would issue bonds for an amount of RMB270 billion, equivalent to approximately US$32 billion, in order to strengthen the equity of state-owned banks, allowing the elimination of some NPLs. In practice, this amounts to taking from the depositors' left pocket to fill their right pockets, since the bonds are likely to deplete the bank deposits and come back to the banks under the shape of fresh capital. Indeed, whoever acquires the bonds will use funds presently deposited with the banks. In anticipation of the liquidity problem this may create, banks will enjoy looser reserve requirements. This sleight of hand is almost similar to the brilliant scheme developed for Bank of Ceylon in 1993 (see Chapter 3 on Bank Accounting).

Potentially more threatening is a string of difficulties China will face in its development. At the time of writing, China had started experiencing a worrying phase of deflation. It is not clear yet whether this is just the last phase of a very successful fight against inflation that started in 1994 when it exceeded 20%. It could also be the sign of a more serious adjustment to a general oversupply of goods and services, stemming from China's unbridled expansion drive of the past few years. There is no doubt that the Asian crisis is adding to the problem. Export growth has fallen in the first quarter of 1998, a result of renewed competition from the other Asian economies, while investment from the rest of Asia is drying up.

The Ministry of Labor and Social Security and the State Bureau of Statistics have released worrying statistics about China's unemployment. At the end of 1997, a total of 150 million people were jobless out of a population of 845 million workers, a rate of employment of about 17%. In 1997 alone, 33 million workers were laid off. Most of the unemployed are in rural sectors, but the cities and industrial regions are in no position to help them.

Why was China not hit by the financial panic? Essentially because there is no capital account convertibility, making it virtually impossible to bet against the renmenbi (also called the Chinese yuan). In addition, China enjoys the strength of a huge surplus, mostly built up in the past four years. The surplus is less impressive when calculated on a per capita basis: Taiwan and Hong Kong each have almost similar absolute surplus figures, but their populations are tiny compared to China's. Yet China's surplus gives it some respite.

Why was China not hit by the Asian crisis? Could its bank implode? The answer is simple: China's banks are firmly in the hands of the state, and seen that way by most depositors, creditors and lenders. Liquidity in local currency is never going to be a problem. Liquidity in foreign currency is a matter of sovereign risk and the creditworthiness of the banks is only a corollary.

The asset deflation seen in China may add to the argument that the renmenbi is overvalued and needs adjusting, although some economists argue that the currency is in fact perennially undervalued and needs no attention. History will tell us, but it seems that China will not be able to withstand for much longer the new competitive pressures born out of the Asian crisis. China needs a road map to measured capitalism, but the current events would make its leaders think twice. Meanwhile, Beijing is getting considerable mileage out of its promise not to rock Asia's boat with a yuan devaluation.

Taiwan

Taiwan is sitting on a huge surplus and its currency is not entirely convertible. This is enough to ensure that the Asian crisis would spare the island. The only side effect has been a modest depreciation of the New Taiwan dollar (Tables 9.1 and 9.2), as a response to competitive pressures from the five countries in distress. Taiwan competes with each of them in one way or another.

TABLE 9.1 CURRENCY TABLE

	1991	1992	1993	1994	1995	1996	1997	15 Jun. 98
US$ per NT$	0.0388	0.0394	0.0376	0.0381	0.0367	0.0363	0.0306	0.0287
Base Dec. 1991 = 100	100	101.55	96.91	98.20	94.59	93.56	79.12	73.97
NT per US$	25.75	25.40	26.63	26.24	27.27	27.49	32.67	34.87
Base Dec. 1991 = 100	100	98.64	103.42	101.90	105.90	106.76	126.41	135.42

Source: Capital Information Services

TABLE 9.2 STOCK EXCHANGE INDEX

	Dec. 90	Dec. 91	Dec. 92	Dec. 93	Dec. 94	Dec. 95	Dec. 96	Dec. 97	15 Jun. 98
Taiwan Weighted Index	4530.16	4600.27	3377.06	6070.56	7124.66	5173.73	6933.94	8187.27	7283.83
Base Dec. 1990 = 100	100	101.55	74.55	134.00	157.27	114.21	153.06	180.73	160.79

Source: Capital Information Services

The Taiwanese industrial structure is much more flexible than that of Korea. While Korea has mobilized its forces around several large conglomerates, Taiwan has built its success on a myriad of small and medium size companies. Such companies, not unlike the manufacturing companies of Hong Kong at the time they still had a significant presence, are extremely creative and versatile. They adapt themselves rapidly to changes and their suffering, if any, will be short.

It would be exaggerated to claim that Taiwan exhibits a very sound banking system. While their efficiency is relatively good, thanks to the geography of the island and the industriousness of its people, the banks are not sufficiently profitable to withstand any serious threat. Fortunately , the guiding hand of the authorities would help them in case of difficulties, and the government has the means to rescue both the banks it owns and those it does not. Among the private sector banks are many new names that belong to wealthy industrial and commercial groups.

Singapore

Singapore measures about 42 kilometers by 23 kilometers. It covers an area of 626 square kilometers and lies approximately 135 kilometers north of the equator. According to the local press,[3] there are several banks in Singapore.

Hong Kong

Hong Kong is a marvellous city. Everybody works hard and efficiency is everywhere. McDonald's serves more hamburgers per outlet in Hong Kong than anywhere else in the world, using the lowest combination of people and space. Hong Kongers eat fast, work fast and think fast. If only they could walk a bit faster in their crowded streets...

Hong Kong was spared by the financial panic, but it suffered from asset deflation, a problem brought by its currency peg. The US dollar, to which the Hong

---

FILTH

Failed in London? Try Hong Kong! "Filth" is the one-word opinion shared by many Asians about the expatriate community hailing from England. In places like Hong Kong, where the "filth" expression was coined, the locals are tired of the often arrogant bunch that has dictated their lives for decades. Most lawyers, many real estate agents, barmen, prostitutes and, alas, some civil servants belong to the "filth" category.[4] Until April 1997, any British citizen could land in Hong Kong and work there without any formality. In a last burst of imperialism, owing to the depressed state of the economy in the early 1990s, Britain sent waves of undereducated workers to Hong Kong, who helped build the new airport — for lower wages than the locals — and sold sandwiches in the streets.

Kong currency has been fixed since 1983, grew steadily against almost every other currency in the region and, for that matter, against most currencies in other parts of the world. Hong Kong always was an expensive city, but the strength of the dollar has made it prohibitive. The ex-colony rejoined China in July 1997, and its economic and financial future depends largely on decisions made in Beijing. This includes the all-important matter of the currency.

Hong Kong runs a tight currency peg, which is akin to a currency board with some important differences: essentially in this case, the authorities allow themselves some latitude in playing with the money supply. By doing so, they take some of the pressure away from interest rates when the parity is under threat. Under a pure currency board, interest rates operate as an automatic regulator, although quite obviously the level of foreign currency reserves backing the peg and a high financial discipline usually act as a deterrent against attacks on the currency. Hong Kong has both huge foreign currency reserves[5] and a comparatively good reputation for financial discipline. But the high value of the Hong Kong dollar is driving the Special Administrative Region (or SAR, the new technical designation of the territory) into serious trouble. Hong Kong essentially sells tourism, trade and financial services and it is slowly driving itself out of competition.

The currency peg is obsolete. It was useful at a time when Hong Kong was shaking under political uncertainty, but this period is now over. Singapore lives pretty happily with a floating currency, and there is no reason why Hong Kong should be different. For obvious political reasons, China does not want to adjust the Hong Kong dollar too soon after the liberation of the territory. The Chinese leaders know that the world is watching and they have very much kept Hong Kong as they received it. The conventional wisdom has therefore been that an elegant way of getting rid of the obsolete peg is to wait for an adjustment to the Chinese yuan. This is a mistake.

On a purchasing power parity basis — comparing currency values on what they actually buy — the Chinese yuan is widely undervalued in comparison to the Hong Kong dollar. The difference is in the region of 50%, meaning that before the two currency can really start moving in concert, the Hong Kong dollar should first lose about one-third of its value. Therefore in the matter of currency adjustments in the wake of Asia's financial panic, the yuan and the HK dollar should be dealt with separately. Since the yuan is not overvalued, the adjustment should come from the Hong Kong dollar.

The stability brought about by a currency peg is worth maintaining. Letting the Hong Kong dollar float freely may send the wrong signal to jittery currency markets, since the financial panic is still on. Therefore the authorities should de-peg the Hong Kong dollar, re-peg it at another rate and defend that rate. If the considerable arsenal they claim to have allows the defense of the peg at 7.80 to the US dollar, then defending a peg at, say, 9.75 to the US dollar will be all the more feasible.

If the peg remains unchanged and the US dollar remains strong against other currencies, the Hong Kong dollar interest rates may very well increase beyond 15% to 20%. If sustained for more than a few months, this level will trigger defaults on mortgage and other loans, and will increase the downward pressure on real estate and stock prices.

Housing has long been madly expensive in Hong Kong, resulting from the collusion between developers and a government that draws a large portion of its revenue from land sales. The new SAR government wants a change, but until recently households would typically divert as much or more than 50% of their income to mortgage repayments on tiny flats. Banks are allowed to finance up to 70% of the value of the flats but there are so many ways around the rules that many flats are financed up to 85% of their value. A fall in property values — at the time of writing, real estate had fallen about 45% from the recent peak — does not necessarily induce borrowers to walk away from a losing investment, as long as they can service their loans and hope for better times. But if interest rates go up,

---

Can Do Better

Bank of Credit and Commerce International (BCCI) is one of the most notorious banking disasters of recent years. It had a subsidiary in Hong Kong called Bank of Credit and Commerce Hong Kong (BCCHK). The bank was not the best in Hong Kong, but it had received a clean bill of health from the authorities. BCCHK had so few financial dealings with the rest of the BCCI group, beyond injections of capital from its parent, that it was almost certainly solvent when the group collapsed. Hong Kong regulators always rightly insist on very high liquidity ratios and BCCHK was sufficiently liquid. If that was in doubt, the bank could have summoned sufficient liquidity against its assets to sustain the heavy withdrawals prompted by the demise of its parent.

On the Friday when Luxembourg, London and other places suspended BCCI's activities, the Hong Kong authorities suspended BCCHK's operations. On the Saturday, they announced that the bank after all was safe and would be permitted to operate, which it did on that day, and in the process received fresh deposits. By Monday, the bank was definitely closed. Nobody will ever know for sure, but it is very likely that BCCHK could have survived perfectly well. It was not the best bank in town, but on a stand alone basis, there was absolutely no indication that it was insolvent. Had the authorities wanted it to carry on operating, it would have been possible. After all, Hong Kong nurtured back to health many a bank in considerably worse shape[6] that BCCHK. The net result is that a large chunk of the bank's assets were wasted in unbelievably high liquidation costs,[7] at the expense of the depositors. Not the colony's finest hour as a financial center.

mortgage repayments soar — most are based on floating interest rates — and borrowers must devote their entire income to servicing the loans.[8] In previous crises, they did not walk away from their loans,[9] partly because the banks would have no better option than to be flexible and to restructure the loans. But this time around, the prospects of a prompt recovery are slimmer than ever.

Banks are therefore in serious danger of recording a growing flow of bad loans. Fortunately, they are highly capitalized — with Cooke (BIS) capital adequacy ratios in the vicinity of 17%, that is twice the norm — meaning that it would take a major disaster for them to collapse. The average ratio conceals differences between good names and weaker names, but even the weak banks are strongly capitalized. However, this protection would be of little use if Hong Kong's economy were to suffer for a prolonged period. Unemployment, high interest rates, slow growth and a continued slump in real estate values would conspire to create NPLs for banks beyond what they can swallow. NPLs could devastate some banks in spite of their strong capital position, and the market may yet see bank failures.

TABLE 9.3   TAIWAN ECONOMIC INDICATORS

	1991	1992	1993	1994	1995	1996	1997	1998p
Currency								
NT$/US$ (end period)	25.75	25.40	26.63	26.24	27.27	27.49	32.55	36.00
Real Exchange Rate (% change)	−8.6	−5.9	1.8	−5.6	−3.9	−2.3	17.2	7.6
Real Economy								
Real GDP (% change)	7.6	6.8	6.3	6.5	6.1	5.7	6.8	5.5
Gross Fixed Investment, as % of GDP	23.5	23.1	22.9	23.3	23.0	23.0	23.2	24.2
Money and Prices								
Consumer Price Inflation (End period)	3.6	4.5	3.0	4.1	3.7	3.1	0.9	3.0
Lending Rate (%)	6.20	8.00	5.50	8.00	7.30	5.50	6.00	7.35
Foreign Reserves (US$ billions)	82.70	87.30	90.00	92.45	90.31	88.00	92.00	75.00
Domestic Savings Rate (%)	25.2	25.9	25.1	25.8	26.0	26.1	26.5	26.2
Balance of Payments								
Exports (US$ billions)	75.54	80.72	81.10	93.05	111.69	118.00	122.07	127.00
Imports (US$ billions)	59.85	68.08	70.50	85.35	103.57	105.00	114.43	121.00
Trade Balance (US$ billions)	15.69	12.64	10.60	7.70	8.12	13.00	7.64	6.00
Current Account Balance (US$ billions)	12.01	8.20	6.70	6.15	5.01	10.43	10.12	5.40
Current Account Balance, % GDP	6.7	3.8	3.0	2.7	1.9	3.7	3.3	2.0
Foreign Debt (US$ billions) as % of GDP	N/A	N/A	N/A	N/A	N/A	31.50	34.60	36.00
Debt Servicing Ratio (%)	N/A	N/A	N/A	N/A	N/A	11.6	12.3	12.8
Governmant Finance								
Gov. Surplus/Deficit as % of GDP	−6.4	−6.7	−7.0	−7.2	−7.4	−8.0	−5.5	−4.8

Source: Thomson BankWatch Inc.

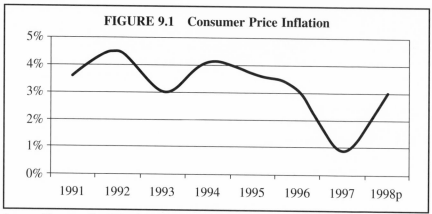

Source: *Thomson BankWatch Inc.*

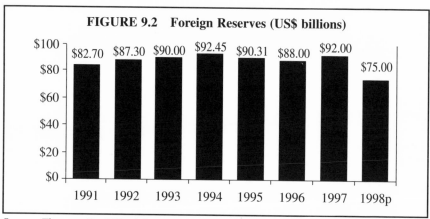

Source: *Thomson BankWatch Inc.*

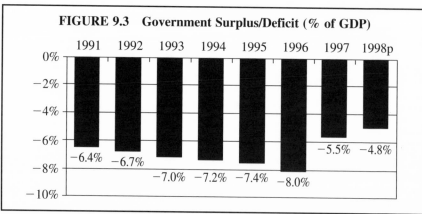

Source: *Thomson BankWatch Inc.*

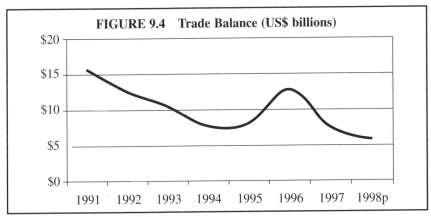

FIGURE 9.4 Trade Balance (US$ billions)

Source: Thomson BankWatch Inc.

TABLE 9.4 SINGAPORE ECONOMIC INDICATORS

	1991	1992	1993	1994	1995	1996	1997	1998p
Currency								
S$/US$ (end period)	1.63	1.64	1.61	1.46	1.41	1.40	1.68	1.7
Real Exchange Rate (% change)	−9.72	−1.69	−4.26	−12.72	−7.19	−2.10	18.0	−1.80
Real Economy								
Real GDP (% change)	6.7	5.8	9.9	10.1	8.8	7.0	7.8	2.5
Fixed Investment as % of GDP	37.0	35.7	34.4	35.0	36.8	34.6	37.3	36.7
Official Unemployment Rate (%)	2.9	2.8	2.7	2.7	2.7	2.7	2.7	N/A
Money and Prices								
Consumer Price Inflation (%)	3.4	2.3	2.5	3.1	1.7	1.4	2.0	3.0
Lending Rate (%)	7.58	5.95	5.39	5.88	6.37	6.26	6.50	6.90
Reserves (US$ billions)	34.13	39.89	48.36	58.18	68.69	78.00	77.00	75.00
Domestic Savings Rate (%)	46.6	48.0	48.9	49.5	50.0	48.7	52.9	50.6
Balance of Payments								
Merchandise Exports (US$ billions)	61.24	67.13	77.80	97.92	118.18	125.08	130.00	135.00
Merchandise Imports (US$ billions)	61.44	68.39	80.59	96.57	124.39	131.82	136.00	141.50
Trade Balance (US$ billions)	(0.20)	(1.26)	(2.79)	1.35	(6.21)	(6.74)	(6.50)	(6.50)
Current Account Balance (US$ billions)	4.88	5.62	4.21	11.28	15.09	13.25	15.35	14.60
Current Account Balance, % GDP	7.8	11.5	9.1	17.4	17.7	14.1	15.6	13.9
Gov. Surplus/Deficit as % of GDP	9.29	7.60	8.70	8.50	5.10	6.70	6.70	1.70

Source: Thomson BankWatch Inc.

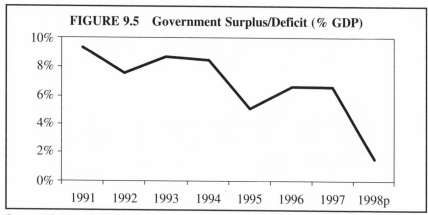

FIGURE 9.5   Government Surplus/Deficit (% GDP)

Source: Thomson BankWatch Inc.

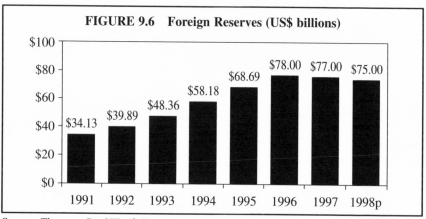

FIGURE 9.6   Foreign Reserves (US$ billions)

Source: Thomson BankWatch Inc.

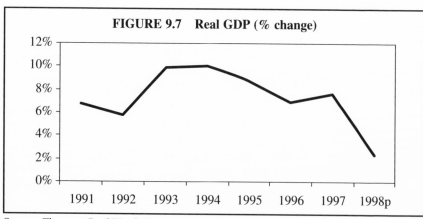

FIGURE 9.7   Real GDP (% change)

Source: Thomson BankWatch Inc.

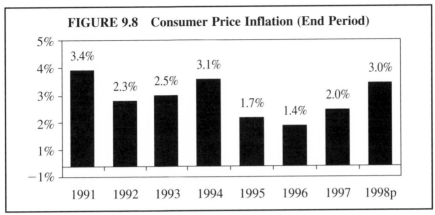

FIGURE 9.8   Consumer Price Inflation (End Period)

Source: Thomson BankWatch Inc.

TABLE 9.5   HONG KONG ECONOMIC INDICATORS

	1991	1992	1993	1994	1995	1996	1997	1998p
Currency								
HK$/US$ (end period)	7.78	7.74	7.73	7.74	7.74	7.73	7.75	7.75
Real Exchange Rate (% change)	−12.3	−9.9	−8.6	−8.0	−8.7	−6.0	−5.8	−4.1
Real Economy								
Real GDP (% change)	5.1	6.3	6.1	5.4	4.6	5.0	5.2	−1.0
Fixed Investment as % of GDP	N/A	N/A	N/A	N/A	30.1	32.4	32.1	31.5
Official Unemployment Rate (%)	3.6	3.4	3.5	3.6	3.5	2.9	2.6	4.5
Money and Prices								
Consumer Price Inflation (%)	11.6	9.4	8.5	8.1	8.7	6.3	5.8	4.1
Lending Rate (%)	8.50	6.50	6.50	8.50	8.75	8.50	9.50	10.25
Foreign Reserves (US$ billions)	29.00	35.00	43.00	49.00	55.00	63.80	70.00	95.00
Domestic Savings Rate (%)	30.5	30.9	31.2	31.7	32.0	32.7	33.0	33.0
Balance of Payments								
Exports (US$ billions)	98.60	119.50	138.00	150.80	172.80	180.80	187.80	193.90
Imports (US$ billions)	100.60	123.80	147.90	161.20	191.80	198.60	208.90	213.00
Trade Balance (US$ billions)	(2.00)	(4.30)	(9.90)	(10.40)	(19.00)	(17.80)	(21.10)	(19.10)
Current Account Balance (US$ billions)	N/A	N/A	N/A	N/A	N/A	N/A	N/A	N/A
Current Account Balance, % GDP	N/A	N/A	N/A	N/A	N/A	N/A	N/A	N/A
Foreign Debt (US$ billions) as % of GDP	N/A	N/A	N/A	N/A	N/A	N/A	N/A	N/A
Debt Service Ratio (%)	N/A	N/A	N/A	N/A	N/A	N/A	N/A	N/A
Government Finance								
Gov. Surplus/Deficit as % of GDP	2.7	2.8	2.2	1.3	−0.2	0.1	1.9	−0.20

Source: Thomson BankWatch Inc.

Japan

Is Japan a distant source of the Asian crisis? The answer is no, but it is probably worth asking the question. Undisputedly, the weakness of the yen is one of the factors since it contributed to a loss of competitiveness for the likes of Korea. But was it that the yen was too weak or the dollar too strong?

Going back further, one could link the crisis to Japan in an elaborate way: the Japanese banks compete internationally for market share and undercut the Western banks; the West retaliates by imposing the BIS capital ratios on OECD banks; Asian banks are led to believe that they, too, should reach high BIS ratios; Asian banks cannot sustain the ratios and gamble in a desperate bid to remunerate capital funds; the Asian banking systems implode. A bit stretched perhaps.

Compared to the rest of Asia, Japan is in a much more advanced phase of a development cycle that started after World War II. Its own crisis started in 1991, with roots established much earlier than that. Japan may have built on the bases of a rural society, like in other parts of the region, but this extraordinary country had a substantial collective wealth in education and management principles well before the war. A combination of hard work, discipline, community and frugality brought wealth and respect for Japan, that culminated with the dizzying height reached by the yen against the US dollar (79 yen for one dollar). By then Japan had the largest banks in the world and was the largest investor in US debt. The bubble burst in the early 1990s and Japan's economy has now been in a sluggish phase for seven years, with no end in sight.

TABLE 9.6   CURRENCY TABLE FOR JAPAN

	Dec. 91	Dec. 92	Dec. 93	Dec. 94	Dec. 95	Dec. 96	Dec. 97	15 Jun. 98
US$ per yen	0.008006	0.008009	0.008941	0.010042	0.008661	0.008643	0.007658	0.006839
Base Dec. 1991 = 100	100	100.03	111.67	125.43	120.66	107.95	95.65	−10.70
Yen per US$	124.90	124.86	111.85	99.58	103.51	115.70	130.58	146.22
Base Dec. 1991 = 100	100	99.97	89.55	79.73	82.87	92.63	104.55	117.07

Source: Capital Information Services

TABLE 9.7   STOCK EXCHANGE INDEX (JAPAN)

	Dec. 90	Dec. 91	Dec. 92	Dec. 93	Dec. 94	Dec. 95	Dec. 96	Dec. 97	15 Jun. 98
Nikkei 225	23848.7	22983.8	16925.0	17417.2	19723.1	19868.2	19361.4	15258.7	14825.17
Base Dec. 1990 = 100	100	96.37	70.97	73.03	82.70	83.31	81.18	63.98	62.16

Source: Capital Information Services

The famous Japanese work ethics seems to have lost ground and creativity has vanished. Japan is now on auto-pilot, guided by a bloated and stubborn bureaucracy. Enough to make BBC's "Yes Prime Minister" series look tame. The Japanese entrenched bureaucrat's only motto is the survival of the species. The economy is still one of the most regulated in the free world. Recent Keynesian decisions to prime the pump, followed by disastrous changes in some tax rates have sent the wrong signals to the Japanese public. Japan is rich, its domestic savers finance the US deficit and it is a major partner — investor, lender, buyer, seller — to Asia. Hundreds of Japanese companies have de-localized production to cheaper Asian countries, Japan dominates the automotive industry in Asia, its banks have US$265 billion on loan to the region. Japan's fate will be the determinant for Asia's survival.

The Japanese banking system has long been in poor condition. The yen has long been a low-interest currency and margins are rather thin. Banks are not highly efficient, so that their ability to generate cash flow is too low to sustain any unusual deterioration of asset quality. The Japanese system of cross-shareholdings, including the incestuous links between banks and major non-financial groups, has made the banks particularly vulnerable when the stock market crashed, as those losses eat away at constituents of bank capital funds.

When NPLs became unbearable, in the past four years, the bureaucrats and the banks took two very Japanese — time will solve it all — decisions. First they created a special vehicle called Cooperative Credit Purchasing Co Ltd (CCPC) to purchase problem loans. In the first four years of its existence (from March 1993), it paid Yen 5.3 trillion for Yen 13.2 trillion of distressed loans (Yen 13 trillion is equivalent to anything between US$100 billion and $150 billion, depending on the exchange rate). The banks took losses at the time of the transfer, but such losses did not depend on the quality of the loans: they were determined by the banks' capacity to write-off the loss, in accordance with the tax authorities. The rationale behind this effort was that, after a 10-year period, most loans would be liquidated and leftovers would be returned to the banks. Unfortunately, after the first four years, only 13% of the original book value of the purchase loans had been liquidated. Meanwhile, the banks finance the CCPC and their advances to it are considered current. Needless to add, it seems likely that the 10-year experiment will be extended for a further period, but this Japan can afford to do.

The second decision pertained to the housing loan companies (Jusen). The story was interesting as it represented one of the world's largest concentrations of dud loans dealt within a single bureaucratic decision. The Jusen were non-bank financial institutions, created at the initiative of the banks principally for the distribution of housing loans, although they ventured disastrously out of their charter as well. The Jusen were financed almost exclusively with funds from Agricultural Cooperatives, which are very powerful groupings of Japanese farmers, a very coveted chunk of the electorate that no politician would want to offend. After the real estate bubble burst, the Jusen had losses of up to Yen 13 trillion. In a normal capitalist country, most of that amount would have to be taken from deposits, but this being Japan and the depositors being the Agricultural Cooperatives, someone else was going to pay. Public funds were used, in a modest way (Yen 0.7 trillion), after screams of protest. The Agricultural Cooperatives were made to lose a minuscule 4% of the loss (Yen 0.5 trillion), and the banks, (almost) innocent[10] bystanders, were made to swallow a loss of Yen 6.3 trillion. For the balance (now Yen 6.8 trillion), a Housing Loan Administration Corporation (HLAC) was created, with many similarities to the CCPC. It will try to liquidate the remaining assets over 10 years. The expected losses are optimistically estimated at a mere Yen 1.2 trillion, but they will ultimately depend on the health of the real estate market. The banks are providing cheap funds to HLAC, under the guarantee of the Deposit Insurance Corporation (DIC). Since the DIC will face substantial calls on its limited funds, the banks will contribute insurance premiums that were raised seven-fold, spreading the pain over several years.

These two examples of very creative accounting have swept Yen 12 billion (US$90 billion at the time of writing) of dud loans under the carpet. This is remarkable. It is equivalent to more than the assets of the entire banking system of Indonesia today. It gives us an idea of the magnitude of the problems faced by the Japanese banks.[11]

Meanwhile, the government is going ahead with the huge reforms collectively known as the "Big Bang", with its Prompt Corrective Action (PCA) destined to assess the banks on the basis of their real capital adequacy ratios.

Japan's Big Bang

The Big Bang can be best described as an overall reform of Japan's money and capital markets in the context of a number of other structural, social and economic reforms planned for the period covering 1998 to 2001 and put together by former Prime Minister Hashimoto. In many ways, Tokyo's growth as a financial center, as would befit the capital city of an economic powerhouse, has been limited. It has long been restrained by a number of negative factors in the shape of high costs, a complicated tax system and a heavy bureaucracy, not to mention subtle — and not so subtle — entry barriers to international players. As a result, Tokyo has lost steam compared to New York, London and other lesser places. The yen is not exactly an international currency: it is held by foreign countries for only about 7% of their total reserves, and business is seldom transacted in yen. The Japanese financial system is segregated into various categories of financial institutions and the lack of real competition makes it highly inefficient. Japan has massive amounts of personal financial assets, and huge funds to recycle. It is the main banker of many countries, among them the USA.

The Big Bang involves the reform of laws in banking, securities, foreign exchange, insurance, taxes, accounting and trade. This is an enormous task. Major aspects of the reform will see the abolition of the ban on holding companies, and the liberalization of the products offered by banks (retail sales of mutual funds and insurance policies, issuance of bonds and asset-backed securities, OTC equity derivatives trading) and securities companies (asset management accounts). The government will provide public funds to the tune of Yen 30 trillion both to protect depositors and to finance the purchase by DIC of preferred shares and subordinated debt issued by banks. Most of the major banks are likely to apply for support.

In June 1995, the government had announced a Financial System Recovery Policy, which was not very different from earlier attempts at addressing the problems of troubled banks. Supervision was to be enhanced and disclosure improved. Japan would make use of public funds when needed and the DIC would help out.

In April 1998, the government reform called PCA was introduced essentially to force an earlier recognition of problem loans. As a result, banks have announced much higher levels of NPLs than previously disclosed. The immediate result of the measure was the recognition by many banks that their real capital adequacy ratio was below the line. Japan's huge exposure to Asia is likely to make matters soon look even worse. The banks have had no other option than to reduce their assets wherever possible. In Asia, this has meant a drastic reduction of their lending in relatively safe markets like Hong Kong and Singapore.

It looks likely that major Japanese financial institutions will benefit from the Big Bang at the expense of smaller and financially weak firms, as is natural in an environment of enhanced competition. The reforms will eventually take place, but their impact — in terms of disclosure more perhaps than in real terms — on some banks will be so severe that it would not be surprising to see the schedule stretched somehow beyond the target dates.

The PCA is a welcomed move that should inspire other Asian countries. But it may very well create secondary problems as the banks, one eye on the Nikkei index (their capital base is partly dependent on its level for hidden reserves)[12] and the other on swelling NPLs, may retreat in a devastating credit crunch. With equity falling, banks have no option but to eliminate assets.

In the past few years, some of Japan's real problems have started surfacing. Several financial institutions have failed, including relatively small banks, but the failures culminated with Hokkaido Takushoku Bank in November 1997 and, in early 1998, with the collapse of giant Yamaichi Securities. The traditional "convoy system" seems to have become obsolete, whereby a financial institution acquires a failed firm in order to postpone the inevitable. The scandals affecting Daiwa, then DKB, the failure of Sanyo Securities and the restructuring of Nippon Credit Bank are other interesting episodes. Less costly, but nonetheless extremely damaging was the recent scandal affecting the Ministry of Finance: in February 1998, local prosecutors accused several banks of bribing government officials with lavish entertainment. Banks involved included major names like Bank of Tokyo Mitsubishi, Sumitomo, Sanwa, Dai-Ichi Kangyo and IBJ. But then, what would business in Japan be without lavish entertainment?

Is everything so bleak in Japan? Perhaps not. After all, some of the pain is suffered at low interest rates: it is obviously less expensive to carry NPLs in banks' books when interest rates are low. This is in sharp contrast, for example, to the high interest rates (around 60%) prevailing in Indonesia at the time of writing, where the funding of NPLs is digging rapidly into equity, and beyond it.

More importantly perhaps, a number of Japanese companies and banks are in fact doing relatively well on a recurrent basis. They generate profits. The weakening of the yen makes up for the loss of some export markets in Asia. Even the banks are generating some good cash flow. No doubt the income is diverted into much needed and never sufficient provisions, but nevertheless some of the banks are doing relatively well. Their operating earnings are still low by international standards, although they would be sufficient for the Japanese investor. This is not to say that the Japanese financial system is any good: even without the huge losses brought about by the asset bubble and the banks' gregarious abandon in financing it, the banks would suffer from inefficiencies and structural weaknesses. Most of the shortcomings of present-day Korean banks did affect the Japanese banks earlier in the decade. The 1997 Asian crisis in fact hit Korea in 1995 and Japan in 1991.

The Future

China and Japan have problems of their own and their developments are likely to affect the rest of the region. Do they hold the key to a solution to the Asian crisis? They do not, but any minor mistake on their side might precipitate further problems in the rest of the region. Not only do China and Japan compete with some of the distressed East Asian countries in the rest of the world, but East Asia also happens to have substantial trade and investment links with them. Japan has invested huge amounts in the region, and may not be willing or able to sustain the pace of its support. There are clear signs that Japanese banks are reducing their activities in Asia, if only because they need to deflate total assets on account of their weak capital ratios. China has received large investments from the rest of Asia, but that source may dry up in the near future. There is a large degree of interdependence between China, Japan and the rest of East Asia, which point at indirect dangers stemming from contagion: problems spread from country to country. The transmission belt can be the currencies, it can be exports, and it can be investment or the lack of it. Clearly the general equilibrium was broken and adjustments are likely to be extremely painful. By not doing the wrong thing — devaluing to stimulate the economy through exports — China and Japan can help the rest of Asia not to fall any further. But there is precious little either China or Japan can do to solve the crisis.

Endnotes

1. A giro is a vast clearing system for payments between economic agents. Many Western countries have long maintained giro systems, usually in the hands of the government postal authorities. The funds maintained in the accounts normally attract no or little remuneration and the surplus balances are lent to the government.
2. Like in India and some other countries, at various degrees, directed lending to subsidized firms and the confiscation of surplus deposits by the state combine to create a hidden fiscal deficit.
3. In general, it is hazardous to make any comment on Singapore banks as there is always a risk that a discrepancy might exist between a commentator's and a bank's notion of what constitutes fair comment. This is why it is wise to limit one's comments to those expressed in the Singapore press, and why the comments are invariably bland.
4. Like expensive English solicitors who, back in London, would barely qualify as junior solicitors, owing to their limited skills, some senior bankers would perhaps qualify, back home, as assistants to the deputy-sub-manager of a high street sub-branch. This, however, is true regardless of national origin.
5. The fiscal surplus is also substantial. The new airport is a white elephant that Hong Kong could afford. It would have been cheaper and easier to expand the international airport of Shenzhen, just across the China-Hong Kong border, and to link it to Hong Kong with fast rail and road connections. The airport was built in Hong Kong, against common sense, for two reasons, it seems. The first reason, often mentioned in the local press, was to allow British firms to receive favors in airport construction contracts way beyond decency. The second reason — not dissociated from the first one, in a shameless quid pro quo — was to deplete for local use Hong Kong's huge fiscal surplus before reunification with China. An airport is an investment that cannot exactly be transplanted somewhere else. An alternative would have been to build 10,000 municipal swimming pools, hardly an option in tiny Hong Kong.
6. The colonial government stood accused of racism in its decision to close a bank whose roots were clearly in Pakistan.
7. Liquidation costs are huge in Hong Kong, essentially because professionals charge exorbitant fees. Accountants and solicitors are among the most expensive in the world. Barristers can easily charge well over US$15,000 per

day. The preliminary liquidation costs of defunct Peregrine have already run into several millions of US dollars.

8. In fact the only serious threat arises when both conditions are met: high interest rates and negative equity. In practice, it is high interest rates that trigger defaults, as servicing the loans swallows a growing portion of household income. Walking away from a mortgage loan in a small place like Hong Kong, on the sole grounds that equity is negative, is not an attractive option. Banks can make life difficult for delinquent borrowers, and personal bankruptcy is not a way out for them.

9. Growing unemployment in 1998 is a new negative factor that barely affected the market in previous crises.

10. It is in fact rumored that the banks may have also used the jusen to park some of their own weak assets.

11. Total NPLs in the system, if properly computed, would probably exceed US$600 billion.

12. Unrealized gains on equity investments are counted towards capital funds. It is fascinating to see that, in Asia, unrealized gains are often taken into consideration while unrealized losses are partly or totally disregarded.

THE CURE

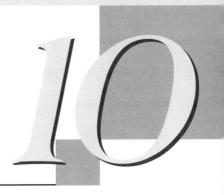

Timeo Danaos et dona ferentes!
(I fear the Greeks, even when they bring gifts!)
— a Trojan citizen upon seeing the horse presented to besieged Troy
by the enemy (Virgil)

There is no easy way out of the Asian crisis. The financial panic has destroyed a number of social, political and economic balances. If there were a simple solution, the respective governments would have found it. However, if governments could be that perceptive, surely they would have noticed the problems before they evolved into a full blown crisis. We should therefore realize that the matter is extremely complex. If it is accepted that this is a crisis of growth and that the unbridled growth is just about the only factor shared by all distressed countries, then it should be perceived that each country would have to find a different solution. No doubt, many similar ingredients will be found in the various recipes. Yet, the symptoms suffered by each of the countries point to at least one major common issue: banks must keep lending so that the entire economy does not grind to a halt. The more elaborate reconstruction of the financial systems is a distinct treatment, where the weaknesses that led to the crisis will be addressed: shallow capital markets and antiquated banking systems.

Can we learn something from the Latin American crisis of the 1980s? There are some similarities. For example, the total debt of Argentina, Brazil, Mexico, Venezuela and Chile to foreign banks was close to the amounts due by the five distressed Asian countries to foreign banks. In both cases, some countries dragged their feet, and others were quick to follow suggestions from outside. But there are also major differences. Inflation hit the South American countries much harder than the East Asian economies, partly because Latin America tried to subsidize exports with monetary expansion. East Asia is largely export-oriented and therefore its debt is a smaller proportion of export earnings. Another major difference is that East Asia's debt was mostly contracted by the private sector. But banks in South America had generally less NPLs in proportion to total assets than the Asian banks. The cost of recapitalizing the banking system was lower than is anticipated for Asia: as a proportion of GDP, the cost was 13% in Argentina and 20% in Chile, against probably 20% to 25% in Asia. It is important to realize that, in the case of Asia, a large chunk of those losses were made prior to the crisis but kept concealed by creative accounting.[1]

Before venturing in the exploration of the IMF rescue efforts, we should first dispel some misgivings about statistics. Do not trust what you see. It is easy to make honest mistakes when preparing or presenting statistics. It is tempting to make dishonest mistakes when nobody will notice. The next few paragraphs will explore figures and statistics in relation to the crisis, but will express no judgment as to what category the possible mistakes belong to.

Foreign Reserves

The IMF rescue packages for Asia were made necessary by the fast disappearance of foreign reserves in the distressed countries. One of the most difficult notions to grasp for the average person is that of foreign reserves. Taxpayers in a large number of IMF member countries have recently been invited to permit their governments to increase their quotas with the IMF, among other things allowing more national assets to be invested in IMF rescue operations. Many taxpayers do not realize that IMF rescue operations are loans, not subsidies. They also fail to realize that foreign reserves are not an accurate indicator of solvency. At best, foreign reserves are an indicator of liquidity.

Foreign reserves are a measure of how much quasi-liquidity in foreign currency is available to a given nation. They are comprised of all foreign denominated assets, including gold, reserves with the IMF and special drawing rights (SDRs). Foreign denominated liabilities are deducted. Off-balance sheet transactions, like swaps, forwards and derivatives come as adjustments. In a number of cases the foreign reserves are just the residual part of a wider amount originally borrowed from the rest of the world. In Asia, only a few countries like Japan, Brunei, Hong Kong and Singapore have foreign reserves that are not someone else's property. Elsewhere, quite a large number of countries in fact owe money to the rest of the world, and there is nothing wrong with that. Many households and companies maintain the same kind of accounts, whereby they hold cash, near cash or quasi-liquid reserves while they separately have liabilities to creditors. As we all know, the name of the game is to maintain a reasonable balance between the two sides and, if reserves are smaller than total debt, to keep creditors in the comfortable opinion that their loans are in safe hands and will eventually be reimbursed.

Table 10.1 shows the total debt, of which some is of a short-term nature, against the official reserves of several Asian countries.

TABLE 10.1 SHORT TERM DEBT AND RESERVES

Dec. 97 Foreign debt (US$ billions)		Jun. 97 Short-term debt (US$ billions)	Jun. 97 Reserves (US$ billions)	Jun. 97 Short-term debt/ reserves (%)
104	South Korea	70	34	206
129	Indonesia	35	20	170
97	Thailand	46	31	145
45	Phlippines	8	10	85
31	Malaysia	16	27	61
93	India	8	26	30
53	Taiwan	22	90	24

Sources: Bank for International Settlements, IMF

It is perhaps important to remind the reader that some countries have recently played with such figures, intentionally or not, by entering into foreign exchange forward transactions which may or may not have found their ways into the nation's books. More on that was explained in Chapter 4 on Thailand.

Among the major factors affecting the reserves are the trade surplus or deficit, the capital inflows or outflows, and large foreign exchange transactions conducted to control the exchange rate. All three categories have considerably influenced net reserves of the five distressed countries during the crisis.

Let us do some arithmetic. According to Table 10.1 as at June 1997, with US$20 billion in reserves, Indonesia would seem to be in worse shape than Thailand, with US$31 billion in reserves. It is true, since Indonesia has borrowed more than Thailand. But if Indonesia were to borrow, say, US$25 billion, from abroad, its reserves would jump to US$45 billion, while its total debt would jump by the same amount. This new level of reserves would make it look better than Thailand, while in reality the relative position would remain unchanged. So the amount of reserves in isolation means very little. A more important indicator is the capacity of a country to obtain and renew foreign deposits and loans. If either Thailand or Korea, with more short-term debt than reserves, were to see their short-term debt not being renewed, for whatever reason, they would be in default since their reserves would dwindle to nothing before they could meet their immediate obligations.

Technically, the crisis in Asia did not stem from the fact that reserves were too low, or total debt incompatible with them. The crisis had other roots. But the mechanisms whereby the crisis unfolded can be linked to the fact that, as many short-term creditors started screaming for their funds at the same time, Asian countries would have exhausted their reserves to satisfy them. Again here, households or companies anywhere in the world could be — and in reality often are — caught in the same predicament if all their creditors wish to be paid at once.

The IMF loans and the bilateral loans offered to Indonesia, Thailand and Korea by Japan and other countries were meant to replenish the reserves with long-term funds, in order for the three countries to meet their short-term obligations. In the case of Korea, this needed such a huge injection of long-term funds that an additional rescheduling of short-term loans was negotiated, postponing their maturity by two months, pending the implementation of other measures. Those measures eventually included the rescheduling of many of the loans. In the case of Thailand and Indonesia, the de facto inability of corporate borrowers to find local funds to acquire US dollars in order to meet their obligations has meant that many short-term loans were rolled-over against the will of the lenders.

Private Sector Foreign Debt

Accurate statistical data about Asia's private sector foreign debt are difficult to come by. The BIS publishes comprehensive figures twice a year, while central banks tend to publish figures on a quarterly basis, or sometimes on a monthly basis. What those figures do not take into account is indirect exposure of various types. Most of the time, foreign borrowings by banks are reported correctly, except in some of the published figures that do not include borrowings by offshore units. Indonesian and Malaysian banks have borrowed through the Cayman Islands or some other tax haven. Nothing wrong with the arrangement, except that conflicting statistical data are published. For example, two different BIS reports estimate Malaysia's bank-related debt as of mid-May 1997 at US$28.8 billion and US$32.8 billion, the difference being funds borrowed in offshore centers.

Discrepancies of that nature are much wider when it comes to corporate borrowings because most countries do not keep track of such transactions. Companies fail to consolidate them, as in many cases the funds are borrowed by associated companies, whose links to the owners' country of origin are not necessarily reported. Thousands of companies from China, Malaysia, Korea, Thailand, Indonesia and the Philippines use ad hoc vehicles in Hong Kong or in Singapore. According to some sources, there would be over 20,000 nominee companies in Hong Kong belonging to Chinese citizens or companies.

The published figures describing the rest of the world's exposure to Hong Kong and Singapore, even allowing for traceable offshore exposure of companies or banks of those two places, is vastly superior to the domestic needs of those two relatively small economies. In other words, it is very likely that a proportion of the world's exposure to Hong Kong and Singapore is in fact an exposure to other countries of the region.

Ching Chi Tao Pao, a magazine published in Hong Kong, has claimed, according to the *Far Eastern Economic Review*, that China has substantial "hidden foreign debt". It claims that Chinese companies use foreign subsidiaries to borrow funds, and that some companies borrow from foreign partners without reporting the matter. This is not surprising. But it suggests another form of liability whereby for example a Chinese party can promise a fixed rate of return to a foreign partner for its investment.

The IMF

Much has been said about the role played by the IMF in this crisis, or rather in the resolution of this crisis. The IMF stepped in as a representative of the international financial community with huge amounts of funds in a gigantic juggling performance. A major reason why Asia is suffering is that, collectively, it borrowed large amounts of international funds and that, in many cases, the repayment is now perceived to be taking more time than anticipated. The IMF is basically consolidating those debts, lending fresh money in order for all debts to be repaid. It is acting very much like small-debt consolidators, offering beleaguered and over-stretched individuals an opportunity to reschedule or restructure the loans they obtained from an array of lenders. There are other similarities between the IMF and the debt consolidators. For example, without the IMF funds, many Asian countries would have to declare a moratorium on their debt, very much like consolidation is the only way out for an over-stretched individual or family; the original lenders would be worse off without the rescue package. Also, typically, the consolidation brings along an increase in the average cost of the funds. The IMF itself may not charge usury levels of interest rates, but those private sector lenders who do restructure loans to accompany the IMF efforts take their pound of flesh.

Sato, president of the Asian Development Bank, may have a point when he implies that the IMF should have adopted another approach. But for all the negative comments about the IMF, there are a number of positive aspects. When a house is ablaze, firefighters intervene to limit the destruction of the house and to prevent an extension of the fire to adjacent properties. If the owner of the house did take excessive risks, an indoor barbecue perhaps, protected as she thought she was by firefighters just across the street, should we deny her our help? Mountain climbers are taking ever-increasing risks as they feel more protected by mobile phones and superior evacuation equipment. Should we deny them our help on the grounds that this would teach them to be more careful? With no support at all from the IMF and its partners-in-help, the Asian crisis could have been worse. If the score is lousy, do not shoot the pianist.

And yet, it seems that the IMF may have put too much cash on the table. Its managers have been acting like bank owners facing a run. The best way to stop a bank run usually is to stack up money on the counter and to extend opening hours. The message is then clear: there are limitless funds available, do not withdraw your support. In Asia, there was a run on the economies, in that billions of dollars of loans were being suspended or were about to be suspended. A bank can hardly declare a moratorium on its liabilities. Unlike a bank manager, an Asian government could easily declare a moratorium. In fact, it can be argued that this is exactly what they did, save that they did not call it that way. The various forms of debt rescheduling signed in Korea and Indonesia are nothing short of a kind of managed moratorium.

In Asia, as indeed almost everywhere, economies depend on external trade to survive. The IMF funds should have been used exclusively to restore financial

IMF Under Fire

Dozen of countries received funds from the IMF in the past 30 years. As a rule, the IMF imposes policy changes in exchange for its support, and its intervention is temporary. Critics have suggested that the IMF support in fact creates more problems than it solves. Here is what they are saying, and some comments on their accusations.

"The IMF imposes conditions to its intervention." It appears that the conditionality has not worked well in the past. It seems that governments make promises in order to receive the funds and only implement them when threatened with a cut in IMF credits. In addition, many countries under IMF perfusion get out of the ordeal in no better shape than they were prior to intervention, the only benefit being a restructuring of the debt.

"The IMF sends the wrong signal." Lenders are encouraged to take excessive risks because they perceive the risk to be mitigated by the potential support of the IMF. Moral hazard operates here on a gigantic scale. Leaving aside the moral aspect of allowing international lenders to escape, this suggests that excessive lending for unproductive purposes would never have taken place had that veiled protection not been in place. The successful rescue of Mexico in 1995 was perhaps seen as a signal that, should Asia meet similar problems, it would be offered a similar rescue package. Indeed, the capital flows to East Asia almost doubled after the Mexico crisis while, by most accounts — as we discussed in the chapters devoted to various countries — several Asian countries were virtually in crisis at least three years before July 1997, at the very time when the Mexican crisis was erupting.

"The IMF tinkers with market mechanisms." It is vain to try and steer economic policies against global tides. Similarly, central banks have long thought that foreign reserves could protect them against market forces. Time and again, the huge amounts transacted in international markets have proved no match for official reserves.

"The IMF neglects structural problems." On May 7, 1998, Mitsui Sato, the president of the Asian Development Bank, speaking at the Asia Society's annual conference in Hong Kong, suggested that the IMF might have mismanaged the Asian crisis. He claimed that the IMF might have neglected structural problems: "Their prescription for these countries has been too much emphasizing the conventional prescription by which I mean the monetary and the fiscal."

flows. In particular, it was essential to prevent disruptions in the flow of funds needed in international trade, as such funding was particularly exposed to market restrictions as the crisis evolved: export-oriented companies need funding as they often rely on imported raw material and semi-finished products before they can export. For everything else, the IMF should perhaps have left the markets to themselves. More banks would have failed and more international lenders would have taken losses, but currencies would have suffered less. More importantly, the person in the street in Bandung or Pusan or Chiang Mai would have been spared some suffering.

We have all heard the accusation that a few hundred IMF economists have been blindly dictating terms and have imposed unacceptable hardship to millions in Asia. The IMF leaders would have done this both in order to rescue international banks heavily exposed to Asian risk, and to prepare local financial markets for the dominance of international giants. This is as simplistic as it is misplaced. One can perhaps argue that the IMF got the volume and timing of the intervention wrong, but this is a delicate matter. If restructuring the Asian debt was the main or the only objective of the maneuver, nothing much would be accomplished. From that angle, the IMF has only substituted its funds for the funds of hundreds of worried lenders. It has taken money from Paul's government to lend to Peter so as to reimburse Paul. This is no cure for the malady Asia is suffering from. Fortunately, the IMF has also suggested a few changes. We all know that governments tend to agree to the suggestions with no intention to follow them all, but this is another story. The IMF was accused of attaching strings to its assistance. To the extent that there were good reasons for the crisis of confidence (the borrowers made a few costly mistakes), it is very natural for the international community to suggest a few changes in the way Asia makes use of its funds. This has put the IMF in an awkward situation where the savior is treated as a censor, responsible for the miseries of millions of people. This is wrong, and unfair to the IMF.

The IMF Prescription

Conceptually, there is nothing odd about the lender imposing conditions on the borrower. Banks all over the world — banks with good credit culture, that is — routinely impose restrictions to the use of the money they lend to households and companies. The borrower's ability to repay principal and interest in a timely fashion is a crucial factor in the lending decision. A lender is often in a position to make constructive suggestions to improve the borrower's repaying capacity. In many cases, those suggestions turn into conditions that must be fulfilled by the borrower before the lender parts with its funds. It is not unnatural for the borrower to disagree with those suggestions and conditions. Depending on the relative strengths of the two parties — there are desperate lenders as well as desperate borrowers — an agreement can be reached that will satisfy both parties. In the present crisis, the borrowers were clearly not in a position to negotiate sweeter terms. Their only strength was in the realization that some help would be forthcoming regardless of their behavior as Korea, Indonesia and Thailand[2] are too important, economically and politically, for the world to let them sink under the burden of their mistakes. A collapse of any of them would have serious repercussions for the stability of Asia, and in turn for the fate of China and especially of Japan. This is a giant chess game where astute politicians can extract more than they are giving away.

Borrowers do therefore have some advantages in their negotiations with the IMF and other international lenders. They can play a game of refusing certain conditions imposed on them, while seemingly accepting other terms, knowing full well that, once the money is in the till, they can always back away from their promises. If this is too embarrassing to engineer, circumstances can always be created which would make the reforms ostensibly untenable. This is well perceived by some of the lenders. The American Congress has played a mirroring game of threatening not to vote for the financial support needed by the IMF. While it is acceptable, as said earlier, that lenders insist on reasonable terms before the loans are disbursed, the American Congress seems to forget that the IMF loans are loans, not grants; they will probably be paid back with interest. On another front, it might perhaps be relevant to remind this particular lender that he is lending borrowed money, ironically from Asia: Japan has long been financing the US deficit. But this of course would not deter from the fact that, as a lender, the US Congress has to satisfy itself that its funds, whether or not in turn it borrowed them from outside, are used as wisely as possible.

What conditions exactly has the IMF been trying to impose on the various Asian countries in exchange for its support? A detailed analysis is not the purpose of this book, so a succinct description of the conditions will suffice. Whether those conditions were reasonable and whether it was justified for some of the countries to try and avoid them is a fruitless discussion.

Here are the terms under which IMF funds were made available to Korea, Indonesia and Thailand. At the time this book was written, Malaysia had yet to reach the point where it would seek help from the IMF, while the Philippines were still under a previous IMF support program whose terms may yet be reshuffled.

In all three countries, major principles were applied as follows:

- Non-financial institutions would not be bailed out under any circumstances on the strength of guarantees, subsidies or any public sector support using IMF funds.
- Financial institutions could be supported if only they have liquidity problems, while they remain solvent.

In the case of financial institutions, liquidity problems often bring them close to insolvency and any public sector support would be submitted to further conditions:

- Shareholders and, as much as possible, creditors of ailing institutions should carry the burden of the losses under appropriate bankruptcy procedures.

- Liquidity support can only be provided if adequate measures were taken to restructure and recapitalize the banks; the authorities would force a capital reduction and assume the management of the institutions.

If the situation warrants the support of the authorities, and commitments were made prior to negotiations with the IMF, the authorities were required to meet their obligations with minimal impact on their medium-term fiscal position. In all cases, the authorities would take measures to strengthen the economy in order to restore confidence and ensure that creditors would maintain their support.

Those general principles translated into specific measures in respect of the financial system of each of the three countries.

The IMF prescriptions included the recapitalization of banks to the standard 8%, and in some cases to higher levels. This is most unrealistic. It would be difficult enough to maintain banks of the distressed countries out of bankruptcy, owing to the mountain of bad loans that have started hitting them. As a result, the only tangible consequence of the IMF requirement was a severe credit crunch. Since fresh equity was difficult to come by, the only way for financial institutions to improve their capital ratios was to reduce lending. Banks were also careful to maintain higher liquidity than usual, owing to the uncertain situation, but the major factor behind the credit crunch seemed to be that strange fascination for high — if incorrect — capital adequacy ratios.

In addition to specific requirements in terms of the rehabilitation of the financial sector, the IMF imposed a number of general conditions, which can be described as follows:

- GDP growth rates must be reduced
- Short-term interest rates must be maintained relatively high
- Inflation must remain low
- Government budgets must be cut
- Financial markets must be more open to foreign investors
- Specific measures are negotiated with each country, for example, labor flexibility in Korea.

The IMF prescriptions are directed at long-term reform as well as at immediate needs. Clearly, high short-term interest rates are needed if currencies are to be stabilized. Inflation must be contained if the countries wish to enjoy the benefits of devaluation. Taking a longer-term view, GDP growth is welcomed but must be accompanied with adequate growth of the capabilities of the financial sector. More controversial is the prescription that governments should cut their budgets and, especially, that they should open financial markets to foreigners.

Many voices in Asia were raised against the IMF conditions and, generally, about its role prior and during the crisis. Many accusations are pitifully simplistic, but some of them did carry weight. In any event, what the Asian person in the street thought of the IMF prescriptions could be regarded very much like the reaction of the average European to the Maastricht Treaty: austerity measures are

IMF in Korea

- Prior to the IMF rescue package, the government had guaranteed deposits made by all domestic depositors. Efforts will have to be made to replace those guarantees with the protection of small depositors only.
- The Korean Asset Management Corporation (KAMC), which buys impaired assets without recourse from distressed financial institutions, will do so at prices reflecting their actual realizable value.
- If institutions are closed, only insured creditors will be compensated, not the shareholders or uninsured creditors.
- All merchant banks must submit rehabilitation plans, especially in respect of solvency and liquidity, and they will be closed if the plans are unrealistic or fail to be implemented. About half of them have actually been suspended pending potential rehabilitation.
- The government has taken control of two commercial banks (Korea First Bank and SeoulBank) with the intention to recapitalize and restructure them, possibly through the merger with other institutions or through an outright sale to foreign investors.

The total amount committed to the support of Korea is US$57 billion, of which:
- US$21 billion is from the IMF
- US$10 billion is from the World Bank
- US$4 billion is from the Asian Development Bank
- US$22 is billion from a group of industrial countries (Australia, Belgium, Canada, France, Germany, Italy, Japan, the Netherlands, Sweden, Switzerland, the UK and USA).

IMF in Indonesia

- There would be no support at all for private sector non-financial corporations.
- The government will introduce a deposit insurance scheme.
- Insolvent banks will be closed. Small depositors (with deposits of maximum Rs 20 million, or about US$1,000) would be compensated, but shareholders, creditors and large depositors would not receive any support, and their claims would be treated according to bankruptcy laws. By April 1998, only 16 such banks had been liquidated.
- Weak banks would be rehabilitated either on their own or through mergers. In April 1998, a number of potential mergers were announced.

- Any liquidity loans provided by the government would be collaterized and submitted to stringent conditions, to include punitive interest rates. Such exceptional assistance would be restricted to situation where systemic risk is a consideration. State and regional development banks would be downsized and gradually privatized.

The total amount committed to the support of Indonesia is US$40 billion, of which:
- US$10 billion is from the IMF
- US$4.5 billion is from the World Bank
- US$3.5 billion is from the Asian Development Bank
- US$17 billion is from a group of countries (Australia, China, Hong Kong SAR of China, Japan, Malaysia, Singapore and the USA)
- US$5 billion is directly from Indonesia's contingency reserves.

IMF in Thailand

- New, stricter loan classification and provisioning rules would apply to all commercial banks.
- Banks that could not meet capital requirements would see a capital reduction and management taken over by the authorities. By April 1998, four of the 15 commercial banks fell into that category.
- 56 out of 91 finance companies were suspended, with shareholders equity and subordinated debt written down and creditors' and depositors' claims restructured.
- The remaining finance companies would see creditors' and depositors' claims honored by the Financial Institution Development Fund (FIDF), a government-owned body.
- No public funds (through the FIDF) would be devoted to the recapitalization of finance companies, and any liquidity support would come at relatively higher interest rates.

The total amount committed to the support of Thailand is US$17.2 billion, of which:
- US$4 billion is from the IMF
- US$1.5 billion is from the World Bank
- US$1.2 billion is from the Asian Development Bank
- US$10.5 billion is from a group of countries (Australia, Brunei, China, Hong Kong SAR of China, Indonesia, Japan, Korea, Malaysia and Singapore).

imposed from the outside world. Naturally, local politicians would play on the misunderstanding and deflect any criticism away from their administration by pointing at the harsh conditions imposed on their citizens by foreign intruders. They would conveniently avoid pointing out that the reforms were necessary in any event.

What are those reforms, all of which are among the prescriptions imposed or suggested by the IMF?

A) Growth reduction

Growth must be reduced. It is the most obvious remedy, as it is at the root of the crisis. This requirement is akin to speed limits on highways. The car might have the power it needs, and be safe at high speeds. The driver might very well be skilled. Her wish to arrive as soon as possible at her destination might be legitimate. Yet the road is winding and narrow and there might be obstacles of all kinds. The driver may have the skill to drive fast on a wide, straight highway, she is simply not used to difficult driving.

It is easy to reduce growth. Central banks can easily control the volume of credit. Generally, authorities have a large arsenal of tools that can be used to penalize growth, such as liquidity, taxes and the constriction of credit transactions in capital markets and the financial sector in general. Much has been said about the negative impact supposedly affecting the markets following the IMF suggestion of lower growth. But in fact, a mechanical result of the crisis is precisely a slowdown, perhaps a contraction of the economies. Countries do not need an IMF prescription to reach that objective as Table 10.2 shows.

TABLE 10.2   GDP GROWTH: 1ST QUARTER 1998

	GDP
Thailand	+0.4
Singapore	+5.6
Hong Kong	−2.0
Indonesia	−6.2
Philippines	+1.7
South Korea	−3.8
Malaysia	−1.8
China	+7.2
Taiwan	+5.9

Source: Capital Information Services

Lower growth might seem to be innocuous. Many OECD countries have posted anemic growth rates for several years. They exhibit a number of structural weaknesses but none of them is the direct result of low growth. It can be argued that, if a relatively low growth rate is tolerable in the OECD countries, it should be the same in East Asia. The situation is not as simple as that, and it has to do with human nature. The bulk of Asia's managers have only known growth. There have been hiccups, like in the mid-1980s, but growth has long been the norm. All individual and collective behaviors have been modeled on a system that promises tomorrow to be bigger and better than yesterday. Expectations have set in that would never imagine a less promising future.

The consumption patterns of late, in all of East Asia, clearly demonstrate this fact. Consumer and credit card lending have exploded. It is as if both the present generation, often born to some wealth and comfort, and the previous one, the generation that built that wealth, have suddenly agreed to enjoy the fruits of the former's labor. The savings rate remains extremely high, but income levels have improved and the absolute amounts available for consumption have grown considerably. Hence the explosion of consumer markets all over East Asia. That growth has brought along a number of dislocations, particularly affecting financial intermediaries specialized in consumer lending. When growth slows down, a number of borrowers at the fringe start suffering and they are responsible for asset quality problems among fringe money lenders, who in turn create liquidity and asset quality problems in the entire banking system. This has been particularly obvious in Thailand and in Malaysia.

The adjustment to low growth will be slow and painful in most East Asian countries. An entire generation, perhaps even two generations must suddenly adjust to the new parameters. Projects and investments that made some sense in a high growth environment will have to be abandoned. Tomorrow's expanded economy will no longer be able to pay for today's optimistic investment decisions.

B) Low inflation

Inflation is generally seen as evil. It creates a number of problems that would require much space if discussed here. High among them is its influence on real interest rates and on the investment decision process. Inflation has not been much of a problem in East Asia during the past 30 years, and certainly not in comparison to other developing regions.

The financial crisis did not only bring negative developments. The substantial devaluation of many currencies should improve the terms of trade in favor of East Asia. Other things being equal, the distressed East Asian nations should build on the situation to increase exports, using the price advantage created by the devaluation. This advantage is eroded by two factors. Firstly, the devaluation has made imports more expensive and, to the degree — rather high in East Asia — that exported products have a high import content, the price advantage is amputated. Secondly, inflation — eventually affecting salaries — will eat away at the competitive advantage. The countries that limit overall inflation will enjoy the maximum impact of the devaluation.

Speed of a Speed

It looks odd and it is wrong to talk about "slow growth". "Low growth" is the correct term in most circumstances. Growth is a speed. GDP growth is the derivative of GDP over time (a measure of how much it changes over a period of one year). If growth is a speed, it can be a high speed or a low speed. The notion of "fast" or "slow" is itself a notion of speed. The speed of a speed is called acceleration. It is the derivative of a derivative. While a high-speed boat moves at high speed, a fast-speed boat would move under a high acceleration, not necessarily at very high speed. A fast GDP growth means a GDP growth that grows, for example from 0.1% last year to 0.2% this year, while a high GDP growth means a GDP growth that is high but not necessarily getting bigger every year, for example 8% last year and 7.8% or 8.3% this year. A fast GDP growth can characterize a low GDP growth that grows quickly over time but remains low.

The level at which currencies eventually stabilize is a very relevant factor in the rehabilitation of the banking system, since most banks must now carry their delinquent borrowers' foreign currency positions. Other competitive factors being equal, inflation tends to eliminate the competitive results of devaluation, and similarly currencies get devalued if inflation creeps in. If one of the distressed economies suffers a domestic inflation of 20% more than that of its neighbors, it will have to see its currency devalued roughly by 20% to maintain the same relative competitiveness. The inflation differential is an important factor in the ultimate relative value of currencies in the region. There are clear signs that Indonesia is facing a situation of overblown inflation, and it is crucial that efforts be made to control it. Without a stabilization of inflation, all the benefits associated with the suffering of devaluation will be wasted.

TABLE 10.3   INFLATION

	1994 (%)	1995 (%)	1996 (%)	1997 (%)
Thailand	5.1	5.8	4.8	8.0
Indonesia	9.2	8.6	6.6	11.6
Malaysia	3.7	3.4	3.8	2.8
Korea	6.2	4.5	5.0	4.5
Philippines	9.1	10.9	5.1	6.0

Source: Thomson BankWatch Inc.

Yet the undesirable effects of inflation might very well be a minor consideration when compared to its advantages. In any situation where inflation is higher than interest rates, borrowers enjoy negative real interest rates: the principal they owe is losing more value than the interest they pay. There is a net wealth transfer from lender to borrower. In particular for governments, it is a painless way out of crippling debts. The trick has been used time and again, in Europe for instance. It seems more probable by the day that East Asian countries will have to nationalize most of their banks, one way or another, transferring huge liabilities from the market to the taxpayer. A government can inflate its currency out of its predicament: its debt burden will be lighter. Putting aside the moral angle, the nationalization of bad debts and the engineering of negative real interest rates, brought about by inflation, would hasten the rehabilitation of the financial systems. The huge debts remaining on the books of highly geared companies would also benefit.

C) Budget cuts

One way or another, whether they guarantee the liabilities of financial institutions or they buy them outright, governments will suffer substantial budget outlays, which are bound to create fiscal deficits. Most East Asian governments have long been models of frugality when compared to Western governments.

TABLE 10.4   GOVERNMENT FINANCE: GOVERNMENT SURPLUS/ DEFICIT AS A PERCENTAGE OF GDP

	1991 (%)	1992 (%)	1993 (%)	1994 (%)	1995 (%)	1996 (%)	1997 (%)	1998p (%)
Thailand	4.7	2.8	2.1	1.8	3.0	1.6	−0.6	−2.0
Philippines	−2.1	−1.2	−1.5	1.1	0.5	0.3	0.0	−0.2
Malaysia	−4.4	−4.2	0.2	2.4	0.5	1.0	1.3	2.5
Korea	−1.6	−0.5	0.6	0.3	0.6	−0.3	−0.5	−2.0
Indonesia	−0.4	0.2	−0.2	−0.5	0.8	0.5	−1.0	−3.2

Source: Thomson BankWatch Inc.

It might seem to be a good idea to suggest budget cuts in preparation for the deficits to come. The fiscal balance will be negatively affected both by a slowdown in the economy and by the private sector liabilities assumed by the governments.

The other side of the coin is that budget cuts have a negative social impact, at a time when selective government support is needed in various sectors of the economies. Therefore it boils down to taking difficult decisions in respect of government expenditure in large projects. This is why governments started downscaling or scrapping several large infrastructure projects, in particular in Indonesia and Thailand.

The IMF is justifiably worried that inflation would increase if deficits are tolerated. But the effects of deficits on inflation pale in comparison to the imported inflation the currency adjustments are bringing with them.

Perhaps it would be interesting to remember that some governments create fiscal deficits without telling the world. When a government uses its state-owned banks as a conduit for subsidies and neglects to reimburse the banks from its current budget, it effectively conceals the deficit in the books of the banks. This situation is obvious in the case of China, for example.

D) High short-term interest rates

Short-term interest rates should remain high for some time. This is a measure destined to slow the devaluation of the currencies and to stabilize them eventually. There is a crisis of confidence that has the mechanical effect of moving considerable amounts out of East Asian currencies and into foreign currencies. This phenomenon not only affects investors and speculators, but also the natural holders of domestic currencies, the person in the street as well as the company treasurer, especially in countries where there are few barriers against holding foreign currency. If the short-term interest rates are unattractive, more funds will flee the currency and considerable efforts will have to be made to attract them back.

Yet this is a very controversial measure as it has a seriously negative impact on the economies. Asian companies traditionally rely more on short-term funding than their counterparts in the rest of the world. Short-term funds are expensive and hard to secure. There is a general credit crunch in Asia at present, prompted by several factors: the Japanese banks must reduce total assets in order to meet capital adequacy ratios, the Western banks lick their wounds and the Asian banks cannot or dare not expand. For any Asian borrower, this is the worst possible time to restructure its liabilities towards the longer term.

High interest rates tend to choke the economy at a time when companies need as much ammunition as possible to make use of the window of opportunity afforded by the devaluation: they have suddenly become much more competitive. Furthermore, high interest rates translate, for delinquent borrowers, into a snowballing burden of compounded interest. Their capacity to repay their loans, ravaged by the crisis, is made worse by the day. NPLs grow much faster. Note that under good accounting practice (not always adhered to in Asia, as explained in Chapter 3 on Bank Accounting), the interest charged to delinquent borrowers is put in reserve rather than counted as income. In that case, NPLs do grow, but so do loan loss reserves. However, the bank's net income falls by the same amount, since the bank does not receive interest while it still has to remunerate — expensively — the funding side.

It is generally said that low interest rates would help banks in distress clear their books. This worked out quite well when US banks ran into trouble in the 1980s. One can even argue that the interest policy of the US at that time was partly geared to rescue the banking system. In Japan, however, perennially low interest rates have failed to rescue the banks, which, it must be stressed, suffer from various ailments not found in the US banks.

There is little doubt that a policy of low interest rates would facilitate the rehabilitation of East Asian banks today. Yet clearly there are superior motives why rates have to be maintained high. The IMF and various governments must find a middle ground between opposing strategies with such dramatically different effects.

E) Financial markets should be opened to foreign investors

The reasoning behind that suggestion is fairly simple: banking systems need reconstruction and only foreign banks can afford such huge amounts of capital. Besides, the banking systems have proven to be unable to behave properly, and only foreign banks are able to instill high standards of good banking. This approach is flawed in many ways, and it is important to give it much attention.

Granted, a major impediment in the implementation of capital market reforms is the lack of skills available in the region. In contrast, when it comes to the simple techniques of money lending, Asia has little to learn from the West. Note that this statement is not incompatible with this book's main message: that greed, cheating and stupidity in commercial banking have brought the systems down. But what Asia ought to do is to develop its capital markets urgently and it needs the West to do a good job of it.

Better capital markets will streamline the access of borrowers to adequately tailored funding, both from domestic and international sources. Yet this will not eliminate some of the problems that brought about the crisis.

In particular, the commercial banking system calls for a considerable amount of attention. Unfortunately, this presents a number of obstacles. It would be too simplistic to assume that a strong foreign bank could step into an Asian country, take over a local institution, and turn it around in the present context. There would be considerable hurdles to negotiate. Cultural differences is one. Accusations of neocolonialism is another.

The entire commercial banking system of Indonesia had assets of approximately US$155 billion at the end of 1996, sustained by about US$10 billion in capital funds. Thanks to the rupiah devaluation, the asset total has probably fallen to approximately US$55 billion in June 1998. The capital funds needed to sustain US$55 billion in assets represent approximately US$3.5 billion. This, we know, is not the going price of all bank shares in the country, since it should be adjusted for goodwill and other factors, but it gives some idea of the amount on a theoretical basis. The amount is in the vicinity of the profits made in one year or two by banking groups like HSBC, Deutsche Bank or Citibank. In theory, they could sign a check and take over the entire banking system of Indonesia in one afternoon. Other figures and comparisons are possible, but one major fact remains: the banking systems of Asia are so small that foreigners can buy them out easily.

Watchdogs

No risk manager would make a business decision without balancing the strengths and weaknesses of the target, and being well-informed is paramount. The decision rests with those who risk their funds, but they tend to rely on the opinion of others, owing to the diversity and the complexity of the investment opportunities. No one is foolish to the point of relying on a single source or a single grouping of sources of information for a risk decision, but bodies like the rating agencies, information and risk monitoring agencies, and the IMF among others, do provide warnings both to the lenders and to the borrowers.

That such warnings are seldom heeded is another matter altogether. Most lenders maintain armies of researchers who draw from a large variety of sources. The market cannot reasonably expect the likes of the IMF and the rating agencies to carry the burden of being right, and look wrong; when everybody else looks right, but is wrong. Had the consensus from all sources been negative on Asia, the lenders would not have expanded their exposure as they did. Singling out the IMF or the rating agencies for their own failures is inappropriate. As a matter of fact, the IMF and some rating agencies did send the correct signals.

The IMF as a Watchdog

Some commentators accuse the IMF of having misread early signs of trouble in Asia and of having done little to avoid difficulties before they got out of hand. The IMF is accused of maintaining a shroud of secrecy around its own decision-making process, and of being accountable only to its own convoluted bureaucracy.

It might appear at first that the IMF did not see the crisis coming. It recently published several excerpts from board discussions. The IMF might have said this: "Directors strongly praise Thailand's remarkable economic performance and the authorities' consistent record of sound macroeconomic policies" and also: "Directors welcome Korea's continued macroeconomic performance... praise the authorities for their enviable fiscal record." But on Indonesia it clearly said: "Directors urged the authorities to address weaknesses in the banking sector..." (See full text in Appendix 1.)

But should the IMF be blamed for getting it wrong, or not sufficiently right? On traditional fundamentals, Asia was doing fine. This crisis has now told the world that fundamentals should not be the only factors in deciding whether a country is humming along well. But is this IMF in charge of rewriting the rules? More importantly, is it in fact true that the IMF was blind to any of the warning signs? It was not. Perhaps it would have been difficult to associate specific warning signs to an impending crisis, but indeed the IMF and some Western governments did suggest to Asian governments that there were unsettling problems.

After the 1994 Mexican crisis, for example, Thailand was told to reconsider the level of short-term borrowings on the books of a weakening financial system, and to attend to its high current account deficit. But the Thai government would not listen. Western governments and the IMF did not insist, as this would create political uneasiness. Even when Thailand became confronted with serious currency problems in early 1997, the reaction of its government was to turn to its neighbors and to hope for a regional solution to what they thought was a manageable problem. In fact, even after the Baht flotation in July 1997, the Thais would not immediately seek any kind of help from the IMF: it took them several weeks to do so. Malaysia has held the same view throughout the crisis. It becomes difficult to blame the IMF for not sending the right signals when the countries do not listen anyway. Perhaps the international community at large is to blame for not insisting on a more sophisticated early warning system, but this would have carried geopolitical implications that are simply not politically correct in this day and age.

The Rating Agencies

On April 18, 1997, barely a few weeks before the collapse of dozens of Thai finance companies triggered the Asian panic, a major rating agency wrote in a published report: "Despite the much talked-about oversupply of housing, we found little evidence, as at February, of significant problems in the finance companies' real estate development loan portfolios. While this form of lending is clearly more risky, on the whole finance companies appear to take reasonable precautions, such as requiring an appropriate level of pre-sales before making a commitment. Most real estate lending is to low rise, stand-alone residential estate developments, which are inherently less risky than condominium developments." The document ended with, "We do not expect a repeat of the mid-1980s banking crisis, when a rash of defaults occurred across the sector."

MIT Professor Paul Krugman said that he was 95% wrong in predicting the crisis, but that the others got it 150% wrong. Have rating agencies failed to warn the world of the impending disaster? This is indeed all a matter of degree. Two of the three major agencies that rate countries accepted that they did not see it coming, while the third one said it was better than its rivals. All three rated the sovereign risk of the distressed countries higher than the pricing of debt would reveal after the crisis had erupted.[3] Did the agencies do anything wrong? Probably not.

It is a fact that, on the basis of the fundamentals normally used in assessing sovereign risk, the rating agencies cannot be faulted. What was wrong, perhaps, was their reliance on those fundamentals. The markets themselves were relying on fundamentals and the pricing of Asia's debt just prior to the crisis confirms that fact. It would be a vain exercise to single out the agencies. Most of the brokerage houses and investment banks were unanimous in praising Asia as a good risk. The truth is that nobody predicted the extent of the crisis, because the contagion that spread from Thailand to other countries had no precedent in the history of such crises.

Thomson BankWatch is usually not mentioned in the various articles and studies lambasting the rating agencies, simply because its focus is on bank ratings. It is in fact the world's largest provider of ratings and scorings on banks, covering over 1,100 names in over 80 countries. Thomson BankWatch does have sovereign risk ratings, but they are used only as caps for bank debt ratings. No sovereign state commissions ratings from Thomson BankWatch, and therefore this rating company does not have access to information other than that available to the public.

But Thomson BankWatch publishes numerous banking system reports and it has assigned scorings and ratings to Asian banks for many years. Well ahead of the crisis, the firm warned its subscribers of the impending problems of the banking systems of now distressed countries. As early as March 1995, calling the circumstances a "lethal cocktail", the analysts noted in presentations and accompanying materials that the Thai banks were mixing low liquidity with an overindulgence for short-term US dollar borrowings. At the end of 1995, they were saying that, on average, the Korean banks — not all of them — were close to bankruptcy. By the end of 1996, they said that most were bankrupt — again not all — and that was well before Hanbo, Jinro and Kia started kicking. Since 1991, they have ranked Indonesian banks among the most risky in the world. They were not generous either when talking about Malaysian banks. The ratings and scorings assigned to banks between 1994 and July 1997 clearly show how negative they were.

Thomson BankWatch warned its subscribers on many occasions at a time when investors and lenders were seemingly blind to potential problems looming in Asian banking systems.

Thomson BankWatch embedded those warnings in ratings and scorings that were very punitive for some banks. In fact the ratings made a clear distinction between good and bad names, to the point that the crisis verified those ratings. Almost all the banks that met with failure or near-failure during the crisis had been poorly rated by Thomson BankWatch for at least three years, and those who survived had consistently been rated highly. This, one might object, is easy: after all everybody knows the strength of Thai Farmers Bank or of Shinhan Bank, and anybody could guess that Korea First Bank was weak. But the difficulty always lies in names that are not so obviously in one camp or the other. This is where Thomson BankWatch did extremely well, an outcome that is attributable to the analysts going beyond the reported numbers in an attempt to understand the underlying dynamics of banking in Asia.

The Credit Rating Agencies

Investors and lenders rely on credit rating agencies in a variety of ways. Those who have their own analytical capabilities require a second or a third opinion on a given risk. Those who would rather subcontract the research, or whose transaction volume would not justify a substantial investment in research tend to rely mostly on one or more rating agencies.

Rating agencies belong to two main categories, along three different criteria: on the basis of the nature of the ratings, in the matter of recognition and following the source of their income.

The nature of the ratings is varied but the two main categories are the debt ratings and the company ratings. The debt ratings apply to a specific debt or category of debt and are very much a measure of risk, with a horizon of several years. The test is: What hope do we hold that the borrowers will honor their commitment to pay in a timely fashion? By contrast, a company rating looks at the firm as a whole and is a mixed measure of risk and performance — not profit only, but all aspects of staying within norms. In this case, the test becomes: Is the company safe for a risk exposure within a 12 to 18-month horizon, meant to capture most current commercial transactions? Sovereign debt ratings fall into the debt ratings category. Most agencies use different scales to distinguish debt ratings from company ratings, and the long from the short term.

The recognition of the rating agencies by regulatory watchdogs around the world will determine whether they are merely domestic, regional, or if their rating have an international recognition. Market recognition is also important, but a certificate of authenticity by the big boys in New York, Tokyo, Hong Kong and London is certainly a minimum for undisputed respect. Only a handful of agencies claim to rate names on a global basis: Moody's, Standard & Poor's, Thomson BankWatch, Fitch-IBCA and Duff & Phelps. All are active in Asia.

The source of income is two-fold: countries and companies pay a rating fee, while investors and lenders pay a retainer fee to receive the rating information. The various agencies tend to focus more on one source or the other, with Moody's and S&P's firmly in the first category and Thomson BankWatch firmly in the second category.

All the agencies have an excellent record for predicting the likelihood of default.

About Thai Banks

The banks cook the books

"The bank's profitability is overstated in its accounts. The bank has taken provisions directly from retained earnings to loan loss reserves on the balance sheet... The amounts transferred equated to 46% and 44% of the after-tax profits for 1994 and 1993 respectively... In itself the transfer is not a major concern... The concern is that this may reflect the bank's management style and that other parts of the accounts are not a true reflection of its position."

Thomson BankWatch report on Siam City Bank, September 14, 1995.

"This is a reflection of how serious the asset quality problem was and is at the bank. Its reported profits are not a true reflection of the underlying profitability of the bank. It makes provisions each year to the extent profits can bear... The impact is that profit has been grossly overstated in the past."

Thomson BankWatch report on Bangkok Bank of Commerce, May 22, 1996.

Asset quality is worse than it appears

" When considering the write-offs and changes in provisions, ...either the bank has not been prudent in determining which assets needed to be provided for or more problems are arising at a fast rate. Neither scenario is comforting for creditors."

Thomson BankWatch report on First Bangkok City Bank, July 12, 1995.

"Given that most collateral is comprised of real estate, in a fragile market with, perhaps, generous appraisal values, the requirements [for loan loss provisions] are arguably too low. Therefore it is no comfort for a bank to claim to have exceeded Bank of Thailand's requirements."

Thomson BankWatch report on Bank of Asia, July 19, 1996.

The banks maintain low liquidity, and they borrow excessively in foreign currency

"This reliance on overseas funds may offer immediate cost savings, but may impact the bank's liquidity in times of financial stress. In early 1995 there was a substantial withdrawal of capital from Thailand. The Bank of Thailand protected the currency and assisted the liquidity of the market. Problems may arise again and if they are more severe, the liquidity of some members of the banking industry will be tested."

Thomson BankWatch report on Bank of Asia, July 15, 1995.

"Generally speaking, external observers have long been tolerant of the low liquidity ratios, drawing comfort from Bank of Thailand's long established practice of offering protection to institutions in trouble. Recent events surrounding the Bangkok Bank of Commerce have eroded confidence in the Bank of Thailand's capacity to identify and address potential problems in the banking industry."
Thomson BankWatch report on Siam City Bank, July 17, 1996.

If the risk perception on Thailand rises, the banks will be in trouble

"The rate of provisioning in the past appeared to be more the result of how much the bottom line can bear rather than a reflection of changing asset quality... Exacerbating the bank's low liquidity is its growing reliance on foreign borrowings... If the capital flight by foreigners in early 1995 is repeated it may test the bank's already slim resources.... If international markets were to withdraw funding on a large scale from Thailand, the bank may have to seek assistance..."
Thomson BankWatch report on Union Bank of Bangkok, June 30, 1995.

About Korean Banks

True ratios are very low

"Korea's banking industry is now emerging from a long period of strict regulatory control, and as has been noted in earlier reports, the banks are ill-equipped to deal with the changes associated with deregulation and liberalization of the financial markets. Poor asset quality, low profitability and comparatively weak capital measures remain fundamental characteristics of many of the country's banks."
Thomson BankWatch Banking System Update on Korea, October 17, 1996.

Credit culture is inadequate

"The traditionally tight management of the banks by the government has had its benefits in the past, yet as deregulation continues, many of the underlying problems facing the banks have surfaced and it is clear that these will not be resolved easily. Perhaps one of the most important is the lack of a strong credit culture... Unfortunately, the government-imposed policy lending of the past has left many of the banks (particularly the old, nationwide commercial banks) with heavy bad debt problems (although documenting the magnitude of these problems is very difficult given the absence of meaningful disclosure). Resolution of these asset quality issues is one of the key hurdles facing the banks in the current environment. Other challenging issues include such structural problems as the relatively weak capital positions of most banks, bureaucratic management systems, overcapacity, and rising labor costs".

Thomson BankWatch Banking System Report on Korea, December 1994.

Asset quality is worse than it appears

"Further, the rising bankruptcy levels are also likely to be indicative of an expansion in substandard loans as well, and... these problem asset totals are believed to be much higher than the "official" figures presented. At this stage it appears that despite the government's efforts to require the banks to improve their reserves against problem assets, the bad debt problem which has long plagued the Korean banking sector will continue to persist, at least in the intermediate term. This is particularly troublesome when one considers that Korea's economy has been generally quite healthy in recent periods. Should the economy show signs of easing, the probability of sharply higher levels of problem assets would likely be high."

Thomson BankWatch Banking System Update on Korea,
September 29, 1995.

"The government's financial sector regulator, the Office of Bank Supervision, has developed a bad debt classification system which is quite similar to that employed by US regulators. However, public disclosure of asset quality data has traditionally been limited to just the amounts included in the two most severe categories... the difference between this definition and one including substandard credit is reportedly a five-fold multiple for most major banks."

Thomson BankWatch report on Dongnam Bank, November 21, 1995.

Risk is highly concentrated

"Nominally, the bank has been able to extricate itself from the debacle over You One's collapse with its loan restructuring agreement with Hanbo but in its place is a potentially worryingly large exposure to the Hanbo group... this massive debt from one company amounts to... a whopping 51% of [the bank's] consolidated equity... To say that this situation is anything but healthy would be an understatement and if the fate of You One and Woosung are anything to go by, a highly distressing picture of the state of the bank's loan book is beginning to emerge."

Thomson BankWatch report on Korea First Bank, August 13, 1996.

About Indonesian Banks

Asset quality is lower than it appears

"Indonesia's economy does not exactly enjoy stable market forces, and the growth of the private sector in terms of banking assets is bound to create the potential for large amounts of bad loans. It is simply not realistic for almost every private sector bank to claim that its loan portfolio is clean, its loans collaterized and its provisions adequate... Furthermore, such rapid portfolio growth continues to raise asset quality concerns."

Thomson BankWatch report on Bank Lippo, December 13, 1995.

"While private banks tend to be more efficient than their state counterparts and do not find their operations hobbled by state directed lending, they are not without their own set of problems. As many are owned by or associated with large business groups they are under enormous pressure to extend credit beyond regulatory limits. In addition, the industry's rapid expansion has resulted in a severe shortage of trained staff, forcing banks to put personnel in decision-making roles with a minimum of preparation. Poor credit decisions have inevitably resulted. While the private sector's NPL problems are a fraction of those faced by the state sector, they do not have the implicit government support that state banks enjoy. Although the authorities have engineered rescues of failing private banks in the past, there is no assurance this will continue in the future."

Thomson BankWatch Banking System Update on Indonesia, June 1996.

"A major area of concern is asset quality. Like most of Indonesia's banks, this bank has grown its portfolio in recent years at a punishing rate. As with portfolios everywhere, the true quality of a creditor does not become apparent to outside observers until well after the bank is aware that problems exist. The experience in Indonesia is that this delay is rather longer than one would find in many other jurisdictions. After posting years of rapid growth, one can only conclude that a major reckoning is at hand... Nothing suggests that this bank will be able to escape this reality."

Thomson BankWatch report on Bank Utama, December 6, 1996.

Banks resort to related-party lending

"There are a number of other changes we would want to see implemented, particularly in the field of bad debt recognition and in the field of related-party lending, where some banks have found convenient but dangerous loopholes in the regulations."

Thomson BankWatch Banking System Update on Indonesia, October 13, 1995.

"It must be stated that it is possible for any bank in Indonesia to report figures in compliance with regulations while actual exposure to intergroup lending or volatile economic sectors, such as real estate, is considerably higher. This can be accomplished through indirect means..."
Thomson BankWatch report on several Indonesian banks, January 1996.

Growth rates and concentration of risk are too high

"Also a cause for concern is that the bank's loan portfolio appears to be heavily concentrated in a few key areas... Given the opportunities offered by Indonesia's diverse economy, it is difficult to see why such an allocation is necessary. The punishing rate of growth that its loan portfolio has sustained in the past few years and the rapid growth in its contingent accounts are but two further areas of concern... Hovering near the industry average for years, its [liquidity ratio] has fallen significantly below the local average and is too low by any standard."
Thomson BankWatch report on Bank Dagang Nasional Indonesia (BDNI),
December 11, 1996.

By 1995, Thomson BankWatch had already assigned to the banks of Thailand, Korea and Indonesia rating or scorings that, on average, were below the line separating the safe banks from the others. Since a number of banks were maintained artificially above the line because of their status as government-controlled institutions, the average for private-sector banks was in fact lower.

Naturally, rating and scoring adjustments took place between 1995 and April 1998, but they were extremely modest: 7/10th of a notch on average for Thailand, 2/10th of a notch for Korea and 3/10th of a notch for Indonesia (there are four notches between the maximum score and the minimum score). This indicates that Thomson BankWatch had discounted the banks' weakness as early as two years before the crisis. Furthermore, in the case of both Thailand and Korea, half — in value, not in numbers — of those minor adjustments took place prior to the crisis. As many as 60% of all ratings in Thailand and 25% of all ratings in Korea did not even require any adjustments after the beginning of the crisis. The adjustments in Indonesia were marginally more severe, owing to the stronger impact of the devaluation of the currency.

In short, the situation in the three most distressed countries did not prompt any substantial adjustments to the Thomson BankWatch bank ratings between 1994 and 1998, in sharp contrast to the sovereign risk ratings. The banks that were rated badly in 1995 all met a cruel fate in the crisis, while almost all the banks that were found satisfactory in 1995 were still kicking in 1998. The ratings were generally low, both before and during the crisis.

None of the rating agencies predicted the crisis through their sovereign risk ratings. But as Moody's rightly suggests:[4] "Looking ahead, we do not believe that any methodology for sovereign risk assessment will ever be precise enough to predict such events." There are lessons to learn from what happened, and perhaps sovereign risk ratings will incorporate other ingredients of a less mechanical nature than the usual fundamentals.

Thomson BankWatch was lucky enough to be involved in the rating of banks in most of the Asian countries and was able to build up a solid understanding of the weaknesses of the banking systems. This translated into low bank ratings that, in conjunction with the warnings expressed in the ratings memoranda, were particularly ominous.

Endnotes

1. One would never emphasize enough the fact that many banks in Asia were doomed well before July 1997 and that a rehabilitation would have been necessary in any event.
2. Malaysia would enjoy less of a leverage due to the modest size of its economy and its population.
3. Long term debt ratings — to include sovereign ratings — are supposed to be just that: giving an estimate of the probability of repayment in the long term. There is a relatively consistent relationship between ratings and the pricing of the debt. After the panic hit Asia, the market started pricing the sovereign and quasi-sovereign debt of some distressed countries at levels that were dramatically more punitive than those suggested by the ratings. This was an overreaction, as demonstrated when spreads subsequently stabilized at a lower level. But that lower level pointed to a serious discrepancy with the pre-crisis pricing suggested by the ratings.
4. In a White Paper published in June 1998, Moody's defended its rating actions prior and during the crisis.

CONCLUSION 11

While Asia sped ahead in a delirium of growth, fueled by abundant liquidity from foreign lenders and investors, very few saw the sinister signs of an impending crisis. The Asia panic, responsible for the financial turmoil, started in July 1997 and, at the time of writing, was still on. But the Asia crisis itself has been brewing for several years. Thailand was ready for an implosion, and the Korean banks were bankrupt. Indonesia was brewing and Malaysia was day-dreaming. It can be argued that the long crisis that has plagued Japan since 1990 is nothing else but just another sign of the Asia crisis. More hiccups must be expected in the next few years and the source, with hindsight, will be traced back to the same origin: Asia grew stupendously since the 1960s and needed a rest. This is nothing short of a growth crisis, which would have affected each individual country at different times, along nature's own internal clock. What is remarkable about the Asia crisis is not that it happened, but that it happened the way it did: hitting five Asian countries — Thailand, Indonesia, Korea, Malaysia and the Philippines — with the same symptoms within a few short weeks.

What did the distressed countries have in common?

We have seen that each of the countries and in particular, Thailand, Korea, Malaysia and Indonesia, had built up the conditions for disaster. One could have imagined that there could be a domino effect among Asian banking systems, the rot in one spreading to the others. But it did not happen that way. The transmission belt was in the currency markets. There was a domino effect, but its roots were in the perception by all players that the ills of Thailand were a symptom of a regional malady. It has become fashionable in fact to predict contagious effects. Seen from a distance, in European or American board rooms and risk committees, some Asian countries look the same and any disruption in one of the economy's balance creates question marks on its neighbors. This is akin to the surprising attitude of the world's financial community when the Mexican peso crisis in late 1994 triggered negative views on most South East Asian currencies. There was some justification in this attitude after all, but it was indiscriminate and therefore more damaging than it should have been.

The contagion effect was compounded by two additional factors that seem to have grown in importance over the past few years: the cynicism of the financial community and the size of the speculative funds it can put into play. The so-called "Japan premium" and "Korea premium" imposed on those weak banking systems had little correlation with the actual incremental risk, very much like the pricing of Thai banks' international debt never made an obvious distinction among the large disparity of underlying risks. Where funds are directed and under what pricing are questions that are often addressed with scant regard for fundamentals. The matter is made worse by a degree of gregarious mentality, with the fate of financial systems remaining dependent on trends and fads. In other words, the markets price the risk in a highly artistic fashion, demanding a premium from relatively safe borrowers while showering funds on shaky names with no compensatory risk premium.

After all, pricing should all be a matter of arithmetic. Lenders need a premium to compensate them for the risk. Each deal carries a risk for which the lender needs a notional provision. Ignoring for a second the remuneration of the underlying equity as well as transaction and underlying costs, the lender must perceive, concealed in the interest spread, a mathematical reserve against default. That reserve is equal to the statistical expectation of default: if three one-year deals out of 100 similar deals are expected to turn sour, the reserve should be equal to 3%. There is no magic in that. In June 1998, right after Suharto's departure, the premium on the Indonesia's sovereign risk was 7%, against 4% on Korea. Theoretically, ignoring costs, this means that the market thinks that Indonesia has a 7% chance of defaulting, while Korea fares better at 4%. One of the difficulties in such pricing lies in the fact that there is hardly a statistical observation period:[1] Indonesia is not facing 100 opportunities to default, out of which it would survive 93 times. We are far from the recurrent observation that, year in year out, car loan defaults hit at a frequency of, say, 3.5%.

International players do not know emerging markets as well as they should, aided by the dismal levels of financial disclosure. As a result, pricing is haphazard. Since the risk perception is not even sustained or confirmed by market pricing behavior, investors and lenders act in a very gregarious fashion. The sheer size of funds searching for interesting plays, coupled with the development of, and easy access to, financial derivatives, has made it possible to devastate a target country's currency and banking system like never before.

It is debatable whether, on fundamentals, the markets had to savage the Thai baht the way they did. Of course, the rigid control maintained for several years over the baht's link to the dollar, made worse by a domestic addiction to dollar borrowing, was bound to designate the baht as a target, ahead of the Philippines' peso, Malaysia's ringgit or Indonesia's rupiah. The baht was defeated, in spite of Thailand's determination and reserves, while the much-trumpeted pact between some of the region's central banks came to nothing.[2] But the peso, for example, was considerably more correctly priced than the baht. Yet the peso was defeated, again not really on fundamentals, but largely because the perception was that it could not be successfully defended. Other currencies went down the same way. Clearly there was a domino effect among currencies.

Does the domino effect apply to the banking systems? It should not. To be sure, the same problems should produce the same results, and indeed some banking systems in the region seemed to be suffering from similar headaches. However, by definition, the domino effect would imply that bringing a banking system to its knees in one country would create the basis for propagation to the next potential victim in the near vicinity.

The domino effect seems likely to occur whenever the fortunes of the banking systems are overly dependent on monetary stability and on foreign currency funding. External observers often think that Asia is very homogeneous, when in fact banking systems are vastly different across the region, more varied than the economies in general. They exhibit strengths and weaknesses that it might be wise to pause for a moment and examine. We have explored several countries separately in previous chapters. Let us look now at the picture from a distance.

An Aerial View of the Banking Systems

The first point to make is that, more in Asia perhaps than anywhere else, sovereign risk and bank risk are often at variance. There are weak banks in low risk countries, like Taiwan and Japan, while higher risk countries like the Philippines or Sri Lanka harbor a number of strong private sector banks. It is in fact remarkable that some of the best banks of Asia on a stand-alone basis are located in high-risk countries. There is perhaps a Darwinian twist here.

The Asian financial systems are largely in the hands of governments. In many countries, there are a number of state-owned banks and banks operating under close government guidance. Such banks usually exhibit performance ratios that are largely artificial, essentially because their asset quality is abysmal. They are used as conduits for government development and fiscal policies. Loan classification and provisioning rules are largely inadequate. Such banks are not relevant to any kind of analytical approach.

In the pure private sector, reasonably good asset quality could only be found in Hong Kong and Singapore, with the Philippines and Malaysia at a distance.[3] Perhaps not surprisingly, those are also the countries where the regulatory authorities enjoy, at various degrees, the best reputations. Banks in Hong Kong, Singapore and the Philippines also have very high capital ratios. At the other extreme, banking systems in Korea, Japan, China, Thailand, Indonesia, Indochina and the Indian sub-continent suffer from low levels of asset quality.

Real estate problems hit the banks in various ways. Direct exposure to real estate borrowers varies largely across the region, with Hong Kong at the top of the list, followed by Thailand, Indonesia, Malaysia and the Philippines. Korea was relatively spared by that particular problem until the crisis hit. In all countries, real estate is used as collateral against most types of lending, compounding problems.

An unfortunate pawnshop mentality is still guiding many banking systems. Loans are extended on the strength of collateral without much regard for the ability of the borrower to repay principal and interest from its main line of activities. The way real estate affects the banks varies vastly. The general oversupply in Thailand and Macau did not immediately affect prices, because a substantial proportion of the surplus was in the hands of owners who did not borrow against their property, and had no pressing need to sell. The markets in Hong Kong, and perhaps in Singapore and Malaysia, were underpinned by genuine demand for more space by a population that was getting wealthier, until that wealth started dwindling. In the Philippines and Indonesia, some property sectors were healthy before the crisis, while others like commercial property and luxury condominiums were close to a stage of distress.

Low liquidity, as often as fraud or bad luck, has historically been responsible for bank failures. On that front, Thailand and Indonesia were always extremely weak, while Hong Kong, Singapore, Korea and the Indian sub-continent were comfortable. Liquidity is the key to survival. A bank can be bankrupt, unprofitable, and at the lower end of the asset quality spectrum, yet it can still be kept alive if the authorities give it enough liquidity and some leeway to cook the books. We are talking here of local currency liquidity. Foreign currency funding is another matter. Some banking systems were also highly dependent on such funding, Thailand, Korea and Indonesia in particular. Malaysia and the Philippines were less affected, while Taiwan, Hong Kong and Singapore were not relying on foreign funds for domestic development.

Efficiency measures the cost of operating the banks. Factors influencing efficiency include salaries, labor laws, industriousness, rent levels, management profligacy, the size of transactions and the number of branches. On that front, only Hong Kong, Singapore, Malaysia and Taiwan appear to remain slim. Korea, Indonesia and the Philippines, by contrast, are extremely inefficient.

Net interest margins remain the single largest source of income for banks in the region, and their level is largely determined by the interest rate structure, by the competition or lack of it, and by established practices. Hong Kong, India, Malaysia, Thailand, Indonesia and the Philippines enjoy high net interest margins, while Taiwan, China, Singapore and Japan have to make do with little raw material.

Interestingly, among inefficient banking systems, those in Indonesia and the Philippines were doing well before the crisis, simply because their interest margins remained high, but this was not to last. Korea has both relatively low interest margins and very low efficiency and this explains why its banks have been struggling for years.

Real operating profitability is seldom correctly measured by profit ratios, essentially because banks tend to prop up their insufficient income with non-recurrent investment gains, as in Taiwan and Korea, and thanks to unrealistic provisioning strategies which are responsible for the perennial presence of non-performing assets on their books. This lack of accounting realism is negatively affecting Japan, Korea, China, Taiwan, Thailand, Indochina, Indonesia and the sub-continent.

Finally, one has to combine all the factors to estimate the likely speed of recovery for a given bank. This would measure the number of years needed, in current circumstances, to generate the cash flow necessary to cover a given deficiency in asset quality. This is the most relevant measure of mitigating factors in bank risk analysis. What is needed is to forget the past, compare the losses to the stream of future profits and decide whether an ailing bank can recover on its own. Hong Kong, the Philippines, Indonesia, and to an extent Thailand, rank high on the list. Korea and Taiwan are at the bottom. This of course works only in the case of banks that have lost their capital only once. Anything beyond that would make natural recovery almost impossible. Some banks have lost their capital funds three or four times and are beyond repair.

In summary, one would be hard pressed to find two banking systems in Asia whose risk characteristics are similar. While it can be said that the currency turmoil has precipitated the bank crisis, and the ensuing slowdown in overall growth has made it even worse, most of the other factors would have affected Asian banks in vastly different ways. The mid-1980s asset quality crisis that affected most South East Asian countries left quite a few weak banking players in Thailand, Indonesia, the Philippines and Malaysia. A number of banks remained strong, but many weaker institutions survived between the two crises thanks to creative accounting and the perception that there was a degree of protection from the authorities.

Thus, the banking systems of the region entered 1997 in various degrees of decay. However, they were all potential victims to one factor: the risk perception of the international financial community, the panic factor. Over the past 15 years, domestic corporations and banks in many Asian countries have been borrowing funds from international lenders, mostly in US dollars. European and US banks have been big lenders, but Japanese and Korean institutions figure prominently on the lending side, while many names, especially from Korea, Thailand and Indonesia, feature on the borrowing side. A shift in perception translated into a liquidity crisis, starting with Thailand, and the rest is history.

But the truth is that the so-called 1997 crisis in fact started in 1988 in Indonesia with the banking reform. It started in the early 1990s in Thailand with the BIBF. It started in the mid-1980s in Korea with the end of the war economy model. It started in 1994 in Malaysia with overheating and grandiose expectations. The Philippines was under brackets for 10 years following the 1983 moratorium and its growth crisis would not have hit until the end of the century.

A Crisis of Growth

We have seen that each country had its own problems, fairly independent from — if at times similar to — the rest of the region, and we have suggested that the only transmission belt was the currency game, led by perception. But what really links all the countries is a growth crisis.

A large spectrum of commentators have pointed at the main causes of the crisis, privileging one cause or another as the *sine qua non* source of the events. They are right to the extent that the crisis would have indeed been less violent, less pronounced and less damaging had one or more of those causes been less substantial. It is suggested that the commentators are wrong if they do not recognize that this crisis has its efficient cause[4] in the inadequacy between financial markets and the growth they were supposed to assist.

East Asia has experienced in the past 40 years an average growth rate that no region of the globe has ever been able to sustain, leaping from poverty and, often, the ravages of war, to relatively sophisticated economies in literally no time. Some of those countries suffered from communism or self-inflicted shades of socialism and many had barely shed the burden of colonist oppression. Busy as they were building an export-oriented economy to pay for the ever-growing needs of a large population, they never paid much attention to establishing a sound financial structure. It is astounding that so high a proportion of the financial sector's assets are in the hands of governments, directly or indirectly, either in an efficient way or in a display of corrupt wastage.

With the exception of Japan, of relatively small Hong Kong and Singapore, and to a degree but with some serious flaws, of Malaysia, capital markets have never grown in tandem with economic growth. When it comes to banking, there is not a single Asian country that has been able to promote the creation of a banking system meeting the minimum standards along all of the following criteria: capital adequacy ratios, liquidity ratios, management skills, credit culture, provisioning rules, single borrower lending, related party lending, directed lending, quality of regulatory supervision and disclosure of financial information. Some countries have approached the minimum requirements, most obviously Hong Kong and Singapore, but for many, this has remained an elusive objective, if it ever was an objective at all.

Why have governments been so inept at creating the basic conditions for a safe banking system, while demonstrating an undisputed ability to promote the general development of their countries? As we saw, the answer is fuzzy, but it can be traced to cultural problems, to a pawnshop mentality and ultimately to greed. There is no simple explanation. There is, indeed, some positive correlation between general corruption levels and banking problems. There is also a negative correlation between the sophistication of the legal infrastructure and banking problems. There is a positive correlation between the influence of government in private sector decisions and banking problems. Less obvious is the correlation with education levels.

Whatever the real source of their weaknesses, banking systems in East Asia were to meet their fate in any event, dragging down whole economies to a grinding halt. We have seen that among the five distressed countries serious problems were bound to happen. The Korean banking industry, on aggregate, was already bankrupt at the end of 1996, before the Hanbo and Kia disasters. The Thai banking system was in a dangerously precarious imbalance as early as the end of 1994. Indonesia had been patching over its banking problems for a long time. Malaysia was inebriated by its apparent success and was indulging in unreasonable investment patterns. Banks in the Philippines were highly profligate, saved only by unnatural interest margins. Many other countries shared some of those weaknesses. We saw why they did not suffer the same fate.

The IMF wrote prescriptions for three of the five distressed countries that received its support following the crisis. The prescriptions give a large part to the rehabilitation of the banking sectors. If indeed they were at the source of the crisis, fixing them is a high priority. Yet one cannot address such substantial questions, and find a solution, in the limited time afforded to the countries by the IMF liquidity support. Undeniably, the process will be slow and governments will be tempted to cut corners. There are so many vested interests involved that one cannot expect to see a thorough rehabilitation of the banking systems. There is indeed a real danger that immediate problems will be fixed, but not fundamental ones, so that the banks will make the same mistakes all over again, leading to a fresh crisis within the next five years. Korea, in particular, could very well see a paralysis, not unlike the one bogging down Japan, simply because fundamental weaknesses like low efficiency are not addressed.

We have seen that the crisis has benefited some people and brought suffering to the masses. Who should pay? There is no time to try and apportion the blame. Swift action is imperative.

Suggestions

Like Cassandra, daughter of Priam, King of Troy, who correctly predicted the fall of the city but received little attention, Thomson BankWatch alerted its subscribers to impending problems in many banking systems well before the 1997 crisis. Many listened, but few would act on the dark predictions embedded in the fairly low ratings and scorings assigned to Asian banks in 1994 and 1995. The low ratings banks deserve today were already there by mid-1995, as more recent adjustments on some names usually did not exceed half a notch. It is easy to be wise after the act, but the old ratings are a testimony of the prescience of some analysts.

Making predictions in treacherous. At the time of writing (early June 1998), we are still largely mired in the crisis. Many developments have taken place, but many more are expected which cannot be factored in my judgment. I do not have the benefit of knowing those ulterior developments. Perhaps the reader will kindly keep this fact in mind.

Rather than making predictions, I would submit some suggestions. I do not claim to have better answers than anyone else. The idea is to share a few ideas. Some of them, by nature, pertain to the short term and are destined to stabilize the financial systems in turmoil. But we said that this crisis was much deeper, reaching back to mistakes built over several years, and some suggestions go beyond the crisis. In fact, I would have made almost all those recommendations even if the 1997 panic had not taken place.

1) Punish the shareholders of failed banks

There is no justification, moral or practical, for taxpayers and creditors to substitute for bank shareholders when capital funds have evaporated. Shareholders must lose the last cent they have invested before others are made to suffer. Furthermore, the authorities should force the shareholders to make good any related party lending found in the books. In practice, however, owing to the complicated company structure and the limited reach of the law, it is often difficult to establish a link between those borrowers and the shareholders.

In a situation where the shareholders have lost everything but the bank can be rehabilitated, several formulae exist that would maintain the shareholders in place, for all or part of their stake.

2) Rehabilitate the banks when possible

Let us examine the arithmetic of rehabilitation. In Chapter 3, we have discussed the notion of solvency and the artificial approaches suggested by various forms of capital adequacy ratios. Assuming the controversial 8% to be a safe and adequate level in the long run, what should be the attitude of regulators whenever a financial institution breaches that minimum level, usually following bad debt provisioning in excess of available current profits and excess equity reserves?

One could basically divide the various cases into three different situations: capital ratios are still positive; capital ratios are moderately negative; or capital ratios are strongly negative. It is naturally assumed here that the shareholders are not able or willing to inject fresh equity funds to cover the losses.

If capital funds are still positive after the mishap, regulators have to decide whether they remain sufficient to absorb the costs of liquidation. If so, they may very well favor rehabilitation over liquidation as this would affect neither taxpayers nor depositors. It would be a simple matter of supervision to ensure that no dividends are paid out and that all profits are retained in the institution until capital ratios are restored to the minimum level. For this rehabilitation to be successful, two conditions should be met, besides the unfettered determination of the regulators. Firstly, the mishap must be the consequence of short-lived problems and no further deterioration should be expected. Secondly, market circumstances — that is, interest rate structure, cost margins and other exogenous factors — should clearly point at a relatively short period of rehabilitation.

In the best of times, Korean commercial banks are unable to generate enough cashflow to restore capital funds in all but the mildest of mishaps. As an illustration, back in 1995 when the Asia crisis was yet to hit them seriously, the Korean banks could barely generate 0.65% of total assets, or about 1% of weighted assets,[5] in ready cash for rehabilitation purposes. Assuming circumstances remain similar, restoring their capital funds from 2% to 8% of weighted assets would take a dangerously long six years. Taiwanese banks are in no better position in that respect. The only countries whose banks exhibited substantial recovery potential were, prior to the crisis, the Philippines, Indonesia, Hong Kong and Thailand.

If capital ratios are moderately negative, perhaps in the vicinity of minus 3%, it can still be argued that careful attention can nurture the bank back to health. This is on the grounds that, as a going concern, the bank has intangible assets that could make up for the missing equity. For example, the bank owns a branch network, a reputation, a securities license or a banking license, all of which have some value. Depending on the circumstances, those intangibles could even be more substantial than the equivalent of 3% of weighted assets, and regulators would have a degree of flexibility in this matter. Somewhere below the zero-equity line, there is a point when, even as a going concern, a bank is worth nothing. Naturally, if it was then to be liquidated, the liquidation costs added to the loss of some or all of the intangible assets would result in losses for depositors or taxpayers. The obvious line of conduct would be to see whether the gap in capital funds is too wide to tolerate the slow rehabilitation process.

The slow rehabilitation process was implemented with success in Malaysia in the mid-1980s. Clear signs appeared in early 1998 that Thailand would follow the same route. Unfortunately, the severity of the 1997 crisis might have precipitated many banks too quickly through the zero-equity line and it looks like few of them would qualify.

3) Merge weak banks into strong ones

Very few strong banks still exist of a sufficient size to allow the consolidation with a small ailing name. Assuming this was possible, one should be careful not to drag the strong bank into fresh problems, as mergers invariably swallow management time. Other types of mergers should be banned: the merger of equals when both are moribund;[6] the merger of a big, bad bank with a small, good bank.

4) Nationalize the banks that are beyond repair

If capital ratios are strongly negative, the institution is clearly beyond repair. The slow rehabilitation is not a realistic option as it would take too long and, most probably, the bank's capacity to generate cashflow would be impaired by the poor quality of some of its assets. In this case, there are only four ways out: merger, creative accounting, liquidation or nationalization. A merger would send the problem to the books of another institution, without solving it. Creative accounting remains by far the preferred option in most Asian countries. Liquidation usually forces a loss on depositors or taxpayers. Nationalization works, at least for some time.

Nationalization is a form of liquidation that minimizes the loss to depositors and creditors at the expense of taxpayers. It reinforces the moral hazard and it is a political minefield. On the positive side, nationalization buys social peace and it avoids systemic shocks. Conceptually, nationalization is a mistake. Most observers will agree that governments are poor industrialists and poor bankers. They should be left out of business altogether. Yet as shareholders they provide an ingredient that often eludes private sector banks in times of crisis: confidence. Depositors and creditors will trust the most fragile financial institution if the government owns it and if it gives clear indications of unfettered support.

Good governments will turn around nationalized banks and, after a few years, sell them back to the private sector. The sad truth in Asia is that most governments do a poor job at running financial institutions. Those banks never prosper and their chances of returning safely to the private sector are very slim. Kookmin Bank and DBS prospered in state hands, but they were not forcibly nationalized at the onset. Some Indian nationalized banks did well, but they were nationalized for ideological reasons, not at a time of distress.

Even the less prosperous countries can resort to nationalization and maintain stability. After all, this is more or less what India, Pakistan, China, Vietnam and other countries have done. It would be overgenerous to credit some of those countries with credible rehabilitation skills. But they are indisputable testimony that it is possible to stretch the life span of solidly bankrupt financial institutions.

Conceptually, what can be done for state-owned banks can also be done for the private sector, without resorting to nationalization. The trick is to maintain a safe level of liquidity, while entertaining the illusion of solvency thanks to creative accounting. But this would not punish the shareholders.

5) Insist on proper corporate governance

The disclosure of information by financial institutions is insufficient. This is tolerable, to a point, in countries where regulators have teeth, as at least depositors and creditors will trust that proper surveillance is exercised. Asymmetry in information remains a serious problem: banks blow their trumpet when they are doing well, but conceal problems as soon as they arise. Banks need clear rules and good rules. Most of their problems stemmed from liberties they took in respect of basic corporate governance.

Regulators must establish rules for early intervention in ailing financial institutions. The winning strategy is to notice early in the game that banks are suffering and to gather the political courage and technical skills to intervene before it is too late. Skills and courage among regulators both lacked in most Asian countries in the 1990s, leading to excesses and failures. However good the rules and inquisitive the regulators, banks will fail, but good controls are likely to minimize the problem.

Central banks must institute stricter rules for the classification of NPLs. Too many tricks are tolerated, that go way beyond the legitimate restructuring of substandard loans. One suggestion would be to make any related party lending beyond 1% of total assets a criminal offense. Bank owners should borrow somewhere else. They should be able to bring non-borrowing business to their own bank, but the bank's exposure to its owners should be minuscule.

Needless to say, command capitalism as a concept is as dead as communism, except for limited intervention. Had Japan and Korea reached that conclusion 10 years ago, their banking systems would be in better shape today.

6) Give up the 8% BIS ratio

Even prior to the crisis, capital ratios were devastatingly low in Asia. For cosmetic reasons, most countries conspired with their banks to give the world the impression that local capital adequacy ratios were satisfying international guidelines. This is a bad joke, and the crisis has made it a pathetic one. Asian countries should declare the implementation of other capital adequacy rules for their banks.

Asian governments should abandon any blind submission to uniform bank capital ratios. They should strike a balance between the prudential approach and market circumstances.[7] Would it not be wiser to face realities? Would it not be better to force all banks to make adequate provisions for their NPLs, in exchange for some leniency in capital adequacy rules? Would it not be reasonable to accept that, unlike in Western economies, no two Asian economies are the same and that they need bank capital ratios compatible with a variety of local parameters?

This is not to suggest that banks should operate with weak capital ratios. If anything, the minimum 8% is probably too low. But in the present circumstances, one should be realistic: most banking systems in Asia operate under negative capital ratios. What the banks are posting as capital ratios is pure fantasy.

There is no arbiter to whom regulators and banks can turn. The BIS made suggestions in 1988 which OECD countries have followed. They were not meant for other countries, but many felt compelled to follow them. It is as if no one wished to be singled out for having different sets of rules. As an example, if a country like Indonesia were to declare unilaterally that its banks henceforth would not follow the 8% rule, most of us, untrained observers, would immediately draw the — correct — conclusion that the banks are more bankrupt than we thought they were. Yet Indonesia should do so and say why it is doing it. It is unlikely that this could do much harm to its already battered financial institutions.

At the same time, still using the same example of Indonesia, the regulators should impose more stringent rules on the recognition of NPLs. This would allow them to create the conditions under which loan loss reserves more closely reflect reality, even at the cost of seemingly weak capital adequacy ratios. Clearly, however weak the resulting capital ratios will be, at least they will be accurate.

Capital ratios should be set at reasonable levels, and should not be dictated by international standards that are irrelevant to Asia. At a time when Asia wishes to create its own version of a Bank of International Settlements, would this not be a good opportunity to establish a fresh set of rules which many of the region's banking systems badly need? Would it not be an ideal time to re-evaluate the basis upon which bank capital adequacy ratios are formulated?

7) Intervene in money markets

Banks should have access to acceptable interest margins, compatible with the rest of the balance sheet. If regulators cannot become flexible on capital ratios, can they at least ensure that banks will be able to generate ample cashflow, for example by allowing them to generate a reasonable amount of interest income? A lot could be said in favor of macro-economic and micro-economic decisions that would result in better interest margins. The wealth of banks is linked to the wealth of the economy, but governments have the power to modulate that relationship. To a large extent, bank profits are a necessary draw on the economy. It is not wise for a banking system to be made to rely on interest margins which, as is the case for many banks in Korea and Taiwan, cannot sometimes provide for the immediate diversion of a small unallocated provision for every fresh loan. At the other extreme, it is morally or socially unacceptable for governments, for example in Hong Kong or in the Philippines, to condone situations where excessive wealth is transferred between bank customers and bank shareholders.[8]

8) Create a deposit insurance system

The small depositor should not be the victim of poor regulations, lax monitoring, fraudulent activities and generally the weaknesses of financial institutions. The person in the street trusts their government, as foolish as that can be. The government licenses the banks and keeps them under supervision. Where else could the person in the street find the comfort to know their money is safe? Certainly not in annual reports, at least not in Asia.

A deposit insurance system protects small deposits against bank failure. All banks contribute to a fund, which is called upon when a bank fails. Such a system penalizes the good banks, which pay as much as the wild ones, when in all probability the good banks' depositors will never need support. Also the good banks would have to compete against bad ones on deposit rates, rather than on safety. This is why the major — and good — banks in Hong Kong have always opposed such a scheme.

But if small depositors were protected, there would be no obstacle for regulators to take swift and harsh decisions on the fate of any ailing institutions. When a bank is liquidated, merged or otherwise dismantled with losses accruing to shareholders or creditors, and not to small depositors, obviously no serious social, political or systemic consideration is an impediment. In no time banks are put out of their misery. This also goes a long way to reduce moral hazard.

9) Restrict off-balance sheet transactions

Let's face it: many Asian banks do not have the skills needed to conduct off-balance sheet transactions beyond the traditional and plain vanilla products. Improvement of their credit culture needs to be a more relevant priority. Derivative products and other sophisticated off-balance sheet transactions allow banks to reduce market risks and sometimes to redistribute other types of risks. But they should be consumed with moderation. Asian banks generally lack the skills and discipline needed to render such transactions reasonably safe. The temptation is always present to use off-balance sheet transactions not only to take speculative positions but also to dissimulate such positions from the scrutiny of regulators. This creates a situation where derivatives may very well increase the exposure of banks to market risks, rather than reduce that exposure.

10) Draft bankruptcy laws

Bankruptcy laws protect both lenders and borrowers and they offer some degree of transparency. I shall argue later in this chapter that the losses to the economies brought about by the crisis cannot be correctly measured by the level of bad loans, thanks to the absence of good bankruptcy laws. But this is not to say that such a situation should be tolerated. Weak bankruptcy laws generate unhealthy transfers of wealth from some economic agents to other agents. This has always resulted in a misallocation of resources that has translated into lower growth. The overhaul of bankruptcy laws in most Asian countries should become an urgent priority.

11) Keep foreigners at bay

Conceptually, or philosophically, is it acceptable to see foreign banks dominate the local scene in Asia? This is a form of neo-colonialism that Malaysian Prime Minister Mahathir rightly fears.

In some Asian countries, for historical reasons, foreign banks have been very active. In Nepal for example, the local banks are still struggling in retail banking while the foreign banks steal away all the rewarding commercial transactions.

The entire banking system in the Philippines is as small as the largest bank in Thailand, in turn 20 times smaller than the largest bank in the world. In fact the profits made by HSBC or Deutsche Bank in one year are equivalent to the entire shareholders' funds of the local banking systems of a country like the Philippines. This is all the more true now that the currency crisis has deflated the dollar value of assets in a number of Asian countries. In addition, if equity were to be adjusted for missing provisions, sending the true price of outstanding shares to minuscule levels, the amount actually needed to acquire entire banking systems in the region would be pocket money to major international names. This is why it is very legitimate for locals to try and protect their banks from foreign predators, as desperate as they may be for fresh funds.

The proponents of foreign ownership of Asian banks suggest that this would achieve a transfer of financial technology to weak banking systems. This may very well be the case, but for every Citibank that does bring such contribution, there are a number of colonial-style banking institutions that keep it all to themselves. They build financial incentives into remuneration, like long-term housing at subsidized rates, that restrict the freedom of employees and therefore the dissemination of financial know-how.

Is it possible to rehabilitate a bank without an injection of fresh capital (from local or foreign investors)? It boils down to the philosophy about capital ratios, explored earlier. If a banking system is sufficiently credible to tell the world that controls and techniques are in place to rehabilitate banks without minimum capital ratios, it is possible. Central banks must then maintain liquidity and strict controls over the banks. East Asia needs huge amounts of capital to resume its growth pattern, but that does not imply that such capital — especially if it is foreign capital — should enter bank balance sheets as shareholders' funds.

Unfortunately, many Asian banks are beyond repair and the capital funds needed often exceed the value of the institution as a going concern, making the additional investment a losing proposition. Foreign banks, in order to secure control of the bank and expand around it, might be tempted to pay that premium,[9] but there should be very few such cases. CommerzBank buying into KEB, or ABN-AMRO into Bank of Asia, belong to a third category, where the investment is poor, but where setting foot in the country creates prospects for future deals.

12) Abandon the Confucian idea that the boss is always right

In earlier times, Asia prospered on the strength of Confucianism that, among many other excellent precepts, gave importance to the respect for elders. Maturity and experience tend to give older people a better grasp of what makes decisions good or bad, in a variety of situations. This concept was valid as long as the children could only learn from their parents, and reproduce and improve on their wisdom.

Times have changed and the new generation now learns lessons from the rest of the world. At present in Asia, children should still learn from their parents, but in business the best bosses are not necessarily those with the longest experience. Corporate seniority still gives too much weight to age, particularly in Japan and in Korea. In a famous recent incident, a Korean airliner crashed as a result of a Korean pilot's mistake. His co-pilot and a subordinate, a Canadian, tried to correct his mistake. Whether the Canadian co-pilot was more qualified than the Korean pilot is not established or relevant. In that particular case, the Canadian was right and the Korean was wrong, but the boss is always right in Korea, and the plane crashed.

13) Develop capital markets, create benchmarks for bond issues

Asia may have overinvested already in some sectors, while other sectors can still grow. Capital formation in the private sector will probably not remain as strong a factor in Asia's growth as it was. But companies need equity. They also need long-term funds[10] and permanent funds, as they must rebalance their books so as to become less dependent on hot money.

14) Allow negative real interest rates

Asia's problem is a debt problem: too many people have borrowed too much. Real interest rates are market rates reduced by inflation rates. Negative real interest rates help the borrower at the expense of the lender.[11] At this stage, borrowers need all the help they can get, if the debt problem is to subside.

15) Follow most of the IMF suggestions

The IMF prescriptions are open to criticism, but the IMF holds the key to the international liquidity most Asian countries lost during the crisis. The IMF and other supporting countries have shown some constructive flexibility in the actual application of their prescriptions.

The Losses

No one can put a figure on the losses associated with the Asian crisis, for two main reasons. First, the dust has not yet settled, and the process of assessing the damage will be slow. Second, some economic agents have gained from the crisis, in such a way that the collective loss is not immediately perceptible.

First of all, let us put to rest the stupid comment that the crisis has cost so many millions to the people of Asia as a result of the collapse of stock markets. The companies listed on the stock markets are still around, with their inventories, their machinery, their people and their markets. What has changed is the price investors agree to pay for them.

Granted, there is a slowdown in the economies, meaning that fewer goods will change hands and fewer services will be rendered. This is turn will slow the expansion of everybody's wealth.

Then there is the vexing matter of the currencies. As explained in this book, some politicians are eager to blame the West for what they call an impoverishment of their people through the collapse of local currencies. This is fallacious. It remains indeed that domestic products and services will, expressed in US dollars, point to a sudden drop in GDP and per capita GDP. But no wealth was stolen or lost, even if the currency crisis has hurt the pride of some.

A common mistake made by external observers is to measure the losses experienced by the various countries as being the losses of the domestic banks, or as being the aggregate amount of bad loans recorded in each of the markets. An NPL is not yet a bad loan, although many banks hide harsh realities behind lenient classifications. Even assuming the worst, a bad loan does not necessarily mean an equivalent amount of wealth destruction.

Someone once wrote to a newspaper in Germany complaining that people buying very expensive wine were disgusting as so many people around the world could not afford to buy enough food. As outrageous as the attitude of the wine buyer might look — because there is indeed immense misery in the lack of food in some places — the reasoning is flawed. When people buy bottles of vintage Bordeaux for a huge sum, they are only transferring a large amount — unreasonable perhaps, but this is another story — of their wealth to the seller of the wine. This gesture does not create nor does it destroy wealth. The price itself is totally irrelevant.

The same holds true for a domestic bad loan. When the lender records his loss by taking a provision against the loan, he simply transfers some of his wealth to the borrower. Yet, there might very well be some wealth destruction. Were it the case, the destruction would be found in the final destination of the funds in the hands of the borrower. Except to the extent that the possible loss is now hurting the lender instead of the borrower — there was a transfer as in the case of the outrageously expensive wine — the wealth destruction must be analyzed as if the borrower had invested his own funds. This particular investment is no different from other investments: there are good ones and bad ones. We are down to the conceptual situation where the quality, or the return, of all investments determines whether there is creation or destruction of wealth.

There is little doubt that a substantial part of recent investment in Thailand has destroyed wealth because it was directed to unproductive real estate. One could say the same in respect of the overcapacity now seen in Korea's semiconductor and automotive industries. Some of Malaysia's grandiose projects also fall into that category, and of course, so does Indonesia's investment in the production of a domestic commercial airliner. But how about the buses and cars that Steady Safe bought in Jakarta with Peregrine's money? Are they not productive? They are. Is that wealth destruction? No, of course not.

Even though Steady Safe may have invested wisely, it will not be able to reimburse the loan, owing to the currency situation. The Peregrine liquidators will probably not succeed in getting much money back, owing to the weak protection offered to lenders by the Indonesian bankruptcy laws. That particular bad loan has apparently destroyed no wealth beyond the fees wasted on lawyers and accountants. One can apply the same reasoning to quite a large number of the bad loans, both domestic and international, generated in the context of this crisis. In Western countries, if a loan cannot be repaid, unless the proceeds were fraudulently diverted, it is probably because the borrowers destroyed wealth by making a poor investment. Beyond the value of the collateral, if any, their loss becomes the bank's loss as they are submitted to established commercial and bankruptcy laws. The bank's loss is approximately, depending on the existence of a collateral, equal to the wealth destruction. In Asia, it does not work that way. Bad loans may result from the unwillingness of the borrower to repay, or from the inability of the lender to obtain repayment through commercial and bankruptcy laws. As a result, we can reach the extraordinary conclusion that, in Asia, the low level of protection against recalcitrant borrowers translates into a limited proportion of bad loans resulting in actual wealth destruction. In other words, adding up all the bad loans in the books of Asian banks to draw an estimate of the losses to the economy is incorrect.

Naturally, some wealth is being destroyed which does not find its way into the books of financial intermediaries. The possibility for an investment to become unproductive is always present, but the Asian crisis has magnified the dangers. It is vain to try and measure the damage, and certainly so on the basis of total bad loans in the banking system.

The banks' losses only give an indication of the amount of fresh funds that should be injected to restore the banking system to its pristine state. That amount may or may not represent the actual losses to the economies. Commercial banks are a necessity, and there is no doubt that the distressed countries will have to rehabilitate their banks one way or another. Among the prescriptions is a restoration of capital funds to minimum levels compatible with international standards. This may not be so wise. Such restoration is not a realistic objective. In East Asia today — with considerable variations across the region — roughly speaking every percentage point of bank capital ratio is equivalent to 1% of the country's GDP. Adjusted capital ratios have been savaged by the crisis. At the end of 1996, they were in a range of 0% at many weak banks to 10% in the few best cases for, say, a weighted average of 3%. By early 1998, they were in a range of negative 15% to positive 5%, for a weighted average of about minus 9%.

Using those averages, one can estimate that sanitizing the banks and restoring their capital ratios, across the board, to 3% is likely to swallow about 12% of GDP. Restoring them to the international level of 8% would swallow 17%

of GDP in the distressed countries. This is a tall order and it has been argued in the pages of this book that a more realistic approach would be welcome. Pushing banks into a high bracket of capital adequacy ratios will inevitably invite them to increase their risk profile, as has been the case throughout the 1990s. It would appear much safer to limit the rehabilitation to a level of 3%, while imposing much more stringent regulatory surveillance. Even so, governments will have immense difficulties in directing 12% of GDP to bank capital, and the temptation is great to open the door to foreign investors.

What are the losses of the Asian crisis? We said that bad loans are not a good indicator, and that there is no way to measure losses with any degree of accuracy. But let us make an assumption. Let us accept that the five distressed East Asian countries have destroyed wealth to the tune of 20% of their combined GDP. How badly is that going to affect them? Well, 20% of GDP is equal to about three years of growth, perhaps the growth registered since July 1994. The crisis has simply brought Asia back to where the region was in July 1994. No big deal. Who would not gladly pay for 25 years of growth with such a modest drawback? Asia is tough. Asia will eat plain rice for a while and will come back to prosperity.

The Lessons

For the price it paid, Asia has learned a lot. The lower GDP growth, even the possible contraction, will ultimately solve a number of problems. Asia will revise its attitude in respect of investment. Excess capacity will disappear. Central banks will be more active in regulating the banks. Corporate governance will improve. And, if nothing else, is such a crisis not a perfect opportunity to eliminate some dictators and improve the political climate? Politicians with limited understanding of business largely ran Asia. One should never listen to them anyway, but Asia will perhaps select them more carefully in the future. From this standpoint, this is the perfect growth crisis.

The rest of the world has also learned from the crisis. It has learned that information circulates quickly in our global village, but the message is often garbled as we suffer from a lack of global information standards. Perception and contagion play immense roles, more devastating than we all thought they were. The world has also learned that greedy, or rather too eager, international lenders are as guilty as avid borrowers in the build-up of debt that was so poorly allocated. The one thing that the world has yet to learn is encapsulated in that famous picture of President Suharto signing an IMF agreement under the watchful eye of Michel Camdessus. The picture shows Camdessus with crossed arms looking over Suharto, like a schoolteacher over a recalcitrant student. This gesture was humiliating for Suharto. We all know that the old general had no intention whatsoever to follow the prescriptions so imposed on him, sure as he was that the funds would be coming anyway. But Westerners have learned nothing if they think they can patronize Asia.

Entropy is a beautiful concept, used in thermodynamics and information systems. It measures disorder, without giving to the word any negative connotation. Building a house is creating disorder in that wood, sand, iron and other raw material are taken from a minimal state of unanimated order to a sophisticated state of functional disorder. Humans are constantly creating disorder, to the point where our environment is negatively affected. Nature also contributes to disorder and it is an accepted concept that the entropy of the universe is constantly growing. Looking at Asia during the past 25 years, there is no denying that entropy has grown tremendously, probably as much as in Europe over a whole century from 1850 to 1950. Is Asia's entropy not growing too quickly? Are we not losing our minds? Probably it is and we are. Asia is the last continent on earth where some people keep religious and spiritual beliefs that are minimalist. Asia is the last continent where more is not necessarily better than less. The minimalists hail from the center of Asia, more precisely from the Indian sub-continent. Their influence on the life philosophies of the rest of Asia has been eroded over the years by a pervasive and destructive mercantilism. This crisis has given Asia a chance to reassess its future. Think of it, Asia, where have you gone?

At the height of the Asian crisis, two young Thais, a man and a woman, total strangers, stumbled across each other on the roof of a Bangkok car park. Desperate, ruined by the crisis, they felt unable to face their friends and families anymore. What Thailand's sudden prosperity had meant for them was an irresistible temptation to run up high consumer debt. They should not worry, they had been told, tomorrow's growth was going to take care of today's debt. But for them as for others, the music stopped. In Asia, you do not go bankrupt. You just lose face and count on friends and family to help you out. That man and that woman simply felt they were not up to that humiliation. They talked for quite a while. I can imagine those eyes, those smiles. Opening their heart to a stranger, they must have talked with that sensual abandon stemming from the knowledge that their words would not be repeated. They spent some time together, holding hands, kissing perhaps, in a last tender encounter. Each then wrote a note to the families, which is how we know what happened. Then together they jumped to their death.

What a waste! There are many reasons why young Thai people would want to put an end to their life before their time is up. But this reason isn't a good one, never was. Stay with us, Asia, the world needs you.

Endnotes

1. Incidentally, credit rating agencies claim that sovereign risk ratings are too recent a product to offer a track record in terms of the predictability of default. This reasoning should, of course, also apply to how spreads are decided by the markets.

2. At one point in 1995, several central banks of East Asia promised to share their foreign currency reserves to help out in the defense of regional currencies. This was symbolic but not taken very seriously by the markets.

3. This comment is made in relative terms and it pertains to the banking systems immediately prior to the crisis.

4. Based on Aristotle's approach.

5. Assets weighted according to the risk they represent, as in the computation of BIS ratios.

6. Korea and Indonesia are likely to select that awkward strategy.

7. See Chapter 3 on bank accounting.

8. This is achieved through a cartel or a quasi-cartel of banks fixing interest rates.

9. In most countries, bank licenses are not easy to obtain, especially so for foreigners. A way around the difficulty is to acquire a local banking institution, however insignificant, and to use it as a base for expansion. Countless banks in Asia have survived for years, feeding only paltry returns to their owners, in the hope that, one day, they would be bought over for their banking license. The premium attached to the license varies over time and across the region. An indication of its high value in a place like Hong Kong can be found in the fact that, in 1996, as a parting gift from the colonial administration to English interests, the only fresh banking licenses given away in decades went to two British-owned non-banks that had absolutely no objective need for them.

10. Even governments that need no funds should issue debt in order to create a market and a benchmark for the pricing of all other debt issued in the country.

11. Note that, ultimately, this penalizes the depositor, not the bank that acts as an intermediary.

CHRONOLOGY

CHRONOLOGY OF THE ASIAN CURRENCY AND STOCK MARKET PANIC

This chronology is based on information from several news sources (Reuters, *Asian Wall Street Journal*, *New York Times*, CNN, *Financial Times*, Bloomberg, etc.).

1997

January   Hanbo Steel, the first bankruptcy of a leading Korean corporation in the past decade, folds under US$6 billion in debts.

Feb. 5   In Thailand, the first substantial company to miss payments on foreign debt is Samprasong

Mar. 10   IMF Managing Director Michel Camdessus says: "I don't see any reason for this crisis to develop further."

March   The failure of Sammi Steel in Korea instigates fear of a potential corporate debt crisis.

May 14–15   Speculators attack Thailand's baht currency because of Thailand's slowing economy and political instability. Thailand is helped by its South East Asian neighbors in its defence of the baht.

The Philippines is also affected and the central bank decides to dump dollars and to raise the overnight rate $1^3/4$ percentage points to 13%.

June 19   Finance Minister, Amnuay Viravan, resigns as Thailand's finance minister. The Prime Minister, Chavalit Yongchaiyudh, says: "We will never devalue the baht."

June 27	In Thailand, the central bank orders 16 cash-strapped finance companies to submit merger or consolidation plans and in the meantime suspends their operations.
June 30	Thai Prime Minister Chavalit Yonchaiyudh once again says that there will be no devaluation of the baht.
July	Kia, Korea's third largest car maker, makes a request for emergency loans after suffering from the credit crunch.
July 1	China resumes sovereignty over Hong Kong.
July 2	The record devaluation of the baht to 28.80 to the dollar results from the Bank of Thailand's announcement that it will abandon the peg. The Bank of Thailand asks for "technical assistance" from the IMF.
	The effects of the devaluation are felt in the Philippines and the central bank is forced to heavily defend the peso.
July 8	Malaysia's central Bank, Bank Negara, is forced to heavily defend the ringgit.
July 11	The Philippines gives up on the peso defense. The peso loses 12% in a few hours
July 14	Malaysia's central bank gives up its defence of the ringgit.
July 24	The ringgit hits a 38-month low of 2.6530 to the dollar. An attack on "rogue speculators" is launched by Malaysian Prime Minister Mahathir Mohamad.
July 25	Thailand and Malaysia seek Japan's help in the creation of a regional rescue fund.
July 28	Thailand calls in the IMF.
Aug. 5	As part of the IMF's suggested policies for a rescue package, Thailand unveils an austerity plan and complete revamp of the finance sector.
	The central bank of Thailand suspends 48 finance firms.
Aug. 11	In Tokyo, the IMF unveils a rescue package for Thailand which includes loans totaling US$16 billion from the IMF and Asian nations.

Aug. 13   In Indonesia, the central bank intervenes in the defense of the rupiah.

Aug. 14   Indonesia's system of managing the exchange rate through the use of a band is abolished, leaving the rupiah to float.

Aug. 15   As speculators attack the Hong Kong dollar, overnight interest rates go up 150 basis points.

Aug. 20   IMF approves disbursement of funds to Thailand.

Aug. 21   IMF Managing Director, Michel Camdessus says "The worst of the crisis is behind us."

Sept. 4   Malaysian ringgit breaks through the 3.00 to the dollar barrier.

    Several multi-billion dollar construction projects are delayed by Malaysian Prime Minister Mahathir Mohamad.

Sept. 16   In an effort to reduce the budget shortfall, Indonesia says that it will postpone projects worth 39 trillion rupiah.

Oct. 1   Mahathir repeats his request for tighter regulation, or a total ban, on FOREX trading. The ringgit falls 4% in less than two hours to a low of 3.4080.

Oct. 8   Indonesia calls in the IMF.

Oct. 17   In an effort to keep the economy from sliding into recession, Malaysia presents a budget intended to decrease the current deficit.

Oct. 20–23   As a result of fears over high interest rates and pressures on the Hong Kong dollar, the Hong Kong stock market loses nearly a quarter of its value in four days. The Hang Seng index falls 23.34% to 10,426.30 at Thursday's close, down from 13,601.01 the previous Friday.

Oct. 27   On Wall Street, the Dow Jones industrial average falls by 7.18% to 7,161.15, its single-biggest point loss ever.

Oct. 31   IMF gives Indonesia a US$23 billion financial support package.

Nov. 6   As the won slides against the dollar, the Bank of Korea is once again forced to intervene. The dollar is quoted at 973.65 won.

IMF Managing Director Michel Camdessus says "I don't believe that the situation in South Korea is as alarming as the one in Indonesia a couple of weeks ago…We are following (the South Korea situation) very attentively and with an attitude of confidence."

Although confidence remains that the IMF's US$17.2 billion dollar bailout will succeed, it is not likely until the political instability is over. Opposition Democrat Party led by former Prime Minister Chuan Leekpai says its government will consist of seven parties encompassing 196 members of Parliament, making it one parliamentary seat short of a majority. However, the ruling coalition of Prime Minister Chavalit Yongchaiyudh announces it would form the next government with a coalition consisting of 198 members of Parliament.

Nov. 7   Asia stocks nose-dive.

Nov. 8   Following the previous day's plunge of 6.9% to 515.63, the Korea Composite Stock Price Index falls a further 3.9%, to end Saturday's half-day trading at 495.70.

IMF Managing Director Michel Camdessus says the IMF is ready to help if needed.

The central Bank of Korea defends the won by selling an undisclosed amount of dollars from its estimated $30.05 billion foreign currency reserves.

South Korea's financial system's deterioration is accelerated as international investors disagree with South Korea's claims that its financial system is sound.

Nov. 10   The Korean won breaks the 1,000 barrier.

Nov. 14   South Korea's majority party vows to pass a reform package that will clean up debt-ridden banks in an effort to ward off a potential financial crisis. By means of a major shakeup of the banking industry, the proposed reform encourages foreign investors to return to South Korea.

Nov. 17   The Hokkaido Takushoku Bank fails, the first of Japan's big banks to collapse under the weight of bad loans.

South Korea abandons its defence of the won, sending the currency down to 1008.60. The sudden weakening of the won sends stocks plunging by more than 4%.

Nov. 19   A proposal following the deputy finance ministers meeting in Manila suggests the formation of a new mechanism that would enhance the IMF's role in identifying possible financial crises in Asia.

                 South Korea's new finance and economy minister says that he doesn't foresee the country requiring assistance from the IMF.

Nov. 20   South Korea acknowledges that it would require outside help, and turns to Japan asking for help in persuading Japanese banks to roll over maturing short-term loans to South Korea. Hoping to attract investors, South Korea allows its currency to fluctuate by up to 10% per day. After half an hour of trading, the won plunges by the daily permissible 10%.

Nov. 21   Following its announcement that it will now seek a rescue package from the IMF, the South Korean won closes 7.9% higher at 1,056 won to the dollar.

                 Bank of Japan governor Yasuo Matsushita and other top officials say they won't allow individual financial collapses to destabilize the overall financial system

Nov. 24   The Central Bank of Japan announces that it will extend special unsecured loans to Yamaichi in order to protect the assets of the securities firm's clients.

Nov. 26   Tokuyo City Bank in Japan fails.

                 Finance Minister Hiroshi Mitsuzuka and Bank of Japan Governor Yasuo Matsushita, in a joint statement, promise that there would be no more major bankruptcies among financial institutions.

Nov. 27   As the unrest in South Korea's market starts to ease, The World Bank and Asia Development Bank express a willingness to join a bailout effort led by the IMF.

Dec. 1   South Korea and the IMF resume talks on a rescue package for the Korean economy.

Dec. 3   The won, rupiah, baht and ringgit are each sent crashing to all-time lows against the dollar.

Dec. 4   Korean officials and IMF Managing Director, Michel Camdessus, sign a letter of intention covering an international accord to provide Korea with US$57 billion.

The militant Korea Confederation of Trade Unions promises to wage "all-out strikes" if concessions to the IMF result in layoffs.

Only one day after the Malaysian cabinet decides to halt all such infrastructure ventures, Dr Mahathir is quoted as saying that a 10 billion ringgit (US$2.7 billion) road, rail and pipeline project would proceed.

Dec. 5   "Ailing financial institutions deemed impossible to recover should close down," a statement from the Korean Finance Ministry says. In addition, South Korea demands that financial institutions speed up the write-offs of non-performing loans.

Malaysia's most sweeping policy changes in a decade are announced, including the reduction of government spending by 18%, restrictions on big-ticket imports, and constraints on bank credits and stock-market fund raising. Deputy Prime Minister, Datuk Seri Anwar, says there will be "no question of any bailout" for financially ailing concerns, adding that Malaysian banks "need to be protected against any excesses" of their customers.

Dec. 8   Halla Group, Korea's 12th-largest conglomerate, announces that it plans to apply for court protection or receivership for some units.

The Indonesian central-bank intervenes to strengthen the rupiah to 3,965 against the dollar, down from 4,020.

During the first week of December, the Korean government suspends the business of nine merchant banks until the end of the year, citing mismanagement and massive withdrawals from investors.

Dec. 9   Southeast Asian currency markets are affected by rumours that President Suharto is gravely ill. Not only is the rupiah affected, but the Korean won plunges to a record low of 1,465.70, down from 1,342.40 won at Monday's close. Stocks go downward as a result of conditions on the money market.

The South Korean government takes a majority stake in Korea First Bank and Seoulbank in an effort to revive them. In both banks, shareholder equity is increased to two trillion won (US$1.5 billion) from 820 billion won (US$615.4 million) and the government takes 59% of the banks' equity.

In Tokyo, there is news that the government may issue 10 trillion yen in new bonds to support the financial system.

Dec. 10   In an effort to remove the bottleneck in the financial system, South Korea's Finance Ministry suspends the business operations of an additional five troubled merchant banks. The five merchant banks are told to submit plans for capital increases or mergers and acquisitions by the end of the year.

An internal IMF document reveals South Korea's foreign-exchange reserves are dangerously low. Official reserves are standing at US$23.9 billion on Dec. 2, down from US$30.5 billion at the end of October. Of the US$23.9 billion, only US$6 billion are in "useable funds", while the rest remain in overseas branches of local commercial banks. The document also states that US$6.2 billion of this reserve is committed to forward dollar contracts which the government bought in its defense of the won in recent months. At the end of September, the country's external liabilities were estimated at about US$100 billion. This is in contradiction to the finance ministry's statement that South Korea's short-term foreign debt at the end of September was US$65.6 billion.

Dec. 11   Despite South Korea's effort to regain foreign confidence in its economy, financial markets continue to slide with currency trading coming to a halt in the first few minutes after the won plunges by its 10% daily limit to 1,719.8 on the dollar. The stock market slumps.

The financial situation in South Korea affects the rest of Asia with currencies and stock prices plummeting.

The turmoil is felt on Wall Street as investors go on a selling spree after three days of sharp losses. The Dow Jones industrial average closes 129.80 points lower at 7,848.99.

Dec. 12   Early in the day, the won falls to its permissible limit of 1891.40 won per dollar. After the central bank sells dollars, the won moves up to 1600 won to the dollar. The central bank is ordered by the Cabinet to extend US$6.3 billion in special, low-interest loans to cash-short banks, securities firms and investment trust companies.

The Indonesian market drops 7.6% amid new rumours concerning the health of the President Suharto.

Dec. 15   The won rises 10% to 1,563.9 against the dollar after tumbling by almost a third inside two weeks. As the Korean benchmark stock index rises 7.22% (its biggest one-day percentage rise ever), its yearly loss decreases to 41%.

Other Asian countries are, however, still on the decline as the Indonesian rupiah plunges as much as 12% to the US dollar, the Philippine peso plunges to the lowest in more than 25 years, the Thai baht plummets 5.3% to 47.35 a dollar, the lowest since the Thai central bank started keeping records in 1969, and the Malaysian ringgit falls 3.7% to its lowest since it was floated in 1973.

Dec. 17   Japan's Prime Minister Ryutaro Hashimoto announces a special two trillion yen (US$15.7 billion) cut in personal income taxes in hopes that it will ease Japan's faltering economy.

Dec. 18   Longtime dissident Kim Dae-jung is elected to serve a five-year term as president, raising concerns that South Korea's financial markets may be further battered.

Dec. 19   The fourth-largest bankruptcy in post-war Japan occurs with the failure of foodstuffs trader Toshoku Ltd. Concerns regarding the uncertain state of Japan's economy results in Tokyo shares dropping 5%, and with it the decline of stocks all over the Pacific Rim.

President-elect Kim Dae-jung promises to faithfully abide by the country's financial agreements with the IMF.

Dec. 23   The Korean won breaks through the 2,000 barrier.

Dec. 24   Amid concerns that Korea's present financial crisis will lead to a debt moratorium, South Korean shares plunge 6%. However, following a recovery of the won, the index closes at 351.45, a fall of 14.91 points.

With around US$15 billion of an estimated US$100 billion in short-term debt coming due this month and another US$15 billion next month, Seoul is in talks with commercial banks about possible debt rollovers.

Dec. 26   The IMF will give out US$10 billion to South Korea by early January to help stabilize its financial markets. In return, Seoul says it has agreed to new reforms set out by the IMF.

Dec. 29   South Korean institutions are given a little more time to pay off their loans by a group of US banks who have agreed in principle to a deal announced in the early afternoon, although no specifics are outlined. Over the next two months, various South Korea banks will be facing about US$30 billion in loan repayments.

Dec. 30   The world's major banks join in the effort to help South Korea by rolling over a mountain of short-term debt due to be paid tomorrow. The effort is expected to help Korea manage its estimated US$100 billion in short-term debt, of which US$15 billion comes due by Dec. 31 and another US$15 billion by the end of January 1998.

1998

Jan. 5   Thailand says it will appeal to the IMF to ease the requirement under the bailout package that the country produce a cash surplus equal to 1% of its gross domestic product in the fiscal year ending in September.

Jan. 7   The Indonesian rupiah falls as much as 12% to 8,400 to the dollar, the Thai baht to 4.2% or 54.75 to the dollar and the Philippine peso to 2.8% or 46.5 to the dollar.

Jan. 8   Indonesian stocks crash 18.5% in mid-afternoon. However, recovery is made in late trade with an overall drop of 11.95%. The rupiah hits a low of 9,900 before recovering to 9,500 late in the afternoon.

Concerns regarding the prospect of a Jakarta debt moratorium are expressed by analysts.

Jan. 9   The Indonesian rupiah recovers nearly 30% to 7,600 against the US dollar from a day low of 10,500. However, by midday, the rupiah is trading at 8,400/9,150.

Although Indonesia's budget, which was tabled in the previous week, fails to outline terms required by the IMF, Suharto pledges his commitment to implement economic reforms attached to a US$40 billion financial aid package negotiated in 1997. In response to this budget, which is widely considered too lenient, there are reports that the IMF has written a "strongly worded" letter to Jakarta.

The IMF agrees on the reduction of several economic targets for Korea. Among these was the lowering of gross domestic product growth from 2.5% to between 1% and 2%. Also, Korea will issue approximately US$25 billion in bonds, of which US$10 billion in bonds sold for new cash. The remaining bonds will be issued to foreign lenders who wish to take them in place of their short-term loans to Korean banks.

Jan. 12   Asian stock markets plunge, with the largest drop of 8.7% taking place in the Hong Kong market.

In Hong Kong, Peregrine Investments Holdings Ltd., once Asia's most powerful, home-grown, investment-banking house, announces that it has moved toward a liquidation.

The Hong Kong three-month interbank rate is 16%.

President Suharto moves to stop 15 costly infrastructure projects.

Jan. 13   After plunging 8.7% the previous day, Hong Kong's benchmark Hang Seng index closes up 7.4%.

Indonesia's stock market rises 9.1% amid new optimism that the IMF and Indonesia appear to be near an agreement over the IMF bailout.

There is speculation in Jakarta that the government is considering, among other options, a move toward some form of currency board like those in place in Hong Kong and Argentina.

Jan. 14   A leaked IMF document, obtained by the *New York Times*, strongly criticizes President Suharto for failing to enact on promised reforms attached to Indonesia's US$43 billion aid package.

Jan. 15   Suharto signs an agreement with the IMF which requires that he dismantle the monopolies and family-owned businesses. Along with the cutting of key monopolies, the agreement includes drastically revised economic forecasts made in a recent budget and promises that the government would not bail-out debt-laden banks.

Jan. 16   President Kim Young Sam assures designated Asian financial troubleshooter Lawrence Summers that South Korea will abide by terms of a US$57 billion IMF bailout.

Jan. 18   President-elect Kim Dae-jung said the worst is yet to come in South Korea's struggle to overcome its economic problems under restrictions from the IMF.

Jan. 19   The merger of Bank Internasional Indonesia (BII), Bank Dagang Negara Internasional (BDNI), Bank Tiara Asia and unlisted Bank Sahid Gajah Perkasa and Bank Dewa Rutji results in the largest private sector bank in Indonesia with US$5.9 billion in assets. With the biggest-ever merger in the nation's private sector, Indonesia displays its commitment to much-awaited bank reform.

Jan. 21   President Suharto confirms that he will seek a seventh five-year term in office, perhaps with big-spending technology minister Jusuf Habibie as his vice-president.

           In order to resolve liquidity and solvency problems in the private banking sector, Indonesia's central bank governor, Sudradjad Djiwandono, says that the government will soon announce new guidelines.

Jan. 22   The Indonesian rupiah plunges below the 15,000 per dollar level to 17,100 as spreads widen and interbank activity dries up.

           As stocks in Jakarta plunge nearly 5% to 443, other Asian countries are also feeling the effects of the declining rupiah. In South Korea, shares are down by 4.47% to 483.99.

Jan. 27   Indonesia announces a big shake-up of its private banks and a temporary debt payment until a new framework is worked out between international lenders and Indonesian borrowers on how to deal with a private sector overseas debt estimated at US$66 billion. Finance Minister Mar'ie Muhammad says the reforms also include government guarantees for debtors and creditors of the country's commercial banks and a new institution to deal with weak banks.

Jan. 29   In a deal expected to end Korea's liquidity crisis, the government and global creditors of 13 leading international banks agree to exchange about US$24 billion of the Asian nation's short-term debt for government-guaranteed loans. Under the deal, Korean banks can exchange their short-term non-trade credits for new loans with maturities of one, two or three years. These loans will be guaranteed by the Republic of Korea for US$20 billion and will bear a floating interest rate of 2.25%, 2.5% and 2.75% over the six-month London interbank offered rate.

           South Korea closes 10 of its merchant banks due to insolvency.

Feb. 6   In a step to aid the return of Japan's banks back to financial health, the nation's lower house of Parliament approves a 30 trillion yen (US$239 billion) bailout package. Of the 30 trillion yen, 17 trillion is allocated to guarantee bank deposits and pay for the clean-up of banks that fail. The remaining 13 trillion yen will be used to buy new preferred stock in Japan's debt-strapped banks.

The Indonesian government's chief debt negotiator says that bankruptcy laws in line with the IMF's requirements will be set up shortly.

In South Korea, the financial market embraces the news of a landmark agreement that makes it easier for companies to shed workers as they restructure. The labor reform legislation includes amending legislation clarifying the circumstances and procedures for layoffs, and relaxing restrictions on private job placements and manpower leasing services.

Feb. 10   With indications that Indonesia may peg the value of its currency to the dollar, Southeast Asian currencies are on the rise.

Feb. 12   Federal Reserve Board Chairman, Alan Greenspan, reiterates that there is a small risk that Asia's financial turmoil could spread to other parts of the world and impact the US economy.

The IMF announces that it will relax a key condition of Thailand's economic bailout requiring it to post a budget surplus equivalent to 1% GDP in fiscal 1998. Thailand will now be allowed to return a budget deficit of 1% to 2% of GDP in the year ending on September 30.

Feb. 13   IMF's Michel Camdessus urges the Indonesian government to delay action on the creation of a currency board and warns that such a move could threaten the nation's prospects of economic recovery. Camdessus says his opposition to the idea has the unanimous backing of the IMF executive board, and his stance is immediately supported by the United States.

John Hopkins University economist Steve Hanke, an adviser to Suharto, after a meeting with the President, declares that the Indonesian leader remains in favor of a currency board.

Rioting is reported by residents and police in the West Java town of Jatiwangi in Indonesia. Violence is also reported in the coastal towns of Pamanukan and Losari. The outbreaks are the result of rising prices.

Feb. 16   Indonesia announces that it is moving towards a fixed exchange rate system, calling on the IMF to come up with an alternative for strengthening the rupiah currency if it objects to the plan.

Feb. 17   President Suharto fires Indonesia's central bank governor, Sudradjad Djiwandono, who is understood to have opposed government plans to create a fixed exchange rate system for the rupiah through a currency board. He is replaced by US-trained economist Sjahril Sabirin.

Feb. 18   J.P. Morgan & Co. files a US$180 million lawsuit against four South Korean financial institutions containing charges of breach of contract on money owed for foreign-exchange swap operations. Diamond is an investment vehicle used by S.K. Securities, LG Metal and Hannam to establish a 20 billion won offshore fund to invest in South East Asian currency derivatives. The fund is believed to have suffered huge losses.

Feb. 20   Indonesian President Suharto announces that the government will guarantee a pay-out on all legal deposits in 16 banks liquidated last year. The government previously said it would cover up to 20 million rupiah in each account of the 16 banks, which amounted to 1.7 trillion rupiah. Finance Minister Mar'ie Muhammad told a parliamentary banking committee that although the government had no legal obligation to do so, the guarantee was a personal decision by Suharto.

Feb. 21–22 Indonesia suspends its plan to implement a controversial currency-board system that would have pegged the rupiah to the US dollar, according to a senior Indonesian monetary official.

            G-7 finance ministers and central bankers put pressure on Japan to spend more on economic growth, as well as to increase world awareness of how the nation's beleaguered banking sector will be energized with public funds.

Feb. 23   Despite severe international criticism of a fixed currency exchange rate system, the Indonesian government states that it is still considering its implementation.

            In Indonesia, riots brake out in about two dozen towns, with many shops being looted and burned.

Mar. 2   Month-to-month inflation in Indonesia jumps to 12.76% in February after a 6.88% rise in January, with the year-to-year rate, as calculated by Reuters, at around 31.74%.

            The main cause of civil unrest is the rising food prices, which are increasing at a much faster rate than official figures show.

Malaysia's central bank says blue chip Sime Darby Bhd's banking unit, one of the country's top 10 banks, needs over a billion ringgit in fresh capital. It also says the capital injections may be required by the country's second largest bank, government-run Bank Bumiputra Malaysia Bhd, as well as two finance companies.

Mar. 4   Steve Hanke, advisor to Suharto, says Indonesia is committed to implementing an "IMF Plus" plan that includes a currency board, banking reforms, debt rescheduling and privatization.

Mar. 6   Indonesia says that it will subsidize imports of food and other essentials to keep prices under control. The move to subsidize imports is a technical violation of an agreement with the IMF on economic reform in return for a US$40 billion bailout package.

           The rupiah falls to a rate of 12,000 to the dollar, down some 25% in the past three days.

Mar. 10   IMF First Deputy Managing Director, Stanley Fischer, says the fund is ready to be flexible on its reform program with Indonesia. Fischer also says that a currency board, an idea criticized by the IMF in the past, could work in Indonesia if the right conditions are met regarding the banking sector and corporate debt problems.

Mar. 14   Ignoring calls for reform from world leaders and the IMF, President Suharto of Indonesia appoints his eldest daughter, his golfing partner and top officials linked to family business interests to a new cabinet.

Mar. 16   Markers indicate that it should be possible to price the planned Korea sovereign issue at 350–400 basis points over treasuries in contrast to the 1000 points at the end of 1997.

Mar. 19   China's new premier, Zhu Rongji, states that Beijing will defend the Hong Kong currency's link to the US dollar at any cost.

Mar. 26   An initial total of 54 domestic banks will be dealt with by the Indonesian Bank Restructuring Agency (IBRA), which has been set up by the Indonesian government to rehabilitate and deal with bad banks. According to bankers, the 54 banks already placed under IBRA include 39 privately owned commercial banks, four state-owned banks, and 11 state-run provincial development banks. The 54 banks have been organized into eight teams.

Mar. 27   A proposal by Indonesia to tackle its mountain of private debt is backed by the IMF. The proposal, modeled after the plan adopted by Mexico in the early 1980s, has merit but still has to be approved by overseas creditors, says the IMF.

Mar. 31   According to the Bank of Korea, more than 10,000 firms have defaulted on debt payment since December 1997.

Apr. 8   Indonesia announces an agreement with the IMF concerning a new package of economic reforms. With IMF agreement, the government will continue subsidies on rice and soybeans, while fuel and power prices would be raised gradually. Further reforms will include the government terminating the granting of monopoly privileges, often given in the past to favor members of Suharto's own family and close associates. The government also plans to sell its stake in five listed companies and to front seven state-owned firms in the current fiscal year in order to increase funds.

Apr. 9   Offered in New York, South Korea's US$4 billion issue is over-subscribed as international investors hurry to buy into South Korea's recovery. South Korea places US$3 billion of 10-year paper at 355 basis points over comparable US Treasuries and US$1 billion of five-year notes at 345 basis points over.

Apr. 16   In Korea, workers at all Kia Motors assembly lines halt production when they down tools in protest against the possible sale of the troubled automaker.

Apr. 23   In Malaysia, after weeks of wrangling over financing, Phileo Allied Bhd steps into the breach to subscribe to one billion ringgit (US$266 million) of preference shares of RHB Capital Bhd, which owns RHB Bank, in order help RHB pay for the takeover of Sime Bank.

May 8   Further student protests in Jakarta, along with continued unrest and looting in cities in north Sumatra, make for uneasy financial markets in Indonesia.

May 13   Six students are killed at a protest rally in Indonesia.

May 14   Trade is once again disrupted by riots in Jakarta, resulting in stocks linked to the family businesses of President Suharto tumbling. The rupiah falls below 11,000 to the dollar. Looters torch buildings in the city center and major banks are virtually empty with scores of staff trapped at home by the riots.

May 15	Jakarta is much quieter as banks and most offices close their doors. Many people are staying at home as there were reports of fresh rioting and looting. Overseas corporations start to close down operations and begin to evacuate staff.
May 19	President Suharto makes a promise of new presidential elections in which he will not run.
	International investors are growing increasingly worried about all emerging markets, resulting in the withdrawal of funds.
May 21	Following his resignation from office, President Suharto hands over power to Vice President Bacharuddin Jusuf Habibie.
	It is unlikely that overseas investors will return to Indonesia as doubts remain that any real change will take place with Habibie, a protégé of Suharto, in power.
May 25	Habibie says the government will go ahead with reforms demanded by the IMF.
	The 55% overseas ownership limit in Korean companies is abolished.
	As local institutions dump blue chips and global investors pay little attention to the removal of overseas stock ownership limits, South Korean stocks tumble to close at an 11-year low.
May 29	The Suharto family is worth an estimated US$40 billion. Indonesians want the family's assets and cash returned to the country as they believe most of the family's fortune has been acquired through nepotism.
June 10	The Taiwan dollar falls to an 11-year low.
	In the wake of the falling yen, China's central bank governor raises fears that a devaluation in China may take place.
June 18	The US and Japan intervene to support the yen.
June 23	A HK$32 billion package to support the economy is announced in Hong Kong.

APPENDIX 1

SUMMARIES OF IMF EXECUTIVE BOARD DISCUSSIONS ON INDONESIA, KOREA AND THAILAND

Indonesia (Board discussion, July 1996):

The board strongly endorsed the authorities' aim to reduce broad money growth in 1996. Directors agreed with the authorities' emphasis on maintaining an open capital account and welcomed the steps already taken to widen the exchange-rate band and give greater flexibility to exchange rate policy...

In the Board's view, further substantial reforms, including financial sector reforms and the development of a strong capital market, were essential for maintaining rapid, sustained growth. Directors urged the authorities to address weaknesses in the banking sector, and in particular to act decisively to resolve problem of insolvent banks and recover non-performing loans. They considered these actions as critical to reduce the vulnerability of the economy to shocks and to lessen moral hazard.

Korea (Board discussion, November 1996):

In their discussion, directors welcomed Korea's continued impressive macroeconomic performance: growth had decelerated from the unsustainably rapid pace of the previous two years, inflation had remained subdued notwithstanding some modest pickup in the months prior to the consultation, and the widening of the current account deficit largely resulted from a temporary weakening of the terms of trade.

Directors praised the authorities for their enviable fiscal record and suggested that fiscal policy could best contribute to strengthening medium-term macroeconomic performance by maintaining a strong budgetary position as much-needed spending on social overhead capital was undertaken. They also welcomed in the recent acceleration of capital account liberalization; although some directors agreed with the authorities' gradual approach to capital market capitalization, a number of them considered that rapid and complete liberalization offered many benefits at Korea's stage of development.

Thailand (Board discussion, July 1996):

Directors strongly praised Thailand's remarkable economic performance and the authorities' consistent record of sound macroeconomic fundamentals. They noted that financial policies had tightened in 1995 in response to the widening of the external current account deficit and the pickup of inflation, and this had begun to bear results, but they cautioned that there was no room for complacency...

The recent increase in the current account deficit had increased Thailand's vulnerability to economic shocks and adverse shifts in market sentiment. On the one hand, Directors noted, economic fundamentals remained generally very strong, characterized by high saving and investment, a public sector surplus, strong export growth in recent years, and manageable debt and debt-service returns. On the other hand, the level of short-term capital inflows and short-term debt were somewhat high. Also, the limitations of present policy instruments constrained the authorities' ability to manage shocks. Caution in the use of foreign savings was warranted, directors observed, and early action was required to reduce the current account deficit. While fiscal policy could play a role in the short-term over the medium-term, the emphasis should be on measures to increase private saving.

Source: IMF

APPENDIX 2

DEFINITIONS OF RATIOS

Asset Quality

Provisioning: Loan Loss Provision/Pre-Tax Operating Profit Before Loan Loss Provision

Capital Adequacy

Leverage: Total (Liabilities & Capital − Total Shareholders' Equity/Total Shareholders' Equity)

Internal Growth Rate of Capital: After-Tax Profit − Dividend/ Total Shareholders' Equity × 100%

Total Equity/Loans: Total Shareholder's Equity/Total Loans & Advances × 100%

Total Equity/Total Deposits: Total Shareholder's Equity/ Total Interbank & Deposits × 100%

Total Equity/Total Assets: Total Shareholder's Equity/Total Assets × 100%

Profitability

Cost Margin: (Administrative Expenses + Depreciation + Other Expenses/ Average of the Total Assets in Current and Last Years) × 100%

Efficiency Ratio: Non-Interest Expenses/Operating Income

Net Interest Margin: Net Interest Income/
(Average of Interbank Assets + Government Securities +
Marketable Securities + Loans & Advances +
Unquoted Securities in Current and Last Years) × 100%

Non-lending Income Margin: {(Fees & Commission Income +
FX Trading Accounts + Other Non-Interest Income)/
Average of the Total Assets in Current and Last Years} × 100%

Profit Handout: Dividend/After-Tax Profit × 100%

Return on Average Assets: (After-Tax Profit in Current Year/
Average of the Total Assets in Current and Last Years) × 100%

Return on Average Equity: (After-tax Profit in Current Year
Average of the Total Shareholders' Equity in Current and Last Years) × 100%

Liquidity

Free Capital Funds on Risk Assets:
{(Total Capital Funds − Fixed Assets − Subsidiaries & Affiliates
Total Deposits with Banks + Total Loans & Advances)/
(Unquoted Securities + Marketable Securities + Total Risk Value)} × 100%

Quasi-Liquid Asset Ratio: {(Cash & Near Cash + Interbank Assets +
Government Securities + Marketable Securities)/
Total Assets} × 100%

Loans/Total Assets: Total Loans & Advances/Total Assets × 100%

Loans/Customer Deposits: Total Loans & Advances/Customer Deposits × 100

Loans/Total Deposits: Total Loans & Advances/
Total Interbank & Deposits × 100%

APPENDIX 3

A SAMPLE OF THE COMPOSITION OF BIS RATIOS

Numerator

Tier I Components: 1) Stockholders Equity (excluding disallowed intangibles and cumulative preferred)
2) Minority Interest

Tier II Components: 1) Subordinated Debt
2) Hybrid Debt/Equity
3) Unallocated Loan Loss Reserve
4) A Portion of Hidden Reserves (Non-US)

Denominator

Balance Sheet Asset:	1) Cash and Certain Government Securities	0%
	2) Assets Secured by Government/ Agency Securities	20%
	3) Residential Mortgages	50%
	4) Commercial Loans	100%
Off-balance Sheet Items:	1) Undrawn Commitment (original maturity > 1 year) to Commercial Customer	50%
	2) Replacement Cost of Interest Rate Swap w/OECD Bank	20%

Source: Thomson BankWatch Inc.

APPENDIX 4

FIGURES AND RATIOS BY COUNTRY

TABLE 1   LEVERAGE

Country average	1994	Rank	1995	Rank	1996	Rank
PHILIPPINES	6.87	2	6.88	2	6.90	1
SINGAPORE	7.74	3	7.37	3	7.55	2
TAIWAN — New Banks	5.32	1	6.82	1	8.13	3
HONG KONG (excl. HSBC)	8.71	4	8.19	4	8.18	4
PAKISTAN — New Banks	11.16	6	9.18	5	10.09	5
THAILAND	11.69	8	11.38	6	10.91	6
SRI LANKA	15.05	13	13.83	12	12.33	7
MACAU	12.59	10	12.81	10	12.37	8
VIETNAM	12.41	9	11.55	7	12.64	9
INDONESIA — Private Banks	11.26	7	12.19	8	12.73	10
INDIA — Commercial Banks	16.82	15	12.98	11	13.65	11
SOUTH KOREA — Old Merchant Banks	11.01	5	12.38	9	13.66	12
MALAYSIA	15.08	12	14.35	13	14.23	13
INDONESIA — State Banks	16.17	14	16.23	15	14.35	14
TAIWAN — Established Banks	18.93	17	18.15	17	15.58	15
CHINA - Hong Kong Incorporated Banks	17.29	16	16.09	14	15.88	16
SOUTH KOREA — Provincial Banks	14.20	11	16.63	16	18.98	17
INDIA — State Banks	28.44	21	27.17	20	25.36	18
SOUTH KOREA — Nationwide Banks	22.24	18	24.83	18	25.99	19
SOUTH KOREA — Specialized Banks	23.78	19	27.22	21	28.35	20
CHINA - Mainland	25.33	20	27.01	19	29.64	21
PAKISTAN — Established Banks	31.46	23	33.00	22	33.53	22
BANGLADESH	31.11	22	36.61	23	35.09	23

Source: Thomson BankWatch Inc.

TABLE 2   RETURN ON AVERAGE ASSETS

Country average	1994	Rank	1995	Rank	1996	Rank
PHILIPPINES	2.12	1	2.06	1	2.06	1
HONG KONG (excl. HSBC)	2.09	2	2.03	2	1.98	2
SRI LANKA	1.63	6	1.61	6	1.74	3
MACAU	1.93	4	1.77	4	1.71	4
PAKISTAN — New Banks	1.97	3	1.84	3	1.69	5
SINGAPORE	1.39	9	1.22	8	1.23	6
MALAYSIA	1.23	10	1.22	9	1.21	7
INDONESIA — Private Banks	1.18	11	1.19	10	1.21	8
THAILAND	1.77	5	1.73	5	1.06	9
SOUTH KOREA — Old Merchant Banks	1.48	7	1.25	7	0.90	10
VIETNAM	1.44	8	0.54	16	0.89	11
INDONESIA — State Banks	0.43	16	0.62	12	0.68	12
TAIWAN — New Banks	0.83	12	0.60	13	0.67	13
TAIWAN — Established Banks	0.72	13	0.64	11	0.65	14
CHINA — Hong Kong Incorporated Banks	0.67	14	0.56	15	0.57	15
INDIA — State Banks	0.27	21	0.57	14	0.46	16
BANGLADESH	−0.06	22	0.07	23	0.33	17
SOUTH KOREA — Provincial Banks	0.44	15	0.39	17	0.31	18
CHINA — Mainland	0.29	20	0.31	18	0.29	19
SOUTH KOREA — Specialized Banks	0.40	17	0.30	19	0.25	20
SOUTH KOREA — Nationwide Banks	0.36	18	0.19	21	0.17	21
PAKISTAN — Established Banks	0.31	19	0.11	22	0.07	22
INDIA — Commercial Banks	−2.09	23	0.23	20	−0.20	23

Source: Thomson BankWatch Inc.

TABLE 3   QUASI-LIQUID ASSET RATIO (%)

Country average	1994	Rank	1995	Rank	1996	Rank
INDIA — Commercial Banks	46.61	2	44.99	1	44.67	1
INDIA — State Banks	46.42	3	44.67	2	43.92	2
PAKISTAN — New Banks	51.98	1	41.85	6	42.63	3
HONG KONG (excl. HSBC)	45.78	4	43.51	4	41.96	4
PAKISTAN — Established Banks	44.82	5	42.32	5	41.94	5
MACAU	35.20	10	44.09	3	39.46	6
SINGAPORE	41.10	6	38.33	7	36.69	7
SOUTH KOREA — Nationwide Banks	35.84	9	37.30	8	34.29	8
CHINA — Hong Kong	36.52	8	36.22	9	33.87	9
SOUTH KOREA — Provincial Banks	34.22	11	34.08	11	32.57	10
CHINA — Mainland	32.00	12	32.60	11	31.08	11
MALAYSIA	38.13	7	32.01	13	29.09	12
SRI LANKA	31.82	13	26.25	15	28.93	13
BANGLADESH	29.11	15	32.22	12	28.34	14
TAIWAN — Established Banks	24.75	16	23.42	17	23.95	15
PHILIPPINES	31.01	14	26.72	14	23.91	16
INDONESIA — State Banks	23.47	17	24.38	16	23.00	17
VIETNAM	22.69	18	21.39	18	22.44	18
INDONESIA — Private Banks	16.05	22	18.61	20	20.78	19
TAIWAN — New Banks	21.07	19	19.87	19	19.67	20
SOUTH KOREA — Specialized Banks	16.11	21	18.41	21	16.68	21
SOUTH KOREA — Old Merchant Banks	17.26	20	13.58	22	15.14	22
THAILAND	9.88	23	9.13	23	7.77	23

Source: Thomson BankWatch Inc.

TABLE 4   BANGLADESH: COUNTRY AVERAGE

	1993	1994	1995
Return on average assets (%)	−0.06	0.07	0.33
Return on average equity (%)	−2.38	2.56	11.97
Leverage (times)	31.11	36.61	35.09
Quasi-liquid assets ratio (%)	29.11	32.22	28.34
Net interest margin (%)	1.38	0.99	1.12
Internal growth rate of capital (%)	−2.38	2.56	11.97
Loans/total deposits (%)	63.83	58.55	61.11

Source: Bank Annual Reports

TABLE 5   CHINA — MAINLAND: COUNTRY AVERAGE

	1994	1995	1996
Return on average assets (%)	0.29	0.31	0.29
Return on average equity (%)	7.3	8.37	8.37
Leverage (times)	25.33	27.01	29.64
Quasi-liquid assets ratio (%)	32	32.6	31.08
Net interest margin (%)	2.01	1.89	1.81
Internal growth rate of capital (%)	7.23	8.34	8.36
Loans/total deposits (%)	64.23	62.63	63.4

Source: Thomson BankWatch Inc.

TABLE 6   CHINA — HONG KONG: COUNTRY AVERAGE

	1994	1995	1996
Return on average assets (%)	0.67	0.56	0.57
Return on average equity (%)	11.89	9.89	9.66
Leverage (times)	17.29	16.09	15.88
Quasi-liquid assets ratio (%)	36.58	36.18	33.87
Net interest margin (%)	1.42	1.32	1.18
Internal growth rate of capital (%)	11.89	9.89	9.66
Loans/total deposits (%)	56.43	57.56	59.76

Source: Bank Annual Reports

TABLE 7   HONG KONG (excl. HSBC): COUNTRY AVERAGE

	1994	1995	1996
Return on average assets (%)	2.09	2.03	1.98
Return on average equity (%)	21.24	19.17	18.24
Leverage (times)	8.71	8.19	8.18
Quasi-liquid assets ratio (%)	45.78	43.51	41.96
Net interest margin (%)	2.64	2.84	2.99
Internal growth rate of capital (%)	11.05	10.10	9.69
Loans/total deposits (%)	54.66	56.62	59.87

Source: Thomson BankWatch Inc.

TABLE 8   INDIA — COMMERCIAL BANKS: COUNTRY AVERAGE

	1994	1995	1996
Return on average assets (%)	−2.09	0.23	−0.20
Return on average equity (%)	−43.96	3.50	−2.88
Leverage (times)	16.82	12.98	13.65
Quasi-liquid assets ratio (%)	46.61	44.99	44.67
Net interest margin (%)	2.98	3.52	3.61
Internal growth rate of capital (%)	−32.09	2.23	−4.06
Loans/total deposits (%)	45.79	48.10	49.70

Source: Thomson BankWatch Inc.

TABLE 9   INDIA — STATE BANKS: COUNTRY AVERAGE

	1994	1995	1996
Return on average assets (%)	0.27	0.57	0.46
Return on average equity (%)	10.25	16.37	12.55
Leverage (times)	28.44	27.17	25.36
Quasi-liquid assets ratio (%)	46.42	44.67	43.92
Net interest margin (%)	3.35	3.91	4.10
Internal growth rate of capital (%)	5.64	11.89	8.56
Loans/total deposits (%)	53.79	56.75	60.44

Source: Thomson BankWatch Inc.

TABLE 10   INDONESIA — PRIVATE BANKS: COUNTRY AVERAGE

	1994	1995	1996
Return on average assets (%)	1.18	1.19	1.21
Return on average equity (%)	14.74	15.18	16.28
Leverage (times)	11.26	12.19	12.73
Quasi-liquid assets ratio (%)	16.05	18.61	20.78
Net interest margin (%)	4.11	3.82	3.66
Internal growth rate of capital (%)	10.96	11.46	12.26
Loans/total deposits (%)	86.20	84.01	81.42

Source: Thomson BankWatch Inc.

TABLE 11   INDONESIA — STATE BANKS: COUNTRY AVERAGE

	1994	1995	1996
Return on average assets (%)	0.43	0.62	0.68
Return on average equity (%)	8.32	10.62	11.02
Leverage (times)	16.17	16.23	14.35
Quasi-liquid assets ratio (%)	23.47	24.38	23.00
Net interest margin (%)	3.03	2.98	2.61
Internal growth rate of capital (%)	8.32	8.56	7.59
Loans/total deposits (%)	98.92	103.23	98.77

Source: Thomson BankWatch Inc.

TABLE 12   KOREA — NATIONWIDE BANKS: COUNTRY AVERAGE

	1994	1995	1996
Return on average assets (%)	0.36	0.19	0.17
Return on average equity (%)	8.08	4.56	4.49
Leverage (times)	22.24	24.83	25.99
Quasi-liquid assets ratio (%)	35.84	37.30	34.29
Net interest margin (%)	1.68	1.64	1.67
Internal growth rate of capital (%)	6.53	3.50	3.38
Loans/total deposits (%)	59.17	56.31	60.63

Source: Thomson BankWatch Inc.

TABLE 13   KOREA — OLD MERCHANT BANKS: COUNTRY AVERAGE

	1994	1995	1996
Return on average assets (%)	1.48	1.25	0.90
Return on average equity (%)	18.71	15.93	12.60
Leverage (times)	11.01	12.38	13.66
Quasi-liquid assets ratio (%)	17.26	13.58	15.14
Net interest margin (%)	6.39	4.83	3.79
Internal growth rate of capital (%)	15.73	14.00	9.74
Loans/total deposits (%)	434.87	408.81	343.90

Source: Thomson BankWatch Inc.

TABLE 14   KOREA — PROVINCIAL BANKS: COUNTRY AVERAGE

	1994	1995	1996
Return on average assets (%)	0.44	0.39	0.31
Return on average equity (%)	6.33	6.44	5.81
Leverage (times)	14.20	16.63	18.98
Quasi-liquid assets ratio (%)	34.22	34.08	32.57
Net interest margin (%)	2.08	2.99	2.98
Internal growth rate of capital (%)	4.32	5.20	4.51
Loans/total deposits (%)	56.74	57.07	59.44

Source: Thomson BankWatch Inc.

TABLE 15   KOREA — SPECIALISED BANKS: COUNTRY AVERAGE

	1994	1995	1996
Return on average assets (%)	0.40	0.30	0.25
Return on average equity (%)	9.76	8.10	7.08
Leverage (times)	23.78	27.22	28.35
Quasi-liquid assets ratio (%)	16.11	18.41	16.68
Net interest margin (%)	2.51	2.29	2.23
Internal growth rate of capital (%)	9.64	7.65	6.63
Loans/total deposits (%)	116.85	107.94	117.57

Source: Thomson BankWatch Inc.

TABLE 16 MACAU: COUNTRY AVERAGE

	1994	1995	1996
Return on average assets (%)	1.93	1.77	1.71
Return on average equity (%)	26.72	24.23	23.17
Leverage (times)	12.59	12.81	12.37
Quasi-liquid assets ratio (%)	35.20	44.09	39.46
Net interest margin (%)	1.48	1.42	1.33
Internal growth rate of capital (%)	21.36	18.48	19.18
Loans/total deposits (%)	60.69	51.97	53.98

Source: Thomson BankWatch Inc.

TABLE 17 MALAYSIA: COUNTRY AVERAGE

	1994	1995	1996
Return on average assets (%)	1.23	1.22	1.21
Return on average equity (%)	20.76	19.10	18.43
Leverage (times)	15.03	14.35	14.23
Quasi-liquid assets ratio (%)	38.13	32.01	29.09
Net interest margin (%)	3.03	3.19	3.47
Internal growth rate of capital (%)	17.48	16.28	15.92
Loans/total deposits (%)	64.43	71.02	72.64

Source: Thomson BankWatch Inc.

TABLE 18 PAKISTAN — ESTABLISHED BANKS: COUNTRY AVERAGE

	1994	1995	1996
Return on average assets (%)	0.13	0.11	0.07
Return on average equity (%)	4.14	3.79	2.46
Leverage (times)	31.46	33.00	33.53
Quasi-liquid assets ratio (%)	44.82	42.32	41.94
Net interest margin (%)	3.15	3.40	3.07
Internal growth rate of capital (%)	4.14	3.45	2.14
Loans/total deposits (%)	48.08	50.11	50.14

Source: Thomson BankWatch Inc.

TABLE 19 PAKISTAN — NEW BANKS: COUNTRY AVERAGE

	1994	1995	1996
Return on average assets (%)	1.97	1.84	1.69
Return on average equity (%)	22.51	19.94	17.99
Leverage (times)	11.16	9.18	10.09
Quasi-liquid assets ratio (%)	51.98	41.85	42.63
Net interest margin (%)	4.89	3.95	3.74
Internal growth rate of capital (%)	19.64	15.20	11.40
Loans/total deposits (%)	49.60	59.27	56.57

Source: Thomson BankWatch Inc.

TABLE 20   PHILIPPINES: COUNTRY AVERAGE

	1994	1995	1996
Return on average assets (%)	2.12	2.06	2.06
Return on average equity (%)	17.14	16.25	16.28
Leverage (times)	6.87	6.88	6.90
Quasi-liquid assets ratio (%)	31.01	26.72	23.91
Net interest margin (%)	4.92	4.79	4.89
Internal growth rate of capital (%)	13.05	13.50	13.99
Loans/total deposits (%)	65.49	71.34	77.14

Source: Bank Annual Reports

TABLE 21   SINGAPORE: COUNTRY AVERAGE

	1994	1995	1996
Return on average assets (%)	1.39	1.22	1.23
Return on average equity (%)	12.52	10.44	10.43
Leverage (times)	7.74	7.37	7.55
Quasi-liquid assets ratio (%)	41.10	38.33	36.69
Net interest margin (%)	2.06	2.03	2.03
Internal growth rate of capital (%)	8.85	7.99	8.19
Loans/total deposits (%)	63.90	67.13	69.03

Source: Thomson BankWatch Inc.

TABLE 22   SRI LANKA: COUNTRY AVERAGE

	1994	1995	1996
Return on average assets (%)	1.63	1.61	1.74
Return on average equity (%)	26.21	24.84	24.33
Leverage (times)	15.05	13.83	12.33
Quasi-liquid assets ratio (%)	31.82	26.25	28.93
Net interest margin (%)	4.99	5.79	5.58
Internal growth rate of capital (%)	21.46	19.69	23.15
Loans/total deposits (%)	66.93	68.47	68.23

Source: Bank Annual Reports

TABLE 23   TAIWAN — ESTABLISHED BANKS: COUNTRY AVERAGE

	1994	1995	1996
Return on average assets (%)	0.72	0.64	0.65
Return on average equity (%)	15.05	12.40	11.51
Leverage (times)	18.93	18.15	15.58
Quasi-liquid assets ratio (%)	24.75	23.42	23.95
Net interest margin (%)	1.60	1.68	1.53
Internal growth rate of capital (%)	12.60	10.09	9.24
Loans/total deposits (%)	78.38	80.38	78.74

Source: Thomson BankWatch Inc.

TABLE 24 TAIWAN: NEW BANKS: COUNTRY AVERAGE

	1994	1995	1996
Return on average assets (%)	0.83	0.60	0.67
Return on average equity (%)	4.33	4.27	5.70
Leverage (times)	5.32	6.82	8.13
Quasi-liquid assets ratio (%)	21.07	19.87	19.67
Net interest margin (%)	2.80	2.29	2.09
Internal growth rate of capital (%)	1.77	2.47	4.08
Loans/total deposits (%)	91.71	88.87	86.18

Source: Thomson BankWatch Inc.

TABLE 25 THAILAND: COUNTRY AVERAGE

	1994	1995	1996
Return on average assets (%)	1.77	1.73	1.06
Return on average equity (%)	22.78	21.69	12.88
Leverage (times)	11.69	11.38	10.91
Quasi-liquid assets ratio (%)	9.88	9.13	7.77
Net interest margin (%)	3.98	3.74	3.61
Internal growth rate of capital (%)	14.99	13.68	5.38
Loans/total deposits (%)	101.76	106.27	107.13

Source: Thomson BankWatch Inc.

TABLE 26 VIETNAM: COUNTRY AVERAGE

	1994	1995	1996
Return on average assets (%)	1.44	0.54	0.89
Return on average equity (%)	18.28	6.97	11.71
Leverage (times)	12.41	11.55	12.64
Quasi-liquid assets ratio (%)	22.69	21.39	22.44
Net interest margin (%)	5.53	4.53	3.85
Internal growth rate of capital (%)	18.28	6.56	11.71
Loans/total deposits (%)	109.10	112.05	105.03

Source: Thomson BankWatch Inc.

REFERENCES

Asian Development Bank, "Critical Issues in Asian Development — Theories, Experiences, Policies," Oxford University Press, 1996.

Asian Development Bank, "Emerging Asia — Changes and Challenges," Asian Development Bank, 1997.

Bank for International Settlements, "67th Annual Report, Bank for International Settlements," 1997.

Bank for International Settlements, "68th Annual Report, Bank for International Settlements," 1998.

Bank for International Settlements, "The Maturity, Sectoral, and Nationality Distribution of International Bank Lending," Bank for International Settlements, January 1998.

Becker, Gary, "Asia May Be Shaken But It's No House of Cards," *Business Week*, February 2," 1998.

Bennett, Adam, "Currency Boards: Issues and Experiences," IMF Paper on Policy Assessment 94/18, International Monetary Fund, 1994.

Claessens, Stijn and Glaessner, Thomas, "Are Financial Sector Weaknesses Undermining the East Asian Miracle?" Directions in Development, World Bank, September 1997.

Dornbusch, R., " Mexico: Stabilization, Reform, and No Growth," Brookings Papers on Economic Activity.

Feldstein, Martin, "Refocusing the IMF," Foreign Affairs, March/April 1998.

Kindleberger, C., *Manias, Panics and Crashes: A History of Financial Crisis*, Third Edition, New York, John Wiley and Sons, 1996.

Kissinger, Henry, "The Asian Collapse: One Fix Does Not Fit All Economies," *The Washington Post*, Op-Ed, February 9, 1998.

Krugman, Paul, "Are Currency Crisis Self-Fulfilling?" Macroeconomics Annual.

Krugman, Paul, "The Myth of Asia's Miracle," *Foreign Affairs* 73(6), November/December, 1994.

Krugman, Paul, (1997) "What Happened to Asia" Paul Krugman's Web Home Page.

Liu, L., Noland, M., Robinson, S. and Wang, Z., "Asian Competitive Devaluations," Working Paper Series 98–2, Washington: Institute for International Economics.

McKinnon, R. and Pill, H., "Credible Liberalizations and International Capital Flows: The Overborrowing Syndrome," in T. Ito and A.O. Krueger, eds, *Financial Deregulation and Integration in East Asia*, Chicago University Press, 1996.

Sachs, Jeffrey, "The Wrong Medicine for Asia," *New York Times*, November 3, 1997.

Sachs, Jeffrey, "The IMF and the Asian Flu," *The American Prospect*, March-April 1998.

Sachs, J., Tornell, A. and Valesco, A., "Financial Crisis in Emerging Markets: The Lessons from 1995," in William C. Brainard and George L. Perry, eds, Brookings Papers on Economic Activity, Brookings Institutions: Washington, DC.

Shultz, G., Simon, W. and Wriston, W., "Who Needs the IMF?" *Wall Street Journal*, February 3, 1998.

Soros, George, "Avoiding A Breakdown," *Financial Times*, December 31, 1997.

Wade, Robert, *Governing the Market, Economic Theory and the Role of Government in East Asian Industrializations*, Princeton University Press, 1990.

Williamson, John, "What Role for Currency Boards? Policy Analyses in International Economics," No. 40, Institute for International Economics, September 1995.

World Bank, *The East Asian Miracle — Economic growth and Public Policy*, Oxford University Press, 1993.

INDEX